JUN 0 2 2005
P9-DGB-916

A Short History of Finland

This is a second edition of the most successful study of Finland in the English language. It presents the reader – whether tourist, student, specialist or business person – with a readable and authoritative introduction to the Finns and the present position of their country in the modern world.

A Short History of Finland traces the historical development of the country from its settlement by the Finns in the first millennium AD to the present time, exploring Finland's earlier connection with Sweden, the complex relationship with Russia which has dominated Finnish history in the past two centuries, and the post-war achievements of the second republic. The author explains how a small nation, placed in an unfavourable geopolitical situation, won its independence and eventually achieved a high material standard of living, together with an enviable degree of social and political stability, by adapting itself to the realities of life in an unpromising environment. This second edition has been revised and updated by Emeritus Professor A. F. Upton, a leading scholar of Scandinavian history, and discusses the impact of the break-up of the Soviet Union and brings events up to Finland's admission to the European Union in 1995. Sadly the author, Fred Singleton, died shortly before publication of the original edition.

A SHORT HISTORY OF

Finland

FRED SINGLETON

Revised and updated by

A. F. Upton

PUBLISHED BY THE PRESS SYNDICATE OF THE UNIVERSITY OF CAMBRIDGE
The Pitt Building, Trumpington Street, Cambridge, United Kingdom

CAMBRIDGE UNIVERSITY PRESS
The Edinburgh Building, Cambridge CB2 2RU, UK
40 West 20th Street, New York, NY 10011–4211, USA
477 Williamstown Road, Port Melbourne 3207, Australia
Ruiz de Alarcón 13, 28014 Madrid, Spain
Dock House, The Waterfront, Cape Town 8001, South Africa

http://www.cambridge.org

First published 1989
Reprinted 1991, 1995
Second edition first published 1998
Reprinted 1999, 2000, 2002, 2003

Typeset in Palatino $9\frac{1}{2}$/13pt [GC]

A catalogue record for this book is available from the British Library

Library of Congress Cataloguing in Publication data applied for

ISBN 0 521 32275 8 hardback First edition
ISBN 0 521 31136 5 paperback First edition
ISBN 0 521 64069 5 hardback Second edition
ISBN 0 521 64701 0 paperback Second edition

Transferred to digital printing 2004

Contents

Maps

This book is dedicated, in accordance
with the author's own wish, to
His Excellency Mauno Koivisto,
President of Finland

Preface

The writing of this book has given the author great pleasure. I hope that the reader may also find enjoyment. Finland is not a major world power and is not on the main trade routes, nor is it a strategic corridor to anywhere. This may be why it has so often been ignored and misunderstood by the rest of the world – especially by the English-speaking world which ought to know better.

During the last twenty years there has been no book comparable to the present volume which attempts to include a summary of Finnish geography and history and an assessment of the country's present position in the modern world: in other words, to *explain* Finland to the rest of the world. The incomparable Bill Mead, to whom the present author owes so much, has given us the picture as he saw it 20 years ago: his *Finland* (1968), his studies of various aspects of Finnish economic geography and agriculture, and his specialist studies of the Åland Islands leave all who follow him in his debt. The present author's '*Economy of Finland in the Twentieth Century* (1987) should logically have followed this volume, but the vagaries of publishing in Britain and the unpredictability of my health made this order of events impossible. However, I have been encouraged by the reception of the *Economy* to feel confident that a reading public awaits a more general historical survey.

As well as trying to dispel the cloud of ignorance and indifference which hangs over Finland in the minds of most readers in the west, I have other, more positive, objectives. One of these is to repay the many friends I have in Finland for the wonderful way in which my steadily growing knowledge of Finland and the Finns has added an extra dimension to my life during the last forty years. The unique beauty of the natural environment; the glow of 'the long white nights' in midsummer and the awesome silence of the snow-covered forests at midwinter; the excitement in season, of setting out for a boating and swimming weekend, with a bagful of crayfish to cook for the picnic meal; the pleasure of packing the dangerous-looking implements needed to cut holes in the two-foot ice cover over the sea, to entice the codling to rise for air and prepare themselves for that night's supper: these are unforgettable experiences – but more than this is the feeling of belonging which Finnish friends have given me whenever I have had the good fortune to 'make myself at home' in their company.

These personal pleasures would not, however, have justified my publishers in producing the present volume. Finland has much to teach the rest of the world: how a small nation can survive in a world of giants and can thrive and prosper by discovering where its true place lies in the community of nations. Finns today are more prosperous than are the citizens of all but a handful of developed industrial countries. They enjoy a lifestyle which is more graceful, and less subject to the stress and paranoia of those who seem to have lived in daily fear of attacks instigated by the evil men of either the Kremlin or the Pentagon. By choosing the path of neutrality, Finland has opted out of the arms race, and if it has taken its share in the duties of 'world policemen' it has done so under the umbrella of The United Nations, sending members of its armed forces to Cyprus, the Middle East and Africa to help the world organization to keep the peace.

Whilst playing its full share in promoting peace Finland has been careful to avoid taking sides. The YYA Treaty with the USSR (see Appendix C), signed in 1948, has often been misunderstood – at times deliberately – by those who find it impossible to comprehend a world in which 'those who are not with us are against us'. The use of the term 'Finlandization' has often been employed by politicians in the United States, West Germany and Britain to depict a country which is the subservient lackey of the Soviet Union, allowed a small amount of rope in order to give others the illusion of freedom of manoeuvre, in order to entice them from their allegiance to the 'western' side in the Cold War.

This book comes out at a time when there appears to be the beginnings of a break in the log jam which has choked the channels of international intercourse. Finland has played a modest part since the Helsinki Summit Conference of 1975 in helping to reduce the militarization of the lines of communication. It appears also at a time when President Koivisto has just embarked on his second six-year term of office. This modest, unassuming man, with a wry sense of humour and a deep understanding of post-war relations in the late twentieth century, is in many ways the embodiment of the Finnish virtues.

I hope that this book will help some of my readers in the English-speaking world to understand how Finland arrived at its present position in the world and why it is that this small country should not be ignored when considering the forces which shape the contours of international relations.

Although I am solely responsible for all that appears between its covers, it would be churlish not to acknowledge the help given by many friends and colleagues in Finland and in Britain. Amongst my Finnish friends I must single out the Möring family, whose never-ending patience and good humour have helped to keep me sane and on the right track, during my many visits to their home – often to stay for long periods at short notice. Ele Alenius, is another good friend, whom I first met when we went together in 1949 to hear the veteran socialist Oskari Tokoi, returned briefly from exile in the U.S.A., give the keynote speech at a rally commemorating the golden jubilee of the Social Democratic Party. Our friendship since then has developed beyond the shared interest in left-wing politics, and my friendship with Finns on the right of the political spectrum, as well as with academics, writers, artists and others in all walks of life, has had only the common denominator of a shared love of Finland and most things Finnish.

Finally I must pay my tribute to others nearer home, whose patience has at last, after too long a period of waiting, been rewarded by the appearance of this book. Mrs Elizabeth Wetton, who commissioned the book for the publishers, has been a model of all that an author should wish for in an editor. Mike Lear has drawn the maps with skill and competence. My long-suffering family know how much the appearance in print of a work which has been so long in the making means to me. In the long struggle against illness they have sustained me and kept me to the promises which I made to myself and to my publishers. To all these, many thanks.

F. S.
Ilkley

Fred Singleton's family helped in various ways towards the completion of this book. They wish to put on record their grateful thanks for the major contribution of Mr J. J. Horton, Deputy Librarian of the J. B. Priestley Library, Bradford University, who corrected the text and compiled the bibliography.

E. A. C. SINGLETON

1
History of Finland

Introduction

The Finns are in many ways a special people. They do not fit into any neat category. Their Finno-Ugrian language is not related to those of their Scandinavian or Slavonic neighbours. For almost seven centuries they were under the rule of the Swedish crown, but the proportion of Finns whose first language is Swedish has been falling steadily from over 10 per cent at the time of independence in 1917 to under 6 per cent today. They were linked to Tsarist Russia for over a century after 1809, but they retained a degree of autonomy which enabled them to nurture an independent spirit, based on a distinctive culture, and to emerge from the chaos of the Russian revolution as a fully fledged nation-state. In 1919 they adopted a republican constitution which incorporated the radical, democratic reforms conceded by the Tsarist government in 1906, which had established an elected, single-chamber parliament (*Eduskunta*), and which made Finland the first country in Europe to give equal voting rights to men and women.

In March 1917 the first democratically elected socialist prime minister in the world, Oskari Tokoi, took office in Helsinki – albeit in charge of a government whose authority was disputed. Finland began its independent life under the shadow of a disastrous civil war, which raged during the first half of 1918. In the 1930s its democratic way of life was challenged by an extreme right wing movement, but the challenge was successfully resisted. In 1939 this little nation of about three and a half million people was invaded by the Soviet Union and for four months fought alone against overwhelming odds before being forced to sue for peace. Despite loss of territory, the independent state survived to join with Germany in 1941 in an attempt to recover the losses of the war with Russia. In 1944 Finland withdrew from the war, made peace with Russia and drove out the German forces from Lapland. Since then Finland has followed a policy of neutrality and of good neighbourliness with Russia. Today it is one of the most prosperous, socially progressive, stable and peace loving nations in the world.

The homeland of the Finns is not, at first glance, a likely base for such a successful state. As the most northerly country on the European mainland, a third of its territory lies within the Arctic Circle. It possesses limited natural resources; it is deficient in fossil fuels and it must import most of its energy requirements. The climate imposes severe limitations on the possibilities of agriculture and the rhythm of everyday life must be adapted to the demands of a long, cold, dark winter.

The Finns have not only survived in these unfavourable conditions – they have flourished. Their economy is one of the most successful in Europe. They enjoy a high material standard of living and they also have a vigorous and progressive cultural life. They have a strong musical tradition and are renowned for their architecture and town planning. Their social welfare provisions, their contributions to medicine, science and technology and even their sporting prowess place them, despite their numerical insignificance, amongst the front runners in the community of nations. Their ability to co-operate with nature in the development of their environment provides an outstanding example of how civilized people may combine material progress with graceful living.

The land of Finland

Finland's geographical position places it on the northern fringe of the European world, outside the mainstream of political, economic and military activities. Throughout history the main currents of European life which have affected the Mediterranean, the north-west coastlands and the heartlands of central Europe have either bypassed Finland or have come to it centuries late and in an attenuated form. Christianity did not appear in Finland until the twelfth century and did not take root until the thirteenth, a millenium after it had reached even the remote offshore islands of Britain. Finnish history can hardly be said to exist in written records before the time in England when King John had been compelled to sign the Magna Carta, or when the Finns' distant linguistic cousins, the Magyars, were defending their Hungarian kingdom against the Mongol invasions. As Professor Wuorinen has written in his *History of Finland* 'Even moderately recognisable contours of Finland's political development and religious and economic life do not in fact appear . . . until the thirteenth century.'

Much of the history of Finland before the twelfth century is either in the realm of archaeology and prehistory or in folklore and legend. There is a brief and dubious reference to the people known as the Fenni in the *Germania* by Tacitus, written in 98 AD, and more reliable geographical descriptions of the land and its climate in the work of the Arab geographer, Idrisi, who served the court of Roger II in Palermo in the early twelfth century, but it is not until later in that century that an authoritative historical document relating to Finland appears. This is the Papal Bull *Gravis admodum*, issued by Pope Alexander III in 1172, which suggests that Christianity was already established in Finland – for it refers to the fact that the Finns were not always as strong in their faith and as obedient to their priests as the Pope would have wished. Tradition rather than historical fact suggest that the Finns were converted by crusaders from Sweden earlier in the twelfth century, one of those involved being the Englishman, Bishop Henry of Uppsala, who later became the patron saint of Finland.

The obscurity and lack of evidence regarding the situation in Finland before the thirteenth century can be explained within the context of its geographical isolation from the rest of Europe. There was little to attract conquerors or traders to this remote land of lakes and forests, with its harsh winters. Finland was not, however, uninhabited during the long millenia during which it lay as a *terra incognita* to the rest of Europe. The archaeological record shows that the first settlers appeared some ten thousand years ago, in the wake of the retreating ice cap. They settled in the lowlands of the southern and southwestern coastlands, between the shores of the Gulfs of Finland and Bothnia and the lake plateau of the interior.

The last ice age had a profound effect on the geography of Finland. It scoured out the lake basins which cover the central regions with thousands of long, finger-like expanses of water and occupy almost 10 per cent of the surface area. These lakes have been important in the history of Finland because they provided routes into the interior which were far more useful than transport by road would have been. In the summer time the Finns took to their boats in order to travel from village to village. In winter, they were able to cross the frozen lakes by sledge or on skis and snowshoes. When the timber industry began to expand, the lakes provided a cheap and easy method of transporting logs to the sawmills. Although the lakes are mainly shallow, the presence of these large expanses of water has a modifying effect on the micro-climate of the lake plateau.

As the ice-cap shrank, it left behind large deposits of material in the form of moraines. Fluvio-glacial deposits washed out from the ice accumulated along the ice margins, creating ridges of sand, gravel and mud. The largest of these, which developed where the ice came into contact with the sea, form the Salpausselkä ridges, which cross the country from the Russian border in the east to the Hanko peninsula, in the south west, and attain heights of over 100 feet. They provide routeways, a source for building materials and even ski slopes. Smaller ridges, which are also derived from fluvio-glacial material and were possibly created when the ice was in retreat, form chains of *eskers* up to 30 feet high, which provide high level causeways across the lakes and swamps of central Finland. The most impressive of these, Jaaman Kangas and Punkaharju, carry roads which are of vital importance to the network of communications in the remote parts of central and eastern Finland.

Much of the farmland in Finland is located on deposits of boulder clay and other morainic deposits, laid down during the last stage of the Ice Age. Although the impermeable character of many of the clays makes them susceptible to the formation of peat bogs, they nurture the forests of Finland and provide the farmers with the basis of the soils on which they grow their crops. The Ice Age was a comparatively recent episode in the geological history of Finland. The changes wrought by it took place on a platform of ancient rocks which have remained relatively stable for hundreds of millions of years, for the bedrock of Finland, a part of the Fenno-Scandian shield, contains some of the oldest and most stable rock formations in Europe. These are the granites, quartzite schists, gneisses and other igneous and metamorphic rocks which were formed in pre-Cambrian times. Virtually no deposition took place during the geological periods in which the sedimentary rocks of Britain and western Europe were laid down. As most of the rocks of Finland are older than the existence of any form of organic life on earth, they do not contain any of the valuable fossil fuels which provide the energy sources for modern industrial societies. There are none of the coal deposits of the Carboniferous period which were the basis for the industrial revolution in nineteenth century Britain, Germany, France and Belgium. Nor are there oil-bearing strata, such as those which occur in sedimentary deposits under the North Sea. When Finland began to industrialize it first relied upon wood from its abundant forests to heat the furnaces and drive the railway engines. Wood is a poor source of energy, with a lower calorific value than coal or oil. Later, in the twentieth century, hydro-electric power was developed and, even more recently, efficient means have been devised for the processing of the abundant reserves of peat. However these domestic energy sources supply only a small proportion of the country's needs and Finland must rely heavily on imported fuels. Coal is imported from Britain and Poland and since the Second World War oil and gas from Russia have become major energy sources.

The ancient rocks of Finland may not produce coal or oil, but they are rich sources of mineral ores. Reference in the national epic, *Kalevala*, to the working of bog iron and copper suggest that these ores were used in the first millenium AD and rock iron ore was mined in Uusimaa province in the 16th century; but the modern exploitation of the mineral wealth of Finland did not begin on a large scale until after independence. The most important source of metal ore is at Outokumpu in Kuopio province, where copper was discovered in 1912. The field was not developed until the 1920s, when the Finnish government took over the ownership of the mine. In addition to the copper ores, the Outokumpu deposits yield iron, zinc, cobalt, nickel, tin, gold, silver and sulphur. The largest nickel deposit, which lies in the Petsamo region on the Arctic coast, was only available to Finland for about twenty years. The Petsamo area was ceded to Finland by the Soviet Union in 1920, under the terms of the Treaty of Dorpat (Tartu), in fulfilment of a promise made in 1864 by the Tsarist government. During the Second World War the nickel deposits came under effective German control, and were totally lost to Finland when the Soviet Union again took the Petsamo area in 1944. There are other nickel deposits which have been developed to replace the lost ores of Petsamo, and as well as producing a range of non-ferrous metals such as copper, lead, zinc and tin, Finland's ancient rocks also contain valuable minerals such as titanium and vanadium which are used in the production of high-grade steel.

Amongst the non-metallic minerals found in Finland are graphite, from the metamorphic schists in the Pori and Kuopio areas, which was exported to Russia during the nineteenth century, the abundant reserves of feldspar and quartz and clay – which have long been used in the pottery and glass-making industries. There is an export surplus of granite for building stone, and Finland can supply its domestic needs of limestone for use in the iron and steel and building industries.

The final melting of the ice-cap, which occurred about 8,000 BC, removed a vast weight which had distorted the earth's crust. The isostatic recovery of the crust is still in progress, and its effect on Finland involves a steady and measurable rise in the land surface. The rate varies from 100 centimetres per century at the head of the Gulf of Finland to 40 centimetres in the Helsinki region. Over the centuries Finland has grown in area as the sea has receded and some towns on the Bothnian shore, which in mediaeval times were ports on the open sea, are now either many miles inland or must be approached along land-girt channels. In order to maintain their seaborne trade, the Finns are compelled to construct, at intervals, new outports, such as that at Mäntyluoto, which serves the former port of Pori, now 20 kilometres inland. The land area of Finland is increasing at the rate of 1,000 square kilometres a century, of which about a third is attributed to the deposition of sediments along the shore; and the rest to the effects of isostatic recovery. The tilting of the land, caused by the differential rate of land uplift, sometimes results in the draining of lake basins. This occasional loss of a lake does not make much impression, as Finland has about 55,000 lakes – a lake being defined as a body of water with its largest surface dimension measuring over 200 metres. The largest lake system, centred on Lake Saimaa, occupies an area of 4,400 square kilometres and provides an inland water route, stretching northward from Lappeenranta through a series of linked waterways to Kuopio, 300 kilometres to the north, and even beyond. The parallel Päijänne system, which lies to the west of Saimaa, provides a similar waterway, linking Lahti to Jyväskylä, a distance of over 170 kilometres.

The rivers which drain the lakes are mainly quite short. The Vuoksi, which flows from Lake Saimaa to Lake Ladoga (which is now in Russian territory), and several of the rapids which provide the power for the generation of electricity benefit the Russian rather than the Finnish economy, although the state-owned power station at Imatra remains in Finnish hands. The Kymi river, which reaches the sea near Kotka, and the Kokemäki, which flows into the Gulf of Bothnia near Pori, both have power stations in the upper reaches of their short courses, where they leave the lake plateau. The longest river in Finland is the Kemi, which flows through 552 kilometres of southern Lapland to enter the Gulf of Bothnia at the town of Kemi. Its potential for the generation of hydro-electricity has been fully utilized in the post-war period, as has that of the Oulu river, which joins the sea some 100 kilometres to the south of the Kemi.

The rivers are of little use for navigation, except along short lengths of their courses, but those which form a link between lakes are used both for navigation and for the floating of logs. Many have been supplemented by short lengths of canal, the first of which, the Murole canal, which was opened in 1854 to extend access to Näsijärvi from the holiday resort of Ruovesi. Two years later, the much more important Saimaa canal, which connects the Saimaa system to the port of Viipuri, was opened. The transfer of territory at the end of the Second World War gave Viipuri to the Soviet Union, but an agreement in 1962, which took five years to become effective, gave Finland the right to use the canal.

The warm waters of the North Atlantic Drift, which surround the northern coasts of the Scandinavian peninsula and reach as far as the Kola Peninsula and the island of Svalbard, exercise a modifying influence on the climate of Finland. Nowhere else in the world do ice-free oceanic waters extend polewards beyond the 70th parallel. This explains why Finland enjoys a considerably milder climate than other countries, such as Alaska, Greenland and Siberia, which lie in similar latitudes. The waters of the Gulfs of Bothnia and Finland which enclose southern and western Finland also have an ameliorating influence on the climate.

The total amount of precipitation – rain and snow – is not high, varying from 500 millimetres rainfall equivalent in the north to 620 millimetres in the south, with only the south-western tip and the Åland Islands recording more than 880 millimetres. The amount of precipitation which falls as snow varies from place to place, as does the incidence of frost. The area with the greatest depth of snow and the highest incidence of frost is along the Russian border in Kainuu and south-eastern Lapland, whilst the south-western coasts and islands experience the mildest climate, with snow usually being confined to the January–March period, although frosts often occur in early December. In an average winter the ports throughout Finland, from Kotka on the Gulf of Finland to Tornio at the head of the Gulf of Bothnia, are hampered by ice. However, with modern ice breakers they can be kept open for shipping. In exceptionally severe winters, about once in a decade, the entrance to the Gulf of Bothnia is completely blocked by ice, reaching to a depth of over three feet; the Åland Islands are frozen in, and it is possible for cars to pass over the ice between Sweden and Finland. In such circumstances the frozen pack ice fills the Gulfs of Finland and Bothnia and shipping is seriously disrupted.

Summers, however, are warm and pleasant, with light winds and clear skies. Because of the high latitudes summer days are long, Helsinki having a daily average of nine hours of sunshine between May and August, and even Sodankylä in the heart of Lapland has eight hours a day. The long days compensate for the low angle of the sun in the northern regions, and the amount of insulation enables a close vegetation cover to grow, despite the fact that the growing season lasts for only a few months. The treeless, barren tundras of northern Canada and Siberia are not found in similar latitudes in Lapland. Even in the far northern fells of Utsjoki and Enontekiö, stands of dwarf birch and willow and shrubs such as mountain heath are to be found.

The growing season for field crops is adequate for the cultivation of temperate cereals. Spring wheat can be grown in most of the area south of Lapland while rye, barley and oats are grown even in central Lapland. Fodder crops like timothy grass can survive in all but the northernmost fells and potatoes are grown virtually throughout the country. In forest clearings in the interior and on the meadows of the south and west, cattle are grazed and dairy farming is a major rural occupation. There are areas of the country, especially in Oulu province, where extensive peat bogs make farming impossible, but wherever soils are adequate the Finnish farmer is not prevented by climatic limitations from obtaining some value from the land. In the recent past, however, agricultural overproduction has been a problem and subsidies which were once paid to encourage the farmers to increase output are now being used to persuade them to leave the land, or at least to grow trees instead of crops.

Although the Finns have shown remarkable resilience in adapting to their environment, there is no doubt that the long, cold, dark winters do exact a heavy price. The exact cost in cash terms is difficult to assess, As Mead and Smeds state in *Winter in Finland*:

> A formula might be devised by adding the costs of protection against winter (heating, food, clothing, medicines) to the costs of the assault on winter (breaking the ice at sea, clearing the snow on land, lighting the darkness) and the costs of damage by winter (from highway and building damage to frost destruction of cultivated plants), and by subtracting from them the cost benefits that accrue from winter (sporting, lumbering and the stimulus to new industrial and technical enterprise).

An attempt to compute the cost of the 1962–3 winter by a Finnish scholar suggested a figure of approximately 4 per cent of GDP, or £17 per capita for each inhabitant, which Mead and Smeds consider to be too low. Whatever the cost to society and to individuals, the Finns appear to have learned to take winter in their stride and to make the most of their often glorious summers.

Geography may have imposed many limitations on Finland, but it has endowed it with one resource in abundance – its forests. More than two thirds of the country is covered with forest and over one half of the forests consists of good quality timber – a greater proportion than in any other European country. The main species of trees are pine, spruce, birch, alder and aspen. Until the nineteenth century, the exploitation of the forests was a haphazard and often wasteful process, with the primitive practice of burn-beating carried out in order to clear forest land for agriculture. The demand for timber increased when the western European nations began to expand their economies in the nineteenth century, and Finland began to exploit its forest resources more systematically. Today the forest industry is conducted on scientific lines, with due attention being paid to conservation.

The ownership of the forests is widely distributed, with more than half the forest area belonging to individual farmers. There are few farmers in Finland who do not own a few hectares of forest, and the income from the timber is an essential element in the rural economy. Wood-based industries – which range from the sale of sawn timber to the manufacture of paper, prefabricated houses and even to the chemical and pharmaceutical industries – constitute the largest single industrial group in the country. In 1985 over one third of the value of Finnish exports was produced by the sale of the products of the wood and paper industries. The forest reserve is continually renewed by nature, and as long as felling does not exceed the rate of growth, it would appear to be an inexhaustible resource. The Finns have learned to co-operate with nature, not only in the development of their forests but also in many other aspects of their national life. This may well explain why, in spite of a comparatively meagre endowment of resources, and with many geographical disadvantages, they have been able to place themselves amongst the most affluent nations in the world.

The people of Finland

The first settlers came to Finland about 7,000 BC when the continental ice sheet had virtually disappeared but the country had not yet assumed its present form. The present Baltic Sea was occupied by the fresh-water Ancyclus Lake. These early inhabitants occupied a bleak, tundra-like terrain and the scant archaeological evidence available suggests that their culture was similar to that of the Maglemosian period in Denmark. These mesolithic settlers occupied scattered sites in the coastal lowlands of southern Finland, which stretch from Ladoga in the east to the Bothnian shore in the west. They lived by hunting elk and by fishing. The discovery of an elk head carved in pine, which appears to be the prow of a boat used by the mesolithic people, is particularly interesting. It was found at Lehtojärvi, north-west of Rovaniemi in Lapland, and dated by radiocarbon techniques to be from about 5,800 BC. Other traces of boat-using people from around 3,000 BC have also been found, notably at Lankaa, near Jyväskylä, where a rock painting depicts an elk head boat which apparently carried a crew of four. Elk head carvings in soapstone are also known from south-west and eastern Finland. The carving of an elk head on a huntsman's club, found at Huittinen in the Kokemäki valley near Pori, may be evidence of a belief in the magical power of an effigy of the hunter's prey.

About 5,000 BC the Ancyclus Lake (named after the freshwater mollusc *Ancyclus fluviatilis* which flourished in its waters) was invaded by salt water through the newly created Danish Sound, and the Ancyclus Lake was transformed into the Litorina Sea, which was the forerunner of the present-day Baltic. About 3,000 BC it appears that a neolithic type of culture flourished in Karelia. Its characteristic was the production of ceramics decorated with a comb pattern, which has affinities with the Comb Ceramic ware, traces of which have been found in an area which extends from the Urals through the Ukraine and the southern Baltic lands to the Bothnian shores and even to Lapland. Unlike the Neolithic peoples of western Europe, these peoples did not practice agriculture but lived by hunting and fishing and the collection of berries, nuts and fungi. Various types of seal – grey, ringed and harp – replaced the elk as a major element in their diet.

The culture which made its appearance in Finland around 2,000 BC probably came from a maritime people who settled along the southern and south-western shores of the mainland and on the Åland

Islands. The characteristic relic of these people is a polished stone axe shaped like a boat, which is found on many coastal sites, but seldom far inland. It would seem that, as early as the second millenium BC, Finland was experiencing cultural influences from both east and west: the eastern regions, especially Karelia, were receiving influences from overland, from what is now Russia, whilst the south-western coastal lowlands were subjected to influences from the south and west which came by sea.

Bronze Age artifacts began to appear in coastal locations near to, but separate from, the Boat Axe remains, dating from about 1,200 BC. Like the Boat Axe people, the Bronze Age settlers appear to have come from the south of the Gulf of Finland and possibly also from Scandinavia, and to have arrived by sea. Pottery from a Bronze Age settlement has been found on one of the Åland Islands, and there are hundreds of Bronze Age sites scattered around the coasts of Finland, which date from about 1,500 to 500 BC.

The knowledge of the use of iron was probably imported into Finland during the last centuries BC. The legends of Kalevala record how Ilmarinen, the smith, taught the *Suomalaiset* (the Finns) to seek iron in 'the footprints of the wolf' in the marshy ground and to smelt the ore 'on a hill of charcoal'. It is not too fanciful to assume that Ilmarinen was related to Wayland, the archetypal smith in Scandinavian mythology, and that both are folk memories of the wandering smiths who spread the knowledge of iron working amongst the peoples of central and western Europe.

Who were these iron-using people who occupied Finland during the first millenium BC? It is thought that they were the ancestors of the modern Finns, but there is considerable doubt about their origins. In a book published in 1946 by an English philologist, R. E. Burnham, *Who are the Finns?* examines the evidence for an Asian origin of the Finns. He notes the relations between the Finnish language and the other Finno-Ugrian languages, which include Lapp, Estonian and Karelian amongst its closest neighbours, and Vogul, Ostiak, Permian, Mordvinian and Magyar amongst its more distant relatives. The Finnish philologist M. A. Castrén, writing in the 1840s, had observed these linguistic affinities and had postulated a Ural-Altaic family of languages, the parent tongue of which was spoken by an Asian people who were the ancestors of the modern Finno-Ugrian speakers, as well as of other non-Aryan speakers, like the Turkic and Mongol peoples. Whether or not the linguistic connections are valid, there is no justification for assuming a common ethnic origin for people who speak related languages. The same mistake was made by the German philologist, Max Müller who, twenty years after Castrén, traced the origins of the Aryan family of languages and made the unwarranted assumption that the 'ancestors of the Indians, the Persians, the Greeks, the Romans, the Slavs, the Celts and the Germans were living together within the same enclosure, nay, under the same roof.'

However, unlike Castrén, Müller lived long enough to become aware of the fallacy of equating race and language, and in 1888 he wrote that 'an ethnologist who speaks of Aryan race, Aryan blood, Aryan eyes and hair is as great a sinner as a linguist who speaks of a dolicephalic dictionary or a brachycephalic grammar.' Müller's disavowal was, unfortunately, ignored by many who followed him, and the Aryan myth provided a philosophical justification for the obscenity of Nazi racism. Nothing as dangerous as this developed amongst the followers of Castrén, but the confusion of race and language has nevertheless clouded the debate about the origins of the Finns. Matti Klinge, a modern Finnish historian writing in 1981, suggests, in the light of the evidence of research into the hereditary nature of blood groups, that three quarters of the present Finnish nation is of western origin, and one third of eastern. 'On the other hand, the linguistic structure of the modern nation shows that the eastern language has been stronger than the western and that a great many inhabitants of Germanic origin have adopted the various dialects of Finnish.' This does not apply, however, to the more recent arrivals from Sweden, whose language survives in present-day Finland.

Contacts between Finland and western Europe during the first millenium AD included the Frisians, who dominated the northern fur trade during the eighth and ninth centuries, and there is evidence of earlier trading relations with the Roman Empire.

In the centuries before Finland entered the period of recorded history, the knowledge of how the Finns lived and what kind of society they had created is derived mainly from archaeology and legend, with occasional references in the records of other peoples who had contact with them. The oral traditions of the folk tales, of which the national epic *Kalevala* is the best known, are an uncertain guide. *Kalevala* itself was not written down until the nineteenth century, although other oral fragments were recorded earlier. Some of the material in Lönnrot's compilation, which dates from 1835, was undoubtedly composed by Lönnrot himself. Nevertheless, used with caution, the evidence gleaned from the oral folk traditions can give a picture of the Finns in their early history. The Estonians have a similar tradition, *Kalevipoeg,* which relates a story of a kindred people who lived in the area to the south of the Gulf of Finland. They present a picture of Iron Age people, who were farmers and fishermen, and who lived in an area where the forests, lakes and an island-studded coast were dominant features of the environment. There are few points at which the impressions gained from *Kalevala* may be directly related to historical events, although Klinge suggests that the Sampo legends, which record the quest of the Finns for a magic talisman, the *Sampo,* may be linked to Finnish participation in plundering raids both into Russia and westward into Scandinavia. The legends relating to the virgin Marjatta who, after swallowing a berry, conceives and bears a child who wields a more powerful magic than that of the great wizard Väinömöinen, may be a poetic allusion to the beginnings of Christianity in Finland.

The people of *Kalevala* refer to themselves as *Suomalaiset,* the name which the Finns still use today. These people lived in the land of Suomi, and the suggestion has been made that the name is derived from the word *suo,* a marsh, but this explanation is contested. The location of Suomi in the legends appears to be in south-west Finland. There were other Finnish-speaking groups who may have been linguistically and ethnically close to the people of Suomi, the nearest relatives being the *Hämäläiset* (Swedish – *Tavasts*). The region of Häme lies inland from the coastal region known as Finland Proper (*Varsinais Suomi*), and in its present form as one of the administrative provinces (*lääni*) of Finland, it extends from Lahti to Tampere, and is governed from the provincial capital of Hämeenlinna (*Tavastehus*). Another group of Finnish speakers, living in the eastern borderlands of Finland and Russia, were the Karelians (*Karjalaiset*) from whom the Kalevalan legends were collected by Elias Lönnrot.

The folk tales recount episodes in a continuous struggle which the people of Suomi wage against the people of *Pohjola*, the North Land, ruled over by the formidable 'Louhi, Pohjola's old mistress, Old and gap-toothed dame of Pohja.' It is possible that the people of the north were the ancestors of the modern Lapps, and that at a time when the Finns were establishing themselves in the southern regions, the Lapps were occupying territory much further to the south of their present homeland. The struggle portrayed in *Kalevala* may represent the driving northward of the original Lapp inhabitants by Finnish invaders.

After about 800 AD Finland was affected by the activities of the Vikings, who sailed eastward from Scandinavia, through the Åland Islands and the archipelagoes of the Gulf of Finland to the Karelian Isthmus and Lake Ladoga. Finnish-speaking tribes lived at this time in Karelia and the area round the head of the Gulf of Finland known as Ingermanland (Finnish – *Inkeri*). Some Finnish speakers accompanied the Vikings in their expeditions into Russia. By 862 AD the Vikings ruled in Novgorod, and twenty years later they were in command of Kiev. In *Decline and Fall of the Roman Empire*, Gibbon suggests that overpopulation in Scandinavia may explain the sudden bursting forth of the Northmen:

> The vast, and as is said, populous regions of Denmark, Sweden and Norway were crowded with independent chieftains . . . Impatient of a bleak climate and narrow limits . . . they explored every coast that promised either spoil or settlement. The Baltic was the first scene of their naval achievements; they visited the eastern shores, the silent residence of Fennic and Sclavonian tribes; and the primitive Russians of Lake Ladoga paid a tribute, the skins of white squirrels, to these strangers whom they saluted with the title of *Varangians*.
>
> (vol. 5, p. 522)

Gibbon later describes how the Varangians formed a guard for the Byzantine emperor:

> With their broad and double edged battle axes on their shoulders, they attended the Greek emperor to the temple, the senate and the

> hippodrome . . . and the keys of the palace, the treasury and the capital, were held by the firm and faithful hands of the Varangians.
> (vol. 5, p. 524)

The Karelian culture, which was stimulated by contacts with Novgorod, was centred on settlements around Lake Ladoga, notably Kexholm (*Käkisalmi*), but it extended into Savo. Karelian traders supplied the market of Novgorod with furs and skins, including those of the white squirrel mentioned by Gibbon. Byzantine motifs influenced the art of the Karelian craftsmen, and the type of jewellery now sold as Kalevalan is derived from models created by them. They also acquired their Orthodox form of Christianity from Byzantium, via Novgorod. Later, Russian monks travelled north to convert the Lapps, and here again it was the Orthodox rite which was adopted, and which survives today amongst the Karelians and the Lapps.

Whilst eastern influences were making headway in these communities, the Finnish speaking tribes in the west – the Suomalaiset and the Hämäläiset – were being influenced by the culture of the west. Missionaries from Sweden visited Finland in the ninth century, and there have been finds of weapons and ornaments bearing Christian symbols which date from the ninth and tenth centuries.

There is little documentary evidence concerning the attempts to Christianize the Finns in the eleventh and twelfth centuries, but fragmentary archaeological evidence suggests that Scandinavian crusaders were at work in Finland. For example, a runic inscription in Sweden, dated from the early eleventh century, refers to a Swedish crusader who died in Tavastland (Häme). There is evidence also of trading activities in which Swedes and Finns participated, especially in the fur trade in Lapland. A group known as the Pirkkalaiset from the village of Pirkkala, now a suburb of Tampere, probably derive their name from a Frisian word, *birek*. The Swedish town of Birca, once more important than Stockholm, was a centre for Frisian fur traders, and the Pirkkalaiset seem to have followed in the same tradition. By the thirteenth century the Pirkkalaiset had a virtual monopoly of trade with Lapland and were given the right by the Swedish crown to collect taxes and to exercise administrative functions in Lapland.

As Finland emerged into the light of European history, it was already an area where competing influences from east and west were at work. And although the western influences were culturally stronger in most aspects of life, the Finns held on tenaciously to their Finno-Ugrian speech, which came from the east.

2

Finland and Sweden

The exact relationship of Sweden to Finland in the twelfth century is not fully understood, as it is based rather on legend and tradition than on historical documents. At this time the Swedish kingdom had been established and in the middle of the twelfth century the throne was occupied by King Erik, a Christian who gave his allegiance to the Roman Church. To the east, the semi-independent state of Novgorod, founded by Vikings in the ninth century and linked to Kiev, was a centre which had commercial ties with the Baltic region and was also a base for a powerful military force. Finland was a buffer zone between the rival powers of Sweden and Novgorod and also came under pressure from the Baltic Germans, who penetrated into the lands south of the Gulf of Finland. The Finns, unlike their powerful neighbours, had not at this time established a state of their own. They were divided between the three main groups – the Suomalaiset, the Hämäläiset and the Karjalaiset who were often in conflict amongst themselves.

The legends tell of a crusade, led by King Erik of Sweden (accompanied by Bishop Henry of Uppsala) in 1155. Henry was an Englishman, originally a monk from Bury St Edmunds, one of three English clerics who had an influence on Finland at this time. The others were Nicholas Breakspear, who was later the first English Pope, and Bishop Thomas, who subdued the Hämäläiset in the early thirteenth century. Henry was left in Finland to consolidate the gains of Erik's crusade when the King was forced to return to Sweden. A popular Finnish ballad recounts how Henry took food from the farm of a certain Lalli, who was away from home when the Bishop called.

Although Henry left money to pay for the supplies he had taken, Lalli was so enraged that he pursued the Bishop, caught up with him as he was crossing the ice on Lake Köyliö in the Kokemäki valley, and killed him. Henry became a martyr in the eyes of the Christian Finns. His body was taken to the church at Nousiainen, near Turku, where it became an object of reverence and of pilgrimages. In the next century a cathedral was built at Turku, the foundations being laid under Bishop Thomas's authority in 1229, and the bones of St Henry were moved there in 1290. The altar is dedicated to St Erik and St Henry and the cathedral houses the offerings brought by Finns to atone for Lalli's crime.

The crusade with which Erik and Henry were associated was not the first attempt to bring Christianity to Finland, but it marks the beginnings of an organized Finnish Church, and there has been a continuous Christian tradition since that time. The crusade was probably prompted by the arrival in Sweden in 1152 or 1153 of Nicholas Breakspear, who was sent by the Pope to strengthen the position of the Church in Scandinavia. Nicholas later became Pope, under the title of Hadrian IV.

A Papal Bull (*Gravis admodum*) issued by Alexander III in 1172 refers to the Finns as part of Christendom, but admonishes them for their lack of obedience to their priests. Apparently they had the reputation of running to the Church for help when their security was threatened by invasion from Novgorod but of forgetting their Christian duty when the danger had passed. Another Papal Bull referring to Finland, *Ex tuorum*, was issued by Innocent III in 1209 and gives instructions to the Archbishop of Lund concerning the appointment of bishops to serve in Finland. The See of Lund was under Danish control and it was the expansionist Danish kingdom which successfully resisted Swedish influence in Estonia, founding the city of Tallinn (Reval) in 1219. The Danes were also in conflict with the Teutonic knights who were encroaching on the eastern coastlands of the Baltic. Finland was subjected to influences from all these sources. There was, for example, a wooden church in Turku, established by the Germans before the founding of the cathedral. However, it was the Swedes who eventually became predominant in all but eastern Finland, where Byzantine influence via Kiev and Novgorod still held sway.

Bishop Thomas, another Englishman, came to Finland from Uppsala in 1220, shortly after the responsibility for the Church in Finland was transferred by the Papacy from the Danish See of Lund. Although nominally under the authority of Uppsala during Thomas's episcopacy (1220–45), the Church in Finland was in fact virtually autonomous, under the direct authority of Rome.

The Finnish Church became independent of the Swedish civil power in matters concerning taxation and the discipline of the clergy. It also acquired some authority over the civil population in the punishment of serious crimes. At about this time the Dominicans established a monastery at Naantali, and although there are today only a few monastic remains in the south-west of the country, the Dominicans had a profound influence on the development of Christianity in mediaeval Finland.

Thomas was Bishop of Turku and until the Reformation the diocese of Turku was in effect the centre of both religious and civil authority in Finland. Thomas encountered some resistance from the people of Häme when he attempted to impose a strict regime upon them, and in 1236 there was a revolt, which was suppressed with some severity.

A Swedish knight, Birger Jarl, a brother-in-law of the King, was called in to subdue Häme and to strengthen Swedish power in central Finland. Birger Jarl built the castle of Hämeenlinna (Tavastehus) in a strategic position, commanding the main east–west route along the Salpausselkä moraine, and the city of Hämeenlinna developed within its shadow. Following Birger Jarl's expedition – sometimes called a crusade – Swedish settlers came to colonize the coastal regions of south-west Finland and the coast of the Gulf of Finland as far as Porvoo (Borgå), and it is from this period that the Swedish-speaking element in Finnish society originated.

The Swedes were well entrenched in Finland when the rulers of Novgorod made sorties into Finland, which were strongly resisted. The Novgorod Chronicles and contemporary Swedish accounts give a confused picture of raids and counter attacks across territory in which there were no clear demarcation lines. Whilst the Russians were preoccupied with the Mongol invasions the Swedes were able to push eastward to the Neva. However, Alexander Nevski, Prince of Novgorod, held them on the line of the Neva in 1240 and went on to defeat the Teutonic knights in Estonia. In 1241 the Mongol horde called off its advance into Europe. Although the Swedes, under Birger Jarl, advanced again in 1249, the Russians held on to the Neva. In 1293 the Swedish Marshal, Tyrgils Knutson, founded a castle at Viipuri in order to hold the eastern marcher lands and especially to dominate the vital isthmus of Karelia, which controls entry to Finland from the east. Even so, in 1311 an expedition from Novgorod reached Häme, and a few years later took Turku. The to and fro movement of armies over the body of Finland was stabilized in 1323 by the signing by Sweden and Novgorod of the Peace of Pähkinäsaari (also known by its Swedish name, Nöteborg and its German name, Schlüsselburg), which fixed the frontier along a line running northwest from a point near the present site of St Petersburg to the neighbourhood of Oulu. The fortress of Viipuri remained in Swedish hands. This treaty, which is one of the oldest written documents in the Swedish archives, defined the eastern frontiers of Finland for over 250 years. It ushered in a period of relative peace, during which it was possible for Swedish influences to establish themselves in the south-western half of Finland. With Swedish rule came Roman Catholicism and trade and cultural links with Western Europe. The area of Finnish territory remaining under the rule of Novgorod (and later of Muscovy and Russia) was subjected to eastern influences, and the Eastern Orthodox Church commanded the allegiance of the Karelians.

Pähkinäsaari did not end the rivalries between the Swedes and the Russians in Finland. Twenty years later, Birgitta of Sweden led a crusade to bring the Karelians within the embrace of the Roman Church. The army of Swedes, Finns and Teutonic knights who joined together in the name of Christendom were ultimately forced to abandon their attempt, not so much because they were defeated by the forces of Novgorod, but because of an outbreak of plague. Peace was signed at Tartu (Dorpat) in 1351, and for two centuries thereafter there was no serious challenge to the supremacy of the Scandinavians in Finland. The frontier agreed upon in 1323 was not a sharp demarcation line, but rather a vaguely defined zone – a no man's land – which was frequently transgressed by traders, fisherfolk, trappers, herders and missionaries. The activities of the Pirkkalaiset (Birkarlar), were often the subject of disputes between the Swedes and the Russians and even between the Bishops of Uppsala and Turku, because the adventurous Pirkkalaiset claimed rights in Lapland which were not always accepted by their neighbours.

The Finns to the west of the Pähkinäsaari line who came under the influence of Swedish culture and the Roman Catholic Church were open to influences from the mainstream of European civilization which penetrated into Finland. These influences came not only from Sweden but also from the German settlers in Estonia, who came under the control of the Teutonic knights in the middle of the fourteenth century. German traders from the Hanseatic League also made contacts with Finland via the Baltic and the Gulf of Finland. Viipuri developed as a staple town, controlling trade between Sweden and Novgorod and there were also Danish traders who sent goods through Finland and Estonia. Some five years after the signing of the Treaty of Pähkinäsaari, an Orthodox monastery was founded on the island of Valamo (Valaam) in Lake Ladoga. It became a centre of piety and learning within the Russian Orthodox Church and remained so for six centuries. In 1944, as a consequence of the frontier changes at the end of the Second World War, the community moved to Finland, taking with it the incomparable treasures of its library.

The fact that the mediaeval Karelians referred to their cousins on the other side of the line as 'Swedes' prompted the modern historian Matti Klinge to suggest that 'administrative and religious factors proved to be stronger than a common ancestry in the shaping of the nation's culture'. The Pähkinäsaari line through southern Karelia remained unchanged for three centuries, shifting eastward in 1617 to incorporate half of Lake Ladoga, including the island of Valamo, in Finland, under the terms of the Treaty of Stolbova, negotiated between Sweden and Russia in 1617. The transfer to Sweden of the area known as Kexholms Län (Käkisalmi Lääni) and of the Inkeri district south of the Neva represented the high water mark of the Swedish advance against Russia.

During the three centuries between Pähkinäsaari and Stolbova Finland became firmly tied to the Swedish Crown. In the early years the influence of the Church was strong, not only in spiritual matters, but also in the civil organization of mediaeval society. During the fourteenth century Swedish laws and administrative practices gradually established themselves in Finland. The right of Finnish representatives to take part in the election of Swedish kings was recognized in 1362 and the Finns, organized in the traditional mediaeval four estates (nobles, clergy, burghers and peasants), were consulted by the king when he found it convenient to do so. There were many changes in the roles of Council of the Realm (*riksråd*) which origially represented the great magnates, the Diet of the Four Estates (*riksdag*), which evolved later and the Swedish Crown. Finland was involved in all these developments and played its part in the elaboration of the Swedish constitution.

The Scandinavian administrative unit adopted from Sweden, the hundred (Swedish *härad*) was first known in Finland in the twelfth century and the continued use of the name Satakunta (*Sata* – hundred, *kunta* – commune) during the next 800 years for the area inland from Pori is a reminder of the beginnings of Swedish rule in Finland. Large-scale Swedish colonization began in the thirteenth century, along the coastal fringes of the Gulfs of Bothnia and Finland, in areas later known as Uusimaa (Swedish Nyland), Varsinais Suomi (Finland Proper), and Pohjanmaa (Ostrobothnia) as well as on the Åland Islands between Sweden and Finland. For the most part the Swedes settled coastlands which were not intensively used by the Finns – whose main centres of population were further inland – and there was little friction between the two linguistic communities. They shared common religious traditions, were under the same administration and complemented rather than competed with each other.

The struggle for supremacy in the Baltic which raged intermittently from the fourteenth to the seventeenth century did not leave Finland unscathed. The chief actors were the Danes, who controlled access to the Baltic via the Sound; Germanic groups, including the Teutonic Knights and the Hanseatic traders; the Swedes, and the Slavs – at first of Novgorod, but later of Muscovy and Poland. The motives which impelled the protagonists were trade, religion and imperial expansion. The battle-ground extended from the southern shores of the Baltic to Estonia, Inkeri (Ingermanland), Karelia and Finland itself.

The territorial expansion of Finland progressed gradually during the fourteenth and fifteenth centuries. The somewhat vague provisions of the Treaty of Pähkinäsaari provided an opportunity for encroachments in Savo, where Finnish-speaking peasants followed a primitive, semi-nomadic form of agriculture, based on the practice of burn-beating. An area of forest was cleared by cutting and burning and the land thus recovered was farmed for a few seasons until its fertility declined. It was then abandoned, and new clearings were made some distance from the original site, which was allowed to revert to scrub and secondary growth. A poetic version of this somewhat wasteful procedure is described in the national folk epic, *Kalevala*. The hero, Väinämöinen has tried in vain to get his barley seeds to germinate, but an eagle comes to the rescue:

> Then the bird of air struck fire,
> And the flames rose up in brightness,
> While the north wind fanned the forest
> . . .
> All the trees were burned to ashes,
> Till the sparks were quite extinguished.
> Then the aged Väinämöinen
> Took the six seeds from his satchel
> . . .
> Then he went to sow the country.

Väinämöinen returns to his newly sown fields, and

> There he found the barley growing,
> And the ears were all six cornered.
>
> (*Kalevala*, Everyman's Library, Rune II, pp. 17 and 19)

When the area of operation had been extended well into the no man's land along the eastern borders, the protection of a powerful magnate would be extended to the newly colonized areas. Thus, in the 1470s, a representative of the powerful Tott family, Erik Axelsson Tott, who was lord of the thirteenth-century castle of Viipuri (Viborg), built the impressive fortress of Olavinlinna, on an island between two branches of the Saimaa lake system. Olavinlinna, magnificently preserved, stands today within the city boundary of Savonlinna, the capital of the historic province of Savo. When it was built it lay in the disputed territory between Sweden and Muscovy, the Slav state which in the fifteenth century took control of the trading republic of Novgorod.

Infiltration across the ill-defined Pähkinäsaari line also occurred in the far north, where Swedish and Finnish settlers moved into Ostrobothnia and Lapland in search of salmon and furs. One group of traders who played an important part in this movement were the people known as *Pirkkalaiset* (Birkarlar). They were fur trappers, hunters and fishermen who came originally from Sweden and occupied the settlement of Pirkkala, on the shores of Pyhäjärvi, a few kilometres to the west of the present city of Tampere. In 1277 the Swedish king gave the Pirkkalaiset the right to tax the Lapps and to fish in the waters of Lapland. In return, the King received payment in furs and skins. The privileges of the Pirkkalaiset were later revoked by the Swedish king Gustavus Vasa in 1550, when he repossessed the rights his predecessors had granted almost three centuries earlier. In their heyday the Pirkkalaiset were a powerful trading guild, and indulged in profitable commercial activities beyond the hunting and trapping activities in Lapland for which they had been licensed by the Swedish crown. The illegal practice of *landsköp* (rural trading), for example, was carried on by the Pirkkalaiset, despite efforts made to stamp it out by successive kings, from the time of Magnus Eriksson in the fourteenth century. Provisions in the law codes (*landslag*) even demanded the death penalty for those who infringed the trading monopolies of the staple towns, especially by trading directly in imported goods, such as salt, spices and cloth, with people living in the countryside.

The same process of infiltration, combined with the building of castles by noblemen in order to consolidate the gains thus achieved, took place in the northern lands beyond the Pähkinäsaari line. The position was complicated in this area by the rival claims of the Swedes and the Danes and between the bishoprics of Turku and Uppsala. A further problem was that the northern shore of the Gulf of Bothnia around the mouth of the Kemi river was claimed by Novgorod, together with an indeterminate area of Lapland. A meeting in 1346 between the two bishops resulted in a division of the area between the two dioceses, in which it was agreed that the boundary between them would run along the watershed between the Kemi river and the Kaakama river, which in its lower course flows parallel to the Kemi, two kilometres to the west. Thus, the whole of the Kemi river belonged to Turku, whilst the Tornio, which enters the Gulf of Bothnia 15 kilometres to the west of the Kemi, was in the area assigned to Uppsala. This boundary, which came to be recognized as the dividing line between Sweden and Finland, remained until the Grand Duchy of Finland was incorporated into the Tsarist Russian Empire in 1809. The two bishops had totally ignored the claims of Novgorod and of the Karelian subjects of the Slav city, and the aggrieved parties refused to accept the settlement. However, they were unable to enforce their claims, although they made frequent forays into the disputed area.

Further north, in Lapland, the claims of the Danes and of Norwegian nobles to exact tribute from the nomadic Lapps conflicted with those of the Swedes and Novgorodians, and there was constant friction during the fourteenth, fifteenth and sixteenth centuries. In 1319 Norway and Sweden were united under a common ruler and in 1397 the Union of Kalmar brought the Danes together with their two Scandinavian neighbours. However, this union did not end the rivalries between the various parties over the right to exploit Lapland and its native Sami inhabitants.

During the fourteenth century a struggle developed in Sweden between the nobility and the king. The Swedish aristocracy elected their kings and, although many of the rulers acted autocratically and rode roughshod over those who had elected them, there was a point beyond which the nobles could not be pushed. Finland became a pawn in the struggle between the crown and the nobles. Magnus Eriksson had greater influence in Finland than did his nobles, and he encouraged the development of the economy of Finland and the settlement of remote areas in the interior, partly as a means of securing for himself an income independent from the powerful magnates, who had greater sway in Sweden. Magnus was also responsible for strengthening the rule of Swedish law in Finland. It had been a practice for Swedish kings to award duchies to leading nobles, especially those of royal blood. These duchies, nominally subordinate to the Crown, often became virtually independent power bases in which the king's law hardly ran. Magnus created a considerable stir in 1353 by awarding Finland as a duchy to a noble who was not a member of the royal family but whom he considered to be a reliable servant who would carry out the king's wishes. The nobles rebelled and forced the king to share his royal authority with two of his sons. In the election of 1362, which raised Magnus's son Haakon to his kingly status, the right of Finland to send its representatives was recognized. The Bishop of Turku came as the voice of the clergy and a member of the Bielke family, who was considered to be a rebel, was chosen as *lagman*, or chief magistrate, to represent the laity. The Bielke family have been described by one writer on Swedish history as being part of 'the high aristocracy, those twenty or thirty families whose names are writ large on every page of Swedish history.'

The power of the nobles showed itself again in 1364, when the unfortunate Haakon and his family were overthrown, and the leading nobles invited a German prince, Albert of Mecklenburg, to ascend the Swedish throne. The new ruler was not welcomed in Finland, and to consolidate their rule, the Germans embarked on a programme of castle building to assist them in subduing the population. After ten years control of Finland fell to a Swedish aristocrat, Grip, who ruled until 1386. Grip acquired, through purchase and diplomacy, the overlordship of provinces in Sweden and Finland as personal possessions, but he also secured the post of *lagman*, which gave him official status under the Swedish constitution. He was able to operate in virtual independence of the king, because of the relative isolation of Finland from Sweden. At this time the main means of contact between Sweden and Finland was by sea, and for long periods in the winter ice in the Baltic and the Gulf of Bothnia made sea transport impossible. With inadequate means of communication the Swedish kings found it extremely difficult to establish their authority in Finland, and they had little choice but to tolerate a considerable degree of *de facto* autonomy. During the fifteenth century it became customary for Finland to hold its own separate electoral assembly in Turku for the swearing of oaths of loyalty to a new king when he could not make an appearance in person – often because the royal progress across the Baltic was prevented by adverse weather.

The formation of the Union of Kalmar in 1397 removed the centre of royal authority from Stockholm to Copenhagen and emphasized the remoteness of Finland. The first sovereign of the united kingdom was Queen Margaret of Denmark, who had overthrown the German dynasty of Mecklenburg in 1389, having intervened at the request of a group of rebellious Swedish nobles. The new Queen awarded the government of Finland to her foster-son, Erik of Pomerania, who was made co-sovereign with his mother, and on her death in 1412 he succeeded to the throne of the joint Scandinavian kingdom.

During Erik's reign Finland's position as a distinct political unit with a degree of local autonomy was enhanced by changes in the administration of justice. A Finnish Supreme Court was established, whose members were made up of the bishop and representatives of the clergy, together with the nobles residing in Finland who were members of the Swedish Council of the Realm (the *riksråd*) and a number of judges from the Finnish courts. Juries could be empanelled from members of the nobility and the peasantry. The authority of the new court extended beyond the dispensing of justice and touched on administrative matters and wider issues of government.

Under the new dispensation, a locally based aristocracy in Finland began to exercise considerable power. Some of its members were military governors of castles – such as those at Turku, Korsholm near Vaasa, and Viipuri on the eastern frontier. Others held positions in the royal administrative machinery – as *lagman* or as justices. One example was the Fleming family, whose rise to the status of a leading magnate dynasty began with the appointment of the founder as Chief Justice of Finland in the fifteenth century. The office was used to build up a family power-base in the province, and in the 1590s Klaes Fleming was the virtual ruler of Finland, powerful enough to attempt the role of king-maker in the dynastic civil war of that decade. Although his faction lost the struggle, his descendants transferred their loyalty to the winners, and a series of Flemings held high office under the Vasa kings of the seventeenth century.

The Fleming family lasted for a longer time at the centre of affairs in Finland and Sweden than did some other nobles who exercised power for a time during the fifteenth and sixteenth centuries. An attempt was made in the 1440s by one called Bonde, son of Karl Knut, to detach Finland from the Scandinavian Union. He did not achieve this, nor did he succeed in making himself master of all Finland. He did, however, accept from King Christopher (Kristoffer) a fiefdom which covered eastern Finland, and in 1442 he took control of Viipuri castle. This was of vital importance to the trade with Novgorod, and provided a useful income as well as being a power base in the defence of the eastern frontier. In 1448, on the death of Christopher, Bonde was elected King, and reigned as Charles VIII.

Charles later abdicated and returned to the throne on three occasions. After his second abdication he retired for a few years to Finland, where he governed as a feudal lord from his castle at Raseborg (Raasepori), which stands on the Salpausselkä ridge, near Tammisaari (Ekenäs) on the south-west coast of Finland.

Charles was replaced as king of the Scandinavian Union by Christian I, a Danish prince, but was returned to the throne for the third and last time with the help of the Tott family, whose power base was in Finland, although their origins were in Denmark. They had briefly supported Christian, but changed their allegiance and successfully supported the restoration of Charles VIII. When Charles died in 1470 the Totts had already become the effective rulers of Finland. One brother, Laurens, took the castle at Raseborg (Raasepori); another, Ivar, received the castle of Korsholm (Mustasaari) near Vaasa as part of his marriage settlement to Charles' daughter; and a third had taken control of Viipuri castle during the earlier troubles in the 1460s.

The reign of the Totts came to an end in the 1480s, following the death in 1481 of Erik Axelsson Tott, the lord of Viipuri. The Swedish regent, Sten Sture, who succeeded Charles VIII, took charge of Finland and for a time re-established royal authority over the powerful lords who had until then behaved as though Finland was independent of Sweden. There were, however, serious threats to the integrity of both Sweden and Finland from neighbouring countries. These pressures were part of the struggle for hegemony in the Baltic, and for control of the lucrative trade routes through the Baltic to Russia.

In 1472 the trading city of Novgorod fell to the forces of Ivan III of Moscow, and the expansionist Muscovites posed a far greater danger to Finland than Novgorod. Sten Sture had problems at home in attempting to assert royal authority over his own nobility. The practice by which a king granted a nobleman the right to administer a district (*län*) nominally in the king's name and to collect taxes within his domain (known as *förläning*), created a class of powerful and virtually independent nobles who could defy the king. In Finland Sten Sture began his reign with an advantage. The powerful Tott family had been removed from power and the king replaced them in their castles with bailiffs who were directly responsible to him. However, faced with pressures from Denmark in the south and Moscow in the east (who became allies in 1493), he was forced to revert to the system of *förläning* in order to muster support. He also sought allies abroad, from as far away as the Netherlands, because Dutch traders were showing a lively interest in the Baltic trade. He encouraged his commander in Finland, Knut Posse, to enlist help from the Teutonic knights and from the Jagellonians of Poland, who were sworn enemies of Moscow.

After the death of Casimir IV of Poland in 1492, Poland endured a period of internal disruption and was also involved in war with the Turks and was unable to participate in what was intended to be a crusade against the Muscovites. In Finland, Bishop Mauno (Magnus) of Turku (known as Särkilahti) was encouraged by Pope Alexander VI to regard the conflict with Moscow as a crusade by Catholic Europe against the Eastern Orthodox, but the bishop and Knut Posse were left very much to their own devices in resisting the Slav onslaught. Although they successfully repelled an attack on the fortress of Viipuri in 1495 – supposedly with the miraculous help of St Andrew – the Russians advanced far into Finland before peace was concluded in 1497. Sten Sture, whose credibility had been undermined by his mismanagement of the campaign in Finland, was overthrown from his regency of the Scandinavian kingdom and was sent into retirement in Finland. His successor, Hans of Denmark, was unpopular amongst the nobles in Finland, not the least because of his alliance with Moscow as well as his attempts to remove the influence of Sten Sture. The Finns turned to the Swedish regents and to their local lords for support against the Danish ruler, and a civil war broke out within the Scandinavian Union. The Danes raided the coasts of southern Finland, capturing the Åland Islands and desecrating Turku.

During the early sixteenth century the effective ruler of Finland was Bielke, son of Erik Ture who, as lord of Viipuri, was responsible for the defence of the eastern frontier. By skilful diplomacy and a strong commercial sense, he managed to keep at bay the pressure from the Hanseatic merchants, Teutonic knights and Swedish and Danish rulers who were attempting to involve Finland in war with Russia. Bielke managed to keep the trade routes to Russia open and to secure from the Muscovites a re-affirmation of the Pähkinäsaari line as far as the eastern boundary of Finland.

Bielke died in 1511, but his successors continued his policies, supported by the new regent (*riksförestandar*) of Sweden, Sten Sture the Younger, who became ruler of Sweden on the death of his father in 1512. Young Herr Sten raised the status of the Riksdag as an instrument of policy making and encouraged the Estates to work with the ruler – sometimes against the senior nobility represented in the *riksråd*. Sture supported the Finnish nobles – amongst whom were the descendants of the Totts – and raised one of them, Åke Tott, to the status of Governor of Finland. The Finns returned their ruler's confidence and when, in 1520, Christian II of Denmark assumed overlordship of Sweden, they rallied round Herr Sten in resisting the Danish invasion. Christian tricked his opponents into accepting a settlement, which he promptly repudiated. Some of the Totts and other supporters of Sture were executed when they went to Stockholm for Christian's coronation, and others were expelled from their castles in Finland, and later executed. Most of the old leaders of Finland were swept away and the way was prepared for the radical changes which took place during the reign of Gustavus Vasa, who came to the throne in 1523 and died in 1560.

Gustavus Vasa and the beginnings of the Reformation

During the reign of Gustavus far-reaching changes were introduced which deeply affected Finland. The new king broke with Rome and launched Catholic Finland and Sweden on the road which led to the adoption of Lutheranism as the established religion of the state. The last Catholic bishop of Uppsala, Magnus Johannes, died in exile. His brother Claus Magnus (1490–1557) established Lutheranism as the official religion.

The Reformation led to the translation of religious texts and other books into the vernacular languages. The break up of the Union of Kalmar separated Sweden–Finland from Norway and Denmark and increased the tendency towards national identification, to which the Reformation gave further cultural and religious impetus. The creation of a Duchy of Finland, governed by one of the king's sons, was a piece of dynastic politics, without any wider significance, although later nationalist historians tried, anachronistically, to present it as an indication that a distinct Finnish national identity already existed in the sixteenth century. Contemporary commentators assumed that Finland, along with Svealand and Götaland, constituted the three core territories of the crown of Sweden, which enjoyed parity of status within the common legal and constitutional structure of the kingdom.

The Finnish language, despite the fact that it was not yet a vehicle for a national literature, was the language of the local parish churches and of the rich oral folk traditions, while Swedish was the language of the nobility and the senior clergy. For a century and a half before the Reformation all the bishops had been born in Finland, although not all were from Finnish-speaking families. The nobility included Swedes, Danes and Germans who had settled in Finland, but a high proportion were born in Finland and many spoke Finnish. Finland, as part of Catholic Europe, shared the common cultural heritage of Christendom. Many Finnish students studied in the universities of western Europe, especially in Paris and later at Wittenberg, Rostock, Giessen and Frankfurt on Oder. The University of Uppsala, originally founded in 1477, ceased to exist in the early sixteenth century and, despite an attempt by the Lutheran theologian Philip Melanchthom in 1539 to persuade Gustavus Vasa to refound it as a Lutheran institution, it was not until 1593 that Uppsala was re-established. Throughout the sixteenth century there was nowhere in the Swedish realm where students from Finland could obtain a university education.

Many of them received scholarships financed from church funds to go to universities abroad. The favourite place for Finnish and Swedish students, especially after the Reformation, was Rostock.

One of the most important Finns to study at Wittenberg was Michael Agricola, who was taught there by Melanchthon and by Luther himself. When Michael returned to Finland he began to translate religious texts into Finnish. In keeping with the Lutheran tradition he felt that the ordinary people should have access to the Bible in their own language, and Agricola's translation of the New Testament into Finnish, published in 1548, 27 years after Luther's appearance at the Diet of Worms, was the effective beginning of the Reformation in Finland and also of Finnish as a literary language. Other Finnish clerics who had been affected by Luther's teachings whilst they were studying in Germany were Pietari Särkilahti and Paavali Juusten. However, it was not until 1642 that the first complete translation of the Bible into Finnish, by Eskil Petraeus, appeared in Stockholm.

In 1554 Finland was divided into two bishoprics. Agricola became Bishop of Turku and eastern Finland was placed in the care of the Bishop of Viipuri. Juusten, who was the first holder of the Viipuri See, translated religious texts into Finnish. Sweden's break with Rome came in 1524, when Gustavus Vasa, during a dispute with Pope Clement VII over the appointment of bishops, filled some vacant bishoprics with nominees of his own without first obtaining papal consent. Gustavus Vasa confiscated church properties, following a resolution of the Västerås Riksdag of 1527, a decade earlier than Henry VIII in England dissolved the monasteries. The establishment of the Lutheran Church as the official religion of Sweden and Finland was not secured until the Uppsala Convention of 1593, and the process of enforcing the Reformation throughout the kingdom lasted well into the seventeenth century.

The succession of Duke Charles (Karl), a son of Gustavus Vasa, who later became King Charles IX, was disputed by the Polish branch of the Vasa family, represented by Sigismund, then King of Poland. Sigismund was a Roman Catholic and was seen by Catholic Europe as being the torch bearer in the north for the Counter-Reformation. Sigismund was accepted by the Riksdag, but his authority in Sweden was undermined by Charles, who in 1595 persuaded the three lower estates of the Riksdag to declare him administrator of Sweden. Charles was believed to have Calvinist leanings, but even if he was not a thoroughgoing Lutheran, he was certainly no friend of the Roman Catholics. Charles had been influential in securing at the Convention of Uppsala in 1593 a declaration of support for the principles of Lutheranism, as set out in the Convention of Augsburg of 1530.

Support for the Catholic cause was stronger in Finland than in Sweden, especially amongst the nobility, who distrusted Charles' centralizing tendencies, and who favoured the link with Poland. Charles supported a rising of Finnish peasants in 1597, known as the Club War (the peasants used clubs to attack their lords), but he was unable to prevent the ruthless suppression of the uprising. The Finnish nobles gave support to Sigismund, when he landed at Kalmar in 1598, but he suffered an initial setback at the Battle of Stangebro and returned to Poland, leaving Charles the master of Sweden. The Finnish fortresses held out against Charles for a time, but were eventually subdued. Sigismund was deposed as king of Sweden in 1599, but Charles, who was thenceforward effectively the ruler of Sweden, was not declared king until 1603 and was not crowned until 1607.

In religious matters Charles was no theologian and was not greatly interested in church doctrine. He was more concerned with the exercise of power. Although the church had won the right to elect its own bishops – the Church Ordinance of 1571 decreed that bishops were to be chosen by 'the clergy and others who may be experienced in these matters' – Charles was quite prepared to act without consulting the clergy if it suited him. In 1607, for example, he appointed Laurentius Gothus to the bishopric of Turku entirely on his own authority.

The long-drawn-out process by which the Protestant Reformation established itself in Sweden and Finland during the sixteenth and early seventeenth centuries had a debilitating effect on the role of the church in social and cultural life. Although there were many prominent individuals in the church – such as Michael Agricola, Mauno (Magnus) Särkilahti and Paavali Juusten – the general cultural level of the parish priests was low. For over forty years, from 1583 to 1625, the leadership of the Finnish church, apart from a break in 1607–9, was in the hands of Bishop Erik Sorolainen, who has been described as 'lacking in energy and administrative talents', and who was unable to give the leadership which an unruly and demoralized clergy needed. There were doctrinal disputes, not only between Catholics and Protestants, but also amongst various factions within Lutheranism and between Lutherans and Calvinists. Sorolainen was timid and conservative in his attitude to the reformed faith, and was unwilling to abandon what strict Lutherans would have regarded as popish rituals. Agricola, in the preface to his Finnish translation of the New Testament, refers to the inadequacies of the Finnish clergy, who were accused of teaching their flocks in 'a manner that is both nasty and lazy'. Forty years later they seem to have become worse, for one historian describes them as being 'drunkards, debauched violators of the laws of man and God, and worse'. Although Sorolainen promoted the publication of religious works in Finnish, it seems that he did little else during his long incumbency to promote the spiritual and material welfare of the church in Finland.

Sorolainen's successor, Isaak Rothovius, who had studied at Wittenberg, was a man of energy and vision who breathed new life into the Finnish church. He was appointed Bishop of Turku in 1627 and died in 1652. During this quarter of a century Lutheranism became firmly rooted in Finnish culture. One of the first tasks which Rothovius set himself was to eradicate superstition, witchcraft and black magic, which appear to have been endemic in Finland, probably being survivals from pagan times, but reinforced by corruption or popish practices. The Finns had an unenviable reputation as magicians, and were believed to have the power to slay their enemies at a distance of hundreds of miles by employing a magic bullet (*Finnskott*), and the shamanistic activities of the Lapps were believed to include the ability to control the winds, to the discomfiture of hostile sailors. Belief in astrology was not confined to the peasantry and their uncouth clergy. Even Charles IX had been impressed by the claims of Laurentius Gothus – who was Bishop of Turku in 1607–9 – to be able to read the future from the behaviour of heavenly bodies.

Rothovius valued education as an instrument of reform, and he did much to enhance the role of the church in education in Finland, both at parish and at university level. Åbo Academy (Turku University) received its royal charter in 1640. The university built up an excellent library and was soon recognized as being the major centre of learning in Finland. It was no longer necessary for Finnish students to travel abroad for their university education. Unfortunately, the university and its library were destroyed in a disastrous fire, which swept through the town in 1827. The following year the national university was reestablished in Helsinki, which had replaced Turku as the capital of Finland in 1819.

Finland and the struggle for supremacy in northern Europe

During more than half of the century from 1550 to 1650 Sweden–Finland was involved in disastrous wars. The issues which particularly concerned Finland were the stability of the eastern frontier and the resolution of the rivalries between several contenders for the lucrative eastern trade which passed through the Baltic. Another struggle which loomed on the horizon was the struggle for supremacy in Europe between the Catholic empire of the Habsburgs, the inheritors of the Holy Roman Empire, and the rising Protestant nations of northern Europe, of which Sweden was the most prominent. Finland, because it was under the Swedish crown, inevitably became involved in the wars which raged in Europe between the Catholic and Protestant powers.

On Finland's eastern frontier the struggle now was primarily with Muscovy, after the absorption of Novgorod by Ivan the Great between 1465 and 1488; although in Lapland Danes and Norwegians vied with Swedes for the right to establish trading posts and to tax the Sami people. Early in the sixteenth century a Russian monk, Trifon, founded an Orthodox monastery at Petsamo (Pechenga) on the Arctic coast, and in 1556 Ivan VI (known to Russians as Ivan Groznii – the Stern – but in English as Ivan the Terrible) gave the monastery a grant of land, covering large areas of the Kola Peninsula and, of more concern to the Scandinavians, territory to the west of the Pasvik river which flows out of Lake Inari. This western area included lands which had traditionally been regarded as belonging to Norway. In 1537 the Danish king became ruler of Norway, so that it was the Danish King Frederick II who took up arms on behalf of his Norwegian subjects in Lapland. He sent two expeditions to the area in the 1580s and in 1586 laid claim to the whole of Lapland. Sweden contested these claims, and extracted from the Russians an agreement that the Swedish-Russian frontier in the Arctic should run through Lake Inari and reach the Arctic Ocean at Varanger Fjord, some 40 kilometres west of the mouth of the Pasvik river.

The position of the Swedish crown had been greatly strengthened in the north lands by the decrees of Gustavus Vasa in the 1550s which extinguished the rights of the Pirkkalaiset and declared all the lands not in private ownership to belong to the crown. The quarrel with Denmark dated back to the break-up of the union of the three crowns in 1523. The attempt of Frederick II of Denmark to restore the Kalmar Union began an invasion of Sweden in 1563, which led to the Seven Years War of the North. Before it was over, Erik XIV of Sweden had been deposed in 1568, being succeeded by John III, who made peace with Denmark in 1570. The Danes had the better of the land fighting, but the Swedes inflicted naval defeats on the invaders. One of the issues which divided the two countries was the control of the trade of the Gulf of Finland. The Treaty of Stettin, which ended the war, would have deprived Sweden of the territory which it had conquered, but the Swedes evaded this condition of the treaty. During the next few years Sweden allied itself with Poland, then ruled by Stephen Batory, and together they overran Estonia and Livonia. Meanwhile the Swedish commander in Finland, Pontus de la Gardie, captured Käkisalmi (Kexholm) on Lake Ladoga in 1580.

At the Treaty of Täysinä in 1595 a long period of war with the Russians came to a temporary halt. Although they relinquished their gains in the Ladoga area, the Swedes won concessions from the Russians regarding the demarcation of the frontier in the Arctic, and the right to tax the Sami people. They also gained recognition of their possession of Estonia. In return they acknowledged Russian rights in the Kola and Fisherman's Peninsulas. Russian claims to a foothold in the gulf of Bothnia were abandoned and Sweden's right of access to the Arctic coast was recognized. Although the Swedes had repulsed the Russians they still had to contend with their Scandinavian neighbours, the Danes.

Russia was at this time preoccupied with internal troubles. Ivan IV's son, Fyodor (1584–98), the last of the Rurikid rulers, has been described as 'a weakling and a bigot.' The Tatar adventurer, Boris Godunov, became Tsar but after his death in 1605 there was a period of uncertainty during which the Polish king, Sigismund III, a member of the Swedish house of Vasa, intrigued in order to secure the Russian throne. A national revolt led by the Russian patriarch resulted in 1613 in the enthronement of the 17-year-old Mikhail I, the founder of the Romanov dynasty who ruled jointly with his father, Patriarch Filaret, until 1633. Thus at the time of the Treaty of Täysinä in 1595, and for some years afterwards, Russia could offer no serious resistance to the Swedes.

The greatest loss which Sweden sustained by the Treaty of Stettin was the loss of the fortress of Älvsborg, near the present site of Göteborg. This was to be returned to Sweden on payment of a ransom, which John managed to settle by raising taxes, through a resolution of the lower houses of the Riksdag in 1571. Sweden and Denmark were again at war in 1611–13 in the Kalmar War – so called because the first Danish victory in the campaign was the fall of the Baltic port of Kalmar, facing the island of Öland. In 1612 the fortress of Älvsborg again fell to the Danes, giving them control of the shipping into the port of Göteborg (founded in 1607), and effectively blocking Sweden's contacts by sea with potential allies in the west, such as Holland and England. This was an inauspicious start to the reign of Gustavus Adolphus, who succeeded his father, Charles IX a few months after the outbreak of war. The Peace of Knäred, which ended the war in 1613, left the Danes in control of Älvsborg and Göteborg until such time as the Swedes paid an indemnity of 10 *tunnor* of gold (one million *riksdaler*), to be paid in four equal instalments, beginning in 1616. Sweden was also obliged to make concessions in the Arctic, which to some extent weakened the position which had been gained at Täysinä in 1595.

The Treaty of Täysinä did not end the troubles on the Russian frontier. In the confused situation following the death of Boris Godunov in 1605, the Poles, supporting the claims of Dimitrii, one of the claimants to the throne, captured the fortresses of Pskov, Ivangorod, Nöteborg (Pähkinäsaari) and Käkisalmi (Kexholm) which gave them control of the frontier region bordering Finland and Estonia. The Polish leader in this area, Lisowski, acted independently of King Sigismund, but this was little consolation to the Swedes, who mistrusted Sigismund's intentions towards both Russia and Sweden. Charles IX entered into an understanding with Vasilii Shuiskii, who overthrew Dimitrii and who reigned as Tsar from 1606 until 1610. One of the first fruits of those contacts was the signing of the Treaty of Viipuri in 1608. Charles pledged to deliver 5,000 Swedish troops, under the command of Jakob de la Gardie in return for a Russian reaffirmation of the Treaty of Täysinä, with the exception that Russia would return the fortress of Käkisalmi, which had been given to Russia in 1595.

Sigismund, the head of the older branch of the Vasa family, saw in the Treaty of Viipuri a potential threat to the Polish position in Russia. Sigismund had ambitions, either to ascend the Russian throne himself, or to see his son Władisław as Tsar. In 1610 it appeared that Sigismund had won. A combined force of Swedish and foreign mercenary troops, under Jakob de la Gardie, and of Russians, led by Tsar Vasilii Shuiskii, was defeated by the Poles at the Battle of Klušino and the Poles went on to take Moscow and depose Shuiskii. The Treaty of Viipuri seemed to be a dead letter. Under Polish pressure the boyars chose Władisław as Tsar, after he had agreed to respect the Orthodox faith. Sigismund dreamt of a Polish–Russian alliance against Sweden which would eventually recover the Swedish throne for his branch of the Vasa family.

The Poles soon became unpopular in Russia and Sigismund's victory proved to be hollow. Within a year, de la Gardie's armies were advancing in Inkeri. Between 1611 and 1613 the fortresses of Käkisalmi, Novgorod, Ladoga and Tikhvin in the area between Lakes Ladoga and Ilmen; and Kopore, Jama and Gdov, which lay along the Estonian frontier between the Gulf of Finland and Lake Peipus, all fell to the Swedes. Gustavus Adolphus arrived in person on the Russian front in 1614, having won a breathing space in the war with Denmark by the Peace of Knäred in 1613. After his failure to capture the citadel of Pskov, Gustavus Adolphus was ready to negotiate, and in the presence of English and Dutch intermediaries, peace talks began in the winter of 1615. A truce was arranged in 1616, during which the king addressed a meeting of the Estates General in Helsinki. He argued that Sweden wanted peace and that the obstacles to a settlement did not come from his side. He knew that his Finnish and Swedish subjects were tired of the strains and financial burdens of the war. After a further year of haggling the Treaty of Stolbova was signed in December 1617. Under its terms Swedish control of the Ingrian fortresses of Pahkinäsaari, Ivangorod, Jama and Kopore was recognized. The Swedish gains under the Treaties of Täysinä and Viipuri were confirmed and Sweden's occupation of Käkisalmi was accepted. Stolbova was the first victory which Gustavus Adolphus could claim after his accession in 1611. Sweden was now in control of both shores of the Gulf of Finland; had mastery of the trade routes to Russia through the Baltic; and had, at least for the time being, scotched the claims of the Poles in Russia and Estonia. During the rest of the seventeenth century Sweden became a major European power, with expansionist ambitions which led its troops to campaign throughout northern and central Europe, and even to the shores of the Black Sea.

Many Finns served in the Swedish armies and earned for themselves a formidable reputation as warriors. The army which fought for Gustavus Adolphus in his long wars in Germany and the Baltic lands was composed partly of conscripts raised within the Swedish realm and partly of mercenaries. In the early years of his reign the king attracted many English and Scottish mercenaries, many of whom settled in their adopted land and their descendants later played an important part in the life of the Swedish–Finnish kingdom. Today the Helsinki telephone directory still lists many Ramsays, who are descended from the Scottish settlers who came via Sweden in the early seventeenth century. After the death of Gustavus Adolphus on the field of Lützen in 1632, an increasing number of German soldiers were recruited to serve in the Swedish army. It has been estimated that out of some 140,000 men under the command of Gustavus Adolphus in 1632, only 13,000 were of native Swedish origin. Swedish soldiers were often employed in garrison duties in Sweden and Finland, whilst mercenaries were engaged to fight in foreign wars.

The system of conscription (*utskrivning*) which Gustavus Adolphus inherited was reformed during the early part of his reign. Commissioners appointed by the king visited each district and chose the conscripts from lists prepared by the parish priest and his vestrymen. It was reported in 1620 that many Finnish peasants took to the woods in order to avoid conscription, and that the deserters were pursued by soldiers who hunted them down and dragged them back to face the wrath of the commissioners. There were complaints of the abandonment of farms in districts where many of the able-bodied men had been forced into the army. The crack cavalry troops, however, were recruited from volunteers, and the Finnish horsemen, mounted on their light but swift and study palominos, were considered to be elite fighting men. They were known as Hakkapeliitta, from their blood curdling war cry, 'hakkaa päälle!' (fall on!) In the 1620s Finland's quota of troops was fixed at three cavalry and nine infantry regiments, which appears to have been a disproportionately high contribution in relation to the population. Sweden had only 23 regiments, each of between 1,000 and 1,200 men. Finland not only supplied men and horses, but also military leaders. Gustav Horn, Count of Pori, became Marshal of Sweden. Åke Tott was a Field Marshal. Torsten Ståhlhandske was the General in charge of the Hakkapeliitta, and Erik Trana was Commissioner responsible for war supplies. Finnish troops were largely responsible for Sweden's great victory at Breitenfeld in 1631.

Gustavus Adolphus spent more than half his reign fighting abroad and he was compelled to delegate authority to others who were responsible for running the state bureaucracy. These included the nobles and the clergy. Although this resulted in the development of an administrative and judicial system which was more in keeping with that of a modern state, in contrast to the more personal rule of the earlier Vasas and their mediaeval predecessors, it also encouraged centralization of authority. The amount of paperwork involved required a standardization of the language of officialdom, and Swedish began to replace Finnish in the governing circles of Finland. Oral Finnish was still used in dealings with the peasantry, by parish priests in their work amongst their flocks and in the Finnish units of the army, but Swedish became the language of the higher courts and the administration. After 1625 Swedish-born bishops were usually appointed to the See of Turku, and in 1649 Swedish replaced Finnish as the language of instruction in grammar schools, alongside classical Latin and Greek. Many officials were recruited from Sweden, and Finnish-born clergy and functionaries adopted Swedish surnames along with the Swedish language.

Finland was not governed as a single unit, but was simply a group of Swedish provinces whose administrative framework resembled that of Dalarna or Norrland, or any other areas in Sweden proper. The boundaries changed to suit the convenience of the Swedish authorities. For example, when Per Brahe first became Governor-General in 1637, the 'Finland' which he administered included the province of Käkisalmi (Kexholm), but not Ostrobothnia; whereas in his second period of office, 1648–54, Ostrobothnia was included but Käkisalmi was not.

The imperial ambitions of Gustavus Adolphus and his successors imposed heavy charges on the Swedish exchequer and the cost had to be borne through taxation. In the early years of his reign, the necessity to discharge the indemnity due to Denmark arising from the Danish occupation of the fortress of Älvsborg imposed an onerous burden. When this had been paid and Älvsborg returned to Sweden in 1619, the Swedes were able to develop the city and port of Göteborg as their 'window on the west', giving access to the North Sea without the risk to their ships from the Danish control of the Sound. However, Gustavus Adolphus soon embarked on the military expeditions in Germany which became part of what was later known as the Thirty Years War.

To the burden of taxation, which bore heavily on the Finnish farmers, were added the imposition of conscription – which deprived many farms of their labour. When war broke out on the eastern frontier, the Finns bore the cost of quartering and supplying the troops stationed in the country, and suffered the destruction which ensued when fighting broke out on the soil of Finland. It has been estimated that, in 1656–57, when the Russians invaded Inkeri and Karelia, some 4,000 Finns abandoned their farms and moved into Russian-held territory partly to escape the ravages of war and the penal levels of taxation, but mainly, as Russian Orthodox believers, because of the persistent persecution and harassment by the Swedish Lutheran authorities.

After the death of Gustavus Adolphus in 1632 a regency was established to govern Sweden during the minority of his six year old daughter, Christina. A Form of Government law, drafted by Chancellor Axel Oxenstierna, and approved in principle by Gustavus Adolphus before his death, was introduced in 1634. It gave power to the upper ranks of the nobility and particularly to the Oxenstierna family, three of whom were amongst the five aristocrats who served as regents until Christina's majority was proclaimed in 1644.

In 1637 a governor-generalship was established for Finland and a Swedish nobleman, Per Brahe, who was thought by the Oxenstiernas to be a potential troublemaker, was appointed to the post in the hope that his energies would be diverted into constructive paths in the outlying fringes of the realm. Per Brahe's first period as Governor-General of Finland, from 1637 to 1640, ended with the founding of the university at Turku. Brahe had large estates at Visingsö in Sweden, covering an area as large as Cornwall which he ruled as a benevolent despot, but he soon identified himself with the aspirations and culture of his new Finnish subjects. Although he relinquished the governor-generalship between 1640 and 1648, he maintained his links with Finland during the interregnum, and continued to draw rents from 1,000 farms. He served for over 30 years as Chancellor of the university which he helped to found at Turku.

During his second period of office, from 1648 to 1654, when Ostrobothnia was included in his domain, he founded the city of Raahe (Brahestad). Brahe did much to encourage the use of the Finnish language and initiated a project to translate the whole of the Bible into Finnish and was responsible for the preparation of a Finnish grammar to be used by Swedish officials who would be posted to Finland. He is also credited with promoting the idea of *Suur Suomi* (Greater Finland) – a concept which was taken up by Finnish nationalists in the nineteenth and twentieth centuries with far from happy results. Brahe was aware that there were groups within the Russian territory who spoke languages related to Finnish, not only in the border regions of Karelia but also further east. He encouraged the idea that these people should be liberated from Slav rule, and that the boundaries of Finland should be pushed forward at least to the White Sea. When he retired from the governor-generalship in 1654 he is reported to have boasted 'I was highly satisfied with this country and the country with me.' He was certainly regarded by the Finns with respect and even with affection as a wise administrator and a friend of Finland. In the troubles which afflicted Finland during the next few decades, the 'Count's time' was thought of as a lost golden age of peace and prosperity. Brahe continued to exercise influence in Sweden and Finland until his death in 1670.

Brahe's retirement from Finland coincided with important changes in Sweden. Axel Oxenstierna died, Queen Christina abdicated, and her successor, Charles X, embarked on a war with Poland. Although Charles gained some initial successes, seizing both Warsaw and Krakow, he soon found himself facing the Russian Armies of Tsar Alexis. Taking advantage of Sweden's involvement in Poland, the Russians were able to advance through Inkeri and Karelia, but after initial reverses, the Finns – under Gustav Horn, Per Brahe's Finnish successor as Governor-General – were able to drive back the invaders. A truce was concluded at Vallisaari in 1658, and a more lasting settlement respecting the pre-war frontiers was reached at Kardis in 1661 by the regents who ruled Sweden after the death of Charles X in 1660.

In the same year as the Treaty of Kardis was signed with Russia, the Swedes also ended the wars with Poland and Denmark which had begun during Charles X's reign. Sweden gained territory, population and influence at the expense of Denmark and Poland. This inaugurated nearly forty years of peace and stability along the eastern borders which inevitably reduced the importance of Finland in the strategic and political thinking of the royal government, whose attention turned southward towards Denmark and the Holy Roman Empire. In this period Finland became something of a provincial backwater.

Charles XI was declared of age in 1672, and for the rest of the reign he and his agents promoted reforms which sought to make Sweden-Finland a model absolute monarchy, with final authority in all matters concentrated in the person of the king. A movement was started to spread Swedish cultural influences in Finland, including the Swedish language in spheres where Finnish was still used – in the army, the courts and in the church. This provoked in some areas a reaction from Finnish speakers, especially in the University of Turku. The Church Law of 1686 was an important part of the programme which required total religious conformity throughout the kingdom, and declared that the king was empowered to appoint bishops and to oversee the government of the church. It was from this period that the church was charged with the responsibility of spreading literacy amongst the mass of the population. The bishop of Turku responded to the challenge with enthusiasm. A powerful sanction in the hands of the clergy was the power to refuse marriage to couples who could not read a catechism. This custom helps to explain why the Finns became one of the most literate nations in the world long before mass literacy became the norm in late nineteenth-century western Europe. Aleksis Kivi, writing about life in rural Finland in the mid nineteenth century, describes how the new vicar of the village of Toukala in southern Häme was 'terribly strict in all that pertained to his office. Especially towards backward readers was he without mercy, harrying them in every way, even confining them in the stocks'. He was referring to a tradition which went back to the reign of Charles XI, in the late seventeenth century.

In the last year of the reign of Charles XI Finland was afflicted by a terrible famine which according to some estimates, killed a third of the population. It was caused primarily by a severe winter in 1696–7, and although the royal government made a considerable effort to bring in relief supplies by sea from its own reserves of grain, this could not prevent the demographic disaster. The government did not escape criticism from the sufferers who knew that while people in Finland were eating bread made from tree bark, or grubbing for roots to survive, other and more fortunate parts of the kingdom got through the crisis years without serious loss. Before long the suffering of the people was made worse by the onset of yet another war.

Charles XII, who succeeded to the Swedish throne in 1697 at the age of 15, refused to rule through a regency council. He crowned himself, refused to take an oath and followed unswervingly the absolutist principles established by his father. War started in 1700, when Augustus II, Elector of Saxony and King of Poland, invaded the Baltic province of Livonia (later to be part of Latvia), but he was stopped by an army mainly composed of Finnish troops advancing from Estonia. The Russians under Tsar Peter the Great then intervened, laying siege to the Swedish-held fortress of Narva on the borders of Estonia and Inkeri. Charles XII took personal charge of an expedition to raise the siege and, despite being outnumbered four to one by the Russians, his troops (half of whom were Finns) succeeded in routing the enemy. The wild adventure at Narva was typical of the headstrong behaviour of Charles. On this occasion the gamble paid off and the 18-year-old king became a legendary hero overnight. He then invaded Poland, deposed Augustus, and went on to conquer Saxony. Whilst he was thus engaged, Peter the Great counter-attacked in Inkeri.

In 1703 Peter captured the Swedish fort of Nevanlinna, at the point where the river Neva enters the Gulf of Finland. It was here in 1704 that he began the building of St Petersburg. In 1704 the humiliation at Narva was avenged and in 1706 the Russian troops stood outside the gates of Viipuri. Because he did not command the sea, Peter did not try to storm the fortress and he waited for four years before he could take Viipuri. When he did so in 1710 he was already in possession of the southern shore of the Gulf of Finland, including the ports of Riga and Reval (Tallinn). Within four years he had occupied the whole of Finland.

The Finnish army, under the command of General K.G. Armfelt, was decisively defeated by the Russians (under Prince Golitsyn) when they met on a bitter February day in 1714, at the village of Napue, in the Kyrö valley, 30 kilometres inland from Vaasa. The battle of Napue, sometimes referred to as the battle of Storkro (Isokyrö), resulted in heavy casualties on both sides. The Russian commander described it as being the hardest fight in which his troops had been engaged since they had defeated Charles XII at Poltava in 1709. It marked the end of organized Finnish resistance and the beginning of a seven-year period of Russian occupation, known as The Great Wrath. Armfelt managed to escape to Sweden and took part in the ill-fated expedition against Norway in 1718, during which Charles XII was shot, probably by one of his own officers.

In the 21 years of his reign Charles was hardly ever in Sweden. After the failure of his attempt to take Moscow in the winter of 1708–9 he was defeated at Poltava, on the Dniester in June 1709 and took refuge in Turkish-held territory for five years, before returning in 1714 to invade Norway. It is incredible that he was able to remain

King of Sweden during his long absence. Instructions which were sent to his officials during his stay in Turkish hands sometimes took a year to be delivered. Obviously, the day-to-day government of the kingdom was left in the hands of local commanders and the leading Swedish magnates. Finland was left very much to its own devices. Following the Russian occupation between 1714 and 1721 the whole system of government was in disarray.

After the death of the king aged 35 and unmarried, it was left to his successors to pick up the pieces and to make peace with the various enemies with whom Charles had been at war. Negotiations with Russia dragged on for three years until agreement was reached with the Treaty of Uusikaupunki (Nystad), in 1721. The Russian occupation of Finland was ended, but Sweden was forced to cede its possessions in Inkeri, Estonia and Livonia. Russia had emerged as a major Baltic power, controlling the coastline from the Neva to the Dvina. There was also a major redrawing of the eastern frontier of Finland. Viipuri and Käkisalmi, the whole of Lake Ladoga and most of Karelia were lost and the balance of power in the Baltic shifted away from Sweden and towards Russia.

The period from the mid 1690s to the 1720s was catastrophic for Finland. The Finns had suffered from famine, pestilence, war and foreign occupation. Their population had fallen from about half a million to under 400,000. The rural economy had been disrupted, the administrative framework was in ruins and the experience caused some Finns to raise questions about the relative benefits and disadvantages of the connection with Sweden. Although modern historians have modified the picture of abject misery and national humiliation which had characterized earlier accounts of The Great Wrath, there is no doubt that Finland suffered greatly under the Russian occupation. There was a systematic devastation of some parts of Karelia, Ostrobothnia and the Åland Islands. Thousands were deported to endure virtual slavery in Russia; others were conscripted into the Russian army and arbitrary acts of cruelty by local Russian officials terrorized some sections of the population.

During the rest of the eighteenth century Finland made a significant demographic and economic recovery from the miseries of the

3

Finland, Sweden and Russia in the eighteenth century

The Peace of Uusikaupunki marked the end of Sweden's role as a major European power and heralded the rise of Russia as the dominant force in the north. Finland, in the front line of the Swedish–Russian confrontation, had no independent input into the politics of the kingdom. The Finnish elites divided politically between the same two political factions, known as the 'Hats' and the 'Caps', as the rest of the kingdom. In foreign policy the Hats advocated alliance with France to counter the ascendancy of Russia. The Caps, accepting the ascendancy of Russia, tried to conciliate 'this dangerous neighbour', hoping that by buying time, it would be possible eventually to look forward to a time when 'the Lord God . . . will mercifully deign to provide circumstances favourable to Sweden'. The Hats had unrealistic expectations that they could push the frontiers of Finland eastward, gaining territory from Russia. Until 1738 they were restrained by the cautious Finnish-born Lord Chancellor of Sweden, Count Arvid Horn. Horn had been a soldier under Charles XII and in his youth had shared the impetous heroism of his royal master, but in old age he was more realistic in his appreciation of what was possible. When he stepped down from the chancellorship in 1738 at the age of 74 years, the Hats became the dominant party in the Swedish–Finnish kingdom. Encouraged by France, who wanted for its own purposes to see Russia's hands tied by a war in the north, the Hats persuaded the Diet to declare war on Russia in July 1741. The defences of Finland had been allowed to fall into decay and the Russians had no difficulty in routing their Swedish opponents. There was only one major battle in the war, at Lappeenranta, although

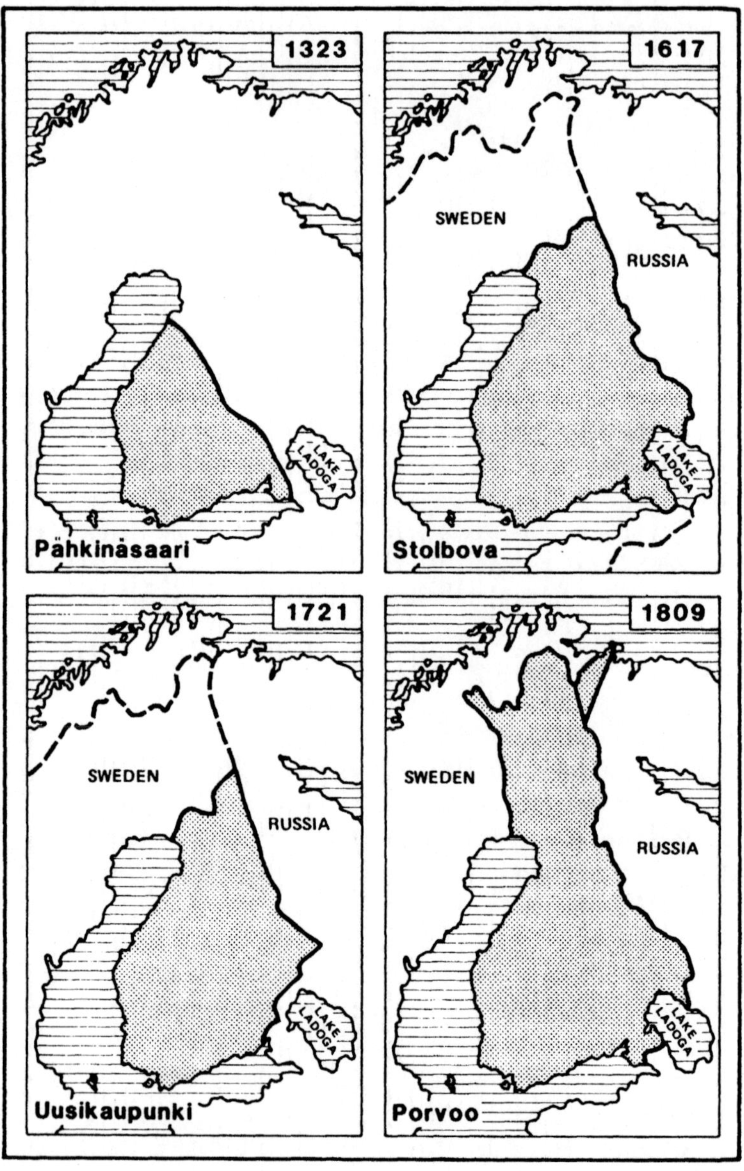

Map 1 Finland: historical boundaries

sporadic resistance by Finnish peasants in Karelia continued after the defeated army had fled westward, Helsinki and Hameenlinna surrendered to the Russians without a fight, and by 1742 Finland was again under Russian occupation. The 'Lesser Wrath' which descended upon the Finns was less traumatic than had been 'The Great Wrath' of the previous generation, but it was nonetheless a bitter blow.

The Peace of Turku which followed in 1743 resulted in further losses of territory in eastern Finland. The new frontier with Russia deprived Finland of the fortress of Olavinlinna and its nearby town of Savonlinna, as well as the towns of Lappeenranta and Hamina. The new frontier followed the course of the Kymi river, which enters the Gulf of Finland near the present-day port of Kotka. The area left to Finland was smaller than at any time since the 16th century.

Despite the loss of territory, the Peace of Turku was relatively mild in its exactions, considering the military strength of Russia and the fact that Russian troops occupied Finland for a long time. Some of the reasons for this are to be found in the policies of the newly enthroned Empress Elizabeth, the youngest daughter of Peter the Great. Elizabeth came to the throne in 1741 after deposing the infant son of Peter's niece Anna Ivanovna. Russia was torn by internal disputes and involved in complicated international problems. Elizabeth was satisfied to see the Finnish frontier pushed back westward, in order to afford greater protection to St Petersburg, but she had no wish to annex Finland. She saw the possibility of weakening Finland's ties with Sweden and also of exercising some influence over affairs in Sweden by claiming the right to nominate the successor to Frederick I of Sweden, who had come to the throne in 1720. During negotiations for a truce in 1742 she sent the Swedish envoy, Colonel Lagercrantz, back to Frederick with a manifesto which, amongst other items, promised a kind of autonomy for a Duchy of Finland, free from either Swedish or Russian domination.

Although Elizabeth probably had no serious intention of encouraging Finnish particularist tendencies for their own sake, her use of the term 'Duchy of Finland' and her apparent encouragement of Finnish autonomy were seen by later historians as an important step in the development of the Finnish national awakening. Her insistence upon choosing Frederick's successor to the Swedish throne bore fruit in 1751, when Frederick Adolphus, a member of the German House of Gottorp and guardian of Elizabeth's nephew, Peter, was chosen as King of Sweden. Peter became Tsar of Russia as Peter III, on the death of Elizabeth in 1762, in the last year of the Seven Years War.

Finland was subjected to two contradictory pressures during the eighteenth century. On the one hand there was a steady growth of Swedish cultural influences, in particular the spread of the Swedish language and the development of closer economic ties with Sweden. On the other hand the Finns were beginning to realize their cultural differences from the Swedes and to develop a taste for 'patriotic' histories of Finland which stressed, often to absurd lengths, the superior virtues of the Finns.

The father of this school of history was Daniel Juslenius, a student in Turku University in the last years of the seventeenth century who eventually occupied a bishopric in Sweden. In his *Vindiciae Fennorum*, published in 1703, he praised the Finnish fatherland, 'the common parent of us all. We must thank her and praise her everywhere and, if necessary, give our lives for her,' The University of Turku and the Lutheran Church in Finland encouraged the interest in Finnish history which Juslenius had stimulated. The movement reached a high point in the second half of the eighteenth century, in the work of the historian Henrik Gabriel Porthan (1739–1804), 'the father of Finnish history'. Porthan became a professor at Turku in 1777, having lectured in the university for the previous 15 years, during which time he published his *Dissertatio de poesi Fennica*. This work, which appeared in five volumes between 1766 and 1778, was a seminal work in the study of the oral folk traditions of the Finnish people. Porthan believed that the distinctive national character of the Finns was expressed in the rich heritage of oral folk culture which had been passed on from generation to generation by the ordinary, unlettered people in the countryside.

Porthan's arguments that the foundation of national identity is to be found in the possession of a common language are clearly similar to those of the internationally renowned German historian and folklorist, J. G. Herder. They have provided the intellectual foundation for the language-based, populist nationalisms that, for better or worse, have played such an important part in the history of nineteenth- and twentieth-century Europe. Porthan was one of many thinkers who explored the roots of folk culture and found there a justification for the awakening of national consciousness. He performed the same work for the Finns that Vuk Karadžić achieved for the south Slavs. Porthan's pioneering endeavours were taken up by other Finnish scholars in the next century and helped to shape the Finnish national movement, which led eventually to the declaration of independence in 1917. Porthan also wrote about the history of Finland from the Dark Ages to the Age of Enlightenment. His interpretation, although now superceded by the work of modern historians, was the *leitmotif* of the Finnish national renaissance.

During the late eighteenth century, literature in Finnish began to be published. It was mainly on ecclesiastical and legal topics, but it also included studies in history, folklore and philosophy. In the 1770s the first Finnish-language newspaper made a brief appearance. The Finnish language was recognized for use in the deliberations of the Diet, and appeared on banknotes.

However, these indications that the elites in Finland were taking an interest in the Finnish language did not mean that they had any thought of weakening Finland's political ties with Sweden. The Swedish language made headway amongst the commercial middle classes in the towns, amongst the professional classes and, of course, as the language of the nobility and the state officials. Finnish continued to be the language of the peasants, the fisherfolk and the mass of ordinary people outside the coastal areas where Swedish speakers had lived for centuries. Many Finns seeking advancement in the ranks of the bourgeoisie not only adopted the Swedish language but also changed their names to Swedish forms.

The period in Swedish–Finnish history between 1719 and 1772 is known as 'The Age of Freedom.' It began with a bargain made between the Council and the Riksdag on the one side and on the other Queen Ulrika Eleanora, who succeeded her brother, Charles XII, following his death in 1718. The nobility wanted to assert their rights over the queen, following the disastrous reign of Charles XII. When the Estates presented her with a new constitution, the queen decided that they had gone far beyond the understanding upon which she had accepted election to the throne. She abdicated in favour of her husband, Prince Frederick of Hesse, who was prepared to accept the restraints imposed on him by the constitution drafted by the estates. A new Council of State composed of 24 nobles was established, over which the king presided. Councillors were chosen by the king from the nominations put to him by the three upper estates of the Riksdag. The Fourth Estate, the peasantry, was excluded from some important decisions, especially those concerning foreign policy and war. The nobles mistrusted the peasant representatives, who were elected by a democratic process, because they tended to side with the king, and the main purpose of the new constitution was to curb the absolutist tendencies of the ruler.

In the middle of the eighteenth century Sweden–Finland had a constitution closer to the parliamentary system of England than to the absolutist monarchies of France, Austria and Russia. The relative freedom of the Swedes and Finns encouraged the growth of political factions who attempted to influence the policies of the government. A complicated political game was played which involved the monarch, the Council and the Four Estates, with foreign intervention from France, Russia, Prussia, Denmark, Holland and England adding to the confusion.

Reference has already been made to the activities of the Hats, who were in the ascendant from 1738 to 1765. Despite their responsibility for the disastrous war with Russia (1741–43), the Hats were not dislodged until the adverse economic consequences of their mercantilist policies began to be felt. It then became the turn of the Caps, who were intermittently in government between 1765 and 1772. They were responsible for important economic changes. The easing of monopolistic trading restrictions enabled Finnish ports to enter directly into foreign trade. The export of tar from Ostrobothnia increased greatly. Although this continued to be known in Britain and other European markets as 'Stockholm tar,' because for centuries it had been exported directly through the staple port of Stockholm, it now became possible to send it directly from places like Pietarsaari (Jakobstad), Vaasa, Raahe (Brahestad) and Oulu, to the benefit of the local economy. The Oulu Trade Company, founded in 1765, commissioned the construction of a Tar Hall (Tervahovi) in 1782 and in the early nineteenth century one third of Finland's tar exports was handled by the Oulu merchants.

Shipbuilding industries were established in the Bothnian ports to supply the vessels needed to carry exports of tar, timber, furs, salmon and other commodities involved in Finland's expanding trade. The philosophy of economic liberalism was associated with the writings of Anders Chydenius, the rector of an Ostrobothnian parish, who later became known as the Adam Smith of Finland. In fact, he anticipated by a generation the ideas of the more famous Scottish political economist.

Despite economic and cultural progress, the political situation in Sweden–Finland in the middle years of the eighteenth century was unstable. The Form of Government which ushered in the 'Age of Freedom' may have given a greater degree of freedom to some subjects of the Swedish crown, but it also opened the doors to foreign intrigues which were designed to keep the kingdom weak and internally divided. After the Peace of Turku in 1743 the defences of Finland had been neglected. Some of the best frontier fortresses had been lost and it was not until thirty years later that new fortifications were completed, to replace those which had been lost. The Swedish nobleman, Count Augustin Ehrensvärd (1710–72), who commanded the Swedish forces in Pomerania during the Seven Years War (1756–63), was responsible for the building of the Svartholm fortress, protecting the approaches to the port of Loviisa. The construction of the fortress of Sveaborg (Swedish Castle) in the entrance to Helsinki harbour occupied Ehrensvärd for 25 years, until 1770. The fortress, which was renamed Suomenlinna (Finnish Castle) after independence, was intended to be a base for a fleet of naval galleys as well as a military redoubt to defend Helsinki against a possible Russian invasion. It became known as the 'Gibraltar of the North', but in fact it played little part in the military history of Finland. The sense of security which the construction of Sveaborg and other coastal fortifications gave was a psychological boost to the Finns, even if its real military value was modest.

The Russians, under Catherine the Great (who deposed her incompetent and probably insane husband, Peter III in 1762), were anxious to preserve the Swedish Form of Government, as were Frederick the Great and several other European rulers. They saw the constitution as a means of weakening the power of the Swedish king, and therefore undermining the ability of Sweden to present a firm front to outside pressures. In 1769 Catherine's Russia and Frederick's Prussia agreed with Christian VII of Denmark that any change in the Swedish constitution which increased the power of the king would be seen by them as a hostile act. They also agreed upon a division of Swedish territory in the event of a joint military intervention by the three powers. Russia's share of the possible spoils was left vague, but it was hinted that Finland might be detached from Sweden and established as an independent state, under Catherine's protection.

King Gustavus III, a young man of 25, was in Paris when his father, Adolphus Frederick, died in 1771. He had previously spent some time in the court of his uncle, Frederick the Great of Prussia. It is not surprising, therefore, that he saw himself standing in the tradition of the benevolent autocrats of the eighteenth-century Enlightenment. The Form of Government which he inherited, and under which Sweden–Finland had been ruled during the Age of Freedom, did not suit his concept of how a kingdom should be governed. Within a year of his return to Sweden to occupy the throne he had abrogated the 1719 Constitution and replaced it with a new Form of Government, which he pushed through the Riksdag in the summer of 1772. The royal coup d'état was achieved with the help of the Finnish colonel, Jakob Magnus Sprengtporten who organized a military revolt in Finland, capturing Helsinki and the almost-completed fortress of Sveaborg. Sprengtporten and his younger step-brother, Göran Magnus, intended to sail from Helsinki to support the king in Stockholm, but unfavourable weather conditions delayed their departure and the king acted on his own, seizing Stockholm in a bloodless coup and intimidating the Riksdag into passing a new Constitution which gave wide powers to the crown.

The venerable Council of the Realm, which had been the main vehicle for the influence of the senior nobility, was reduced to an administrative rubber stamping machine and the Riksdag was stripped of most of its powers. Between 1772 and the murder of the king in 1792 it was summoned only four times, and although it was officially supposed to have joint authority with the crown over legislation and the raising of taxes and had a veto over the king's power to wage war, it was easy for Gustavus to circumvent its rights. The rival parties, the Hats and the Caps, were proscribed, but at first the king leaned heavily on the support of former Hat nobles. This later proved to be a political expedient rather than a matter of principle.

In 1789 a new constitutional law, the Act of Union and Security, was passed by the three lower Estates, the king having ordered the nobles to leave the throne-room when it became apparent that they would oppose his plans. The new constitution abolished the Council of the Realm and further reduced the powers of the Riksdag, including their right to be consulted when war was declared. Some gestures were made towards the lowest Estate – the peasantry – whose status, if not their powers, was enhanced. Henceforward, the king would have virtually unfettered powers in all matters of state, except over the levying of taxes, where the consent of the Riksdag was required in certain circumstances. The members of the lower Estates were flattered by being given access to posts in the local and national bureaucracy and in the judiciary, which had previously been the preserve of the nobility; and restrictions on the right of peasants to buy land were also removed.

The Act of Union and Security was introduced at a time when Gustavus was involved in an unnecessary war of his own choosing with Catherine's Russia. Although the formal declaration of war in 1788 came from Russia, Gustavus had deliberately provoked the conflict at a time when Catherine was preoccupied with a war in Turkey. The plan was to send a group of men disguised as Cossacks to attack a Finnish farm. In retaliation, the Finnish army would move on Hamina, but this land attack was conceived as a diversion from the real thrust – a seaborne landing at the Russian capital, St Petersburg. Gustavus III came to Helsinki to take charge of the operation despite warnings that he might be taken prisoner by dissident Finnish officers. The invasion plan misfired. Hamina held out for two weeks against a siege by Gustavus' forces. The fleet did not reach St Petersburg, but was halted at Suursaari (Hogland), an island 160 kilometres west of the Russian capital. Catherine persuaded the Danes and Norwegians to invade southern Sweden in order to create a diversion from the Finnish front.

The intervention of Frederick William II of Prussia and Prime Minister William Pitt brought the war with Denmark to an end in the autumn of 1788, but hostilities with Russia on the Finnish front continued until 1790. In July 1790 the Swedes suffered a major naval defeat off Viipuri, but Vice-Admiral K. O. Cronstedt gained his revenge a week later by sinking over fifty Russian ships at Ruotsinsalmi (Svensksund), between Hamina and the mouth of the Kymi river. Peace was signed at Värälä in August 1790. The Treaty of Värälä, negotiated by G. M. Armfelt, a Finn in the service of Gustavus, left the Finnish–Russian frontier unchanged. However, Gustavus believed that it had removed the threat of Russian interference with Sweden's internal affairs, which had existed since the Tsarina Elizabeth had concluded the Peace of Turku in 1743.

The Anjala League

The idea that Finland's future lay with the rising power of Russia rather than with the declining fortunes of Sweden began to be talked about by some Finnish officers during the early years of the reign of Gustavus III. J. M. Sprengtporten was one of the first to use it. He had personal reasons for being dissatisfied with Gustavus' autocratic rule. He and his step-brother, G. M. Sprengtporten, had taken an active part in the coup of 1772 which had consolidated the king's authority, but once the reins of power were firmly in his hands Gustavus brushed aside his former supporters. In the early days of the war of 1788–90 a group of officers camped near the manor of Anjala, in the Kymi valley, entered into secret correspondence with Catherine the Great, hoping to bring the war to an end. One of their grievances was that Gustavus had acted unconstitutionally in not consulting the Riksdag before committing his forces to the attack upon Russia. Gustavus, who was with his troops in Finland, learned through his friend Armfelt of his officers' treasonable conduct and demanded assurances of their loyalty. Instead, they sent him a document, the Covenant of Anjala, signed by 113 Finns and Swedes, in which they accused him of waging a war of aggression for which neither they nor their men had any stomach, and which they feared they would lose. They added, however, that if Catherine rejected their proposals for an honourable peace, they would feel justified in fighting against her with all their strength. G. M. Sprengtporten, who had crossed into Russian territory in 1786 and was acting as adviser to Catherine during the war, was elected as the representative of the Finnish nation by a so-called Diet of gentry living in the border areas which met at Paaso, near Heinola, in December 1788.

Gustavus, faced with this formidable challenge to his authority from the men upon whom he had to rely for the defence of his realm, is said to have contemplated abdication, but the situation was transformed by the declaration of war by Christian VII of Denmark. Gustavus hurried back to Sweden, where he successfully held off the Danish attack and forced the Danes to agree to a truce. He left his brother, Duke Charles, in charge of his forces in Finland, but there was little fighting on the Russian front until the following summer, when the Russians attacked in Savo. In an engagement at Porrassalmi, near Mikkeli, in June 1789, Sprengtporten – who was fighting on the Russian side – was wounded but escaped capture. Another member of the Anjala League, J. A. Jägerhorn, attempted without much success to raise the peasantry of Savo in support of the Russians. When it appeared that the army of Sweden–Finland was holding its own in the land fighting – they even had a famous victory at Parkumäki, near Savonlinna – the opposition to Gustavus began to dwindle. Many of the signatories of the Anjala Covenent were not Finnish separatists, and the Finnish peasantry was more royalist and more anti-Russian than were their nobles. The Act of Union and Security, which was passed in February 1789, had given greater powers to the king but had also made concessions to the lower Estates because the King had appealed to the peasantry and burghers over the heads of the recalcitrant nobility.

The signing of the Peace of Värälä effectively killed for the time being any hope of a separation of Finland from Sweden. It only remained for Gustavus to come to a reckoning with the men of Anjala. Some of them had fled to Russia and were beyond the reach of Swedish justice. Others had remained with the army and fought against the Russians. Eighty seven of the 113 signatories of the

Covenant were sentenced to death but only one, Colonel J. H. Hästesko, was actually executed. The others received a royal pardon. The Anjala League was part of a widespread movement of opposition amongst the Swedish nobility against the autocracy of Gustavus, but it did not represent a significant demand for Finnish independence. This was to come later.

The nobility exacted their revenge on Gustavus when, in 1792, the king was mortally wounded by J. J. Anckarström, during a masked ball in Stockholm. He lived long enough to propose the establishment of a five-member Regency Council, which was to include his brother, Duke Charles, and his trusted Finnish councillor G. M. Armfelt, who would exercise the royal prerogative until Gustavus' son, then 14 years old, would come of age. Charles ignored the provision and ruled as sole Regent until the young prince was declared to be of age in 1796. He ruled as Gustavus IV Adolphus until he was deposed in 1809. Armfelt appealed to Tsarina Catherine, alleging that Charles's chief adviser, the Finnish landowner baron G. A. Reuterholm, was a Jacobin. Armfelt, under threat of trial for treason, fled to Russia.

Gustavus IV at first attempted to keep Sweden–Finland out of the wars which were raging across Europe during the period of Napoleon's ascendancy in the last years of the eighteenth and the first years of the nineteenth century. In 1805, however, he launched an ill-fated attack on the French from Swedish-held territory in Pomerania and was only saved from total humiliation through the good offices of his Russian ally. Following the Pomeranian debacle he resisted French pressure to join the Continental System and to ally his country with Napoleonic France.

In 1807 Napoleon defeated Russia and then made a bargain with Tsar Alexander I, which brought Russia and France together as allies. The Treaty of Tilsit of July 1807 recognized French supremacy in western and central Europe but gave Russia a free hand in the Baltic. Alexander also agreed to act as a mediator in offering peace terms to England. If these were refused, Russia would join in the war on Napoleon's side and would also compel Sweden to close its ports to English ships. When the terms were not accepted Alexander duly declared war in November 1807. The British fleet had been withdrawn from the Baltic shortly before the declaration of war, and Alexander knew that it would not return until the spring thaw of 1808 had set in. In order to forestall the return of the British he attacked in February 1808, and by November Finland was again under Russian occupation. The surrender of the fortress of Sveaborg without a fight by Vice-Admiral Cronstedt, the hero of Ruotsinsalmi (Svensksund) in 1790, in the early summer of 1808 was a bitter blow to the defenders of Finland. Cronstedt has had a bad press from Finnish historians, who took their line from the national poet, J. L. Runeberg, whose poems under the title *Ensign Ståhl's Tales* (*Fänrik Ståls Sägner*) gave a romantic account of the role of the Finnish army during the campaigns of 1808. Cronstedt is described as a base coward who was guilty of treason. This seems to be an unfair portrait of the man, although his surrender of the fortress at a time when he might have held on until the Swedish fleet came to relieve him has never been satisfactorily explained. General Klingspor, the commander of the land forces, has also been harshly treated by Finnish historians, who seem to have been influenced by Runeberg's account of a man who had 'two chins, one eye and only half a heart'.

The Finnish army retreated to Ostrobothnia in the early weeks of the war in accordance with a prearranged plan, and then counterattacked in the summer, recovering much of the territory which they had evacuated in the winter. Their victory at Lapua on 14 July is still celebrated as a public holiday by patriotic Finns in parts of southern Ostrobothnia. Klingspor concluded an armistice in September, shortly before he was removed from his command, and before the winter was over all Finland lay under Russian control. Peace was concluded at Hamina in September 1809. Swedish rule had gone forever after almost seven centuries and Finland embarked on its long road to independence. The first stage on that road involved over a century as an autonomous Grand Duchy within the Tsarist Empire.

Finland under the Tsars: the Grand Duchy of Finland

Dissatisfaction with Swedish rule had been growing amongst the nobility and the educated classes in Finland for some time. The autocratic behaviour of Gustavus III and the involvement of Sweden in disastrous wars with Russia, which were fought out over Finnish territory during the reigns of both Gustavus III and Gustavus IV, convinced many Finns that there was more hope for the country in a separation from Sweden. Russian rulers from the time of Elizabeth in the 1740s had hinted at the possibility of some kind of autonomy for Finland under Russian sovereignty. The survivors of the Anjala League – Sprengtporten, Klick and Jägerhorn – had worked during their exile in Russia to keep alive the idea of a Finland divorced from Sweden, although they were not in agreement concerning the exact constitutional relationship which might be worked out with Russia. There is little evidence, however, that the mass of the Finnish people were anxious to come under Russian rule. The peasants had shown a touching loyalty to the Swedish crown despite the behaviour of the last two Swedish kings and Finnish soldiers had fought bravely against the Russians, even if the officers had at times appeared to have dubious loyalties.

The formal annexation of Finland which had been proclaimed by the Russian commander in chief in 1808 was formally ratified on 29 March 1809 at a meeting of the Finnish Diet, which had been hastily convoked to hear a declaration by Tsar Alexander I, known as the Act of Assurance. In it the Emperor acknowledged the right of the Finns to the practice of their religion and the preservation of their traditional rights and privileges which they 'have hitherto enjoyed according to the Constitution' (see Appendix A). The meeting was held in the Lutheran Cathedral of Porvoo (Borgå), an ancient seaport founded in 1346, which lies on the coast of Uusimaa, 50 kilometres east of Helsinki.

In return for the guarantees of internal autonomy implicit in the Tsar's declaration, the Finnish Estates took an oath of allegiance to the Tsar as Grand Duke of Finland. A week later Alexander issued a decree, which stated (in French):

> When We convoked Finland's Estates to a General Diet, and received their oath of allegiance, We desired . . . by means of a solemn act . . . to confirm and secure to them the maintenance of their religion and fundamental laws, together with the 'liberties and rights that each Estate in particular and all of Finland's inhabitants in general, have hitherto enjoyed . . . We consider the oath

> of allegiance of the Estates in general, and of the Deputies of the Estates of the Peasants in particular . . . to be good and binding on all the inhabitants of Finland.'

The Diet remained in session in Porvoo until July 1809, during which time it discussed important administrative matters arising from the new status of Finland. At the closing session, Alexander again attended in person and to reassure the Finns of his trust in them, he urged the members of the Diet to 'impress on the minds of your fellow citizens the same confidence which has presided over your deliberations here'.

The final act of transferring Finland from Sweden to Russian sovereignty came in September 1809, with the peace treaty signed at Hamina (Fredrikshamn), by which Sweden assigned Finland, including the Åland Islands, to its old enemy. In Alexander's words, Finland was now able to take its place 'in the rank of nations, governed by its own laws'.

The settlement arrived at in 1809 was not unique in Russian history. The Baltic provinces which had earlier been annexed to Russia had also been allowed to retain some of their former institutions, and in 1815 the Congress of Vienna agreed to the formation of a Kingdom of Poland under Russian sovereignty which retained some degree of internal autonomy. There was some evidence that the liberal-minded Alexander saw the future of the multi-national Russian Empire in terms of a grouping of semi-autonomous national units under the sceptre of the Tsars. In fact, Finland was the only such unit which survived until the collapse of Tsardom. Poland's limited form of autonomy, which covered only a small proportion of Polish territory – the so-called Kingdom of Poland – was treated as occupied territory after the abortive Polish insurrection of 1863, and the Baltic provinces were also incorporated into the Russian system of government. Finland, however, retained its special status and was able to develop a degree of political and cultural autonomy which provided a springboard for the leap into full independence which was achieved in 1917.

Local government in Finland remained much as it had been under Sweden, but at national level changes were introduced to bring the administration into line with the new dispensation. A government council, which was known after 1816 as the Imperial Senate of Finland, was in effect the government of Finland. The number of senators increased from 14 to 20 in 1820 and the majority of members discharged departmental responsibilities in such matters as finance, agriculture, education, industry and public works. There was even a War Department until 1903, although its powers were constrained by the overriding authority of the Tsar's government in St Petersburg. A group of senators constituted a Supreme Court, which dealt with cases originating in the lower courts which had survived from the Swedish period. An independent official, the Procurator, acted as a kind of Ombudsman whose responsibilities involved investigating the actions of senators and public officials to ensure that they carried out their functions in accordance with the law.

Relations between Finland and Russia were regulated by a Secretary of State, based in St Petersburg, who was assisted by a secretariat. For most of the nineteenth century there was also a Committee on Finnish Affairs based in the Russian capital. Its function was to process submissions to the Tsar which came from Finland. This enabled the Finns to have access to the Tsar without having to go through the official channels of the Russian administrative machine. The personal representative of the Tsar in Finland was the Governor-General, who for the whole of the period of Russian rule from 1809 to 1917 was a Russian-speaking official (discounting the brief tenure of office of G. M. Sprengtporten, which ended in 1809). One of the functions of the Governor-General was to preside at meetings of the Senate, the proceedings of which were conducted in Swedish, the official language of government. As most of the Governors-General did not know Swedish, the practice grew up for the Vice-Chairman of the Senate, who was a Finnish subject to preside at meetings of the government. He became the *de facto* prime minister of the Finnish government. This was a similar situation to that which existed in England in the early eighteenth century, when the German-speaking George I found it impossible to take the chair at meetings of the Cabinet and was forced to delegate this responsibility to his chief minister, Robert Walpole, who became in effect the first British Prime Minister.

The Governor-General was appointed by the Tsar without consultation with the Finns and had direct access to the Tsar when he wished to raise any matters concerning the government of Finland. He was also commander of the Russian garrison stationed in Finland.

Most Governors-General until the turn of the century did not attempt to interfere with the day-to-day government of Finland. The Finnish government (the Senate) had in practice wide executive powers over the internal affairs of Finland, and this degree of autonomy enabled Finland to preserve its culture and religion, and to develop a sense of separate national identity. The taxation system as it existed in 1809 was subject to the same rules as had applied under the Gustavian constitution of late eighteenth-century Sweden. Some aspects of government went back further, to the Swedish 'Law of 1734', especially in regard to civil law, inheritance, commerce and land ownership.

Although Alexander was considered to be a liberal in the climate of contemporary Europe outside the constitutional monarchies of Britain and a few countries of Western Europe, he still regarded himself as 'Emperor and Autocrat of all the Russias,' and had been accepted as such by the Porvoo Diet. He was prepared to promise certain rights and privileges to his Finnish subjects and to keep his promises, but he could not bind his successors. The Finnish Diet, which under Swedish rule had been part of the combined Diet of Sweden–Finland, was a purely Finnish institution after 1809. It was a survival from the world before 1789: only the Peasant Estate was chosen by a numerous electorate of free peasant farmers, and this excluded the tenants and labourers. The Clergy Estate represented an elite of bishops and beneficed clergy, together with the academics, all of whom were state employees. The Burgher Estate was chosen by the tiny administrative and commercial oligarchies of the corporate towns and the Nobles' Estate was a mix of hereditary landowners and the senior military and civil servants of the crown. After the Gustavian coup d'état, however, the powers of the Diet were greatly circumscribed and Alexander's assumption of the title of Grand Duke of Finland did not alter this situation. Alexander, like Gustavus III, saw the Diet as a purely advisory body which could be called upon at the discretion of the ruler, but which had no constitutional rights to restrict the absolute power of the divinely appointed monarch. After 1809 Alexander saw no reason to call a Diet, and his successors did not feel the need to do so, until Alexander II summoned one in 1863 and attended the opening ceremony in person. Thereafter it met on a regular basis and acquired further powers, including a limited right to initiate legislation. There were, of course, no Finnish representatives in a Russian Diet, because, unlike Sweden, Russia had no elected body of legislators until the early twentieth century, when Nicholas II was forced to summon the first Duma.

The Finns fared better under the paternalistic rule of the Tsars – at least until the end of the century – than they had done under the last of the Gustavian kings. There were some Finns who were unwilling to accept the settlement of 1809. They included some members of the nobility and some army officers who were loath to break their oath of allegiance to the Swedish crown and a number of peasants who remained loyal to Sweden. Resistance to the Russian rule continued in parts of Finland for a few years after 1809, but the majority of the population were prepared to accept the separation from Sweden. The accession of the first of the royal line of Bernadottes, who was crowned King Charles XIV of Sweden in 1818, effectively released those who had scruples about their oaths to the former royal house from their obligations of fealty. There were some servants of the Swedish crown who shared the view of King Charles XIII (1809–18) that 'Finland will return to us yet.' Even Bernadotte, who had been nominated Crown Prince in 1810, hoped for Napoleon's help in restoring Finland to Sweden, but when the French invaded Russia, Sweden had changed its posture. In return for a promise of Russian support for Bernadotte's claim to Norway, he was prepared to accept the idea of the loss of Finland.

In 1812, a few months before Napoleon's troops crossed the Memel river into Russian territory, Alexander made a conciliatory gesture to his new Finnish subjects when he handed back to the Grand Duchy the territory which had been annexed to Russia in 1721 and 1743 by the Treaties of Uusikaupunki and Turku. This restored to Finland the port of Viipuri, the Karelian isthmus, the Karelian district around Lappeenranta, and the Kymi valley. It has been suggested that the main reason for Alexander's generosity was his fear that Sweden, with Napoleon's help, might try to recover Finland. The territorial concessions of 1812 might help to secure the loyalty of the Finns and encourage them to resist Swedish blandishments. The frontier line fixed in 1812 remained the boundary between Russia and Finland until the Peace of Moscow in 1940, when Russia took back the Karelian isthmus and parts of Karelia to the west and north of Lake Ladoga.

Alexander need have had no fears concerning Finland during the war with France. Finland was one of the societies on the European periphery which was not penetrated by the French Revolution. Its ruling elites had been almost unanimous in their abhorrence of the ideas and practices of the Revolution, and they had no problem about changing their status to subjects of the Tsar, once it was clear that their local hegemony would become stronger rather than weaker as a result. Many of them later served in the Russian army, helping Alexander's successors to suppress the revolts in Poland in 1830 and 1863, and serving in wars against Turkey in the Crimea and the Balkans. Alexander felt sufficiently confident of the Finns in 1812 to accept the proposal of G. M. Armfelt, who had returned to Finland, to permit the formation of Finnish military units to serve alongside the Russians.

Helsinki as capital of Finland

Another important development in 1812 was the decision to relocate the capital of Finland, removing it from Turku to Helsinki. The ancient capital of Turku was associated with the period of Swedish rule. It lay on the western limits of Finnish territory, facing the Åland Islands and beyond to the Swedish capital of Stockholm. Helsinki was more centrally placed within the main inhabited area of the Grand Duchy, and 165 kilometres closer to St Petersburg than Turku. In 1812 Helsinki was a small garrison town and seaport, with a population of 4,000. The fortifications of Sveaborg on an island guarding the approaches to the harbour gave it an impressive defensive bulwark against sea-borne attack. The task of converting this small settlement into one of the most impressive architectural monuments of the nineteenth century was entrusted to J. A. Ehrenström, a former servant of the Swedish Crown. The German architect C. L. Engel, who settled in Finland in 1815, was employed to design the main public buildings, conceived in the neo-classical style. The original design was not completed until the 1870s, but even by 1830 enough had been accomplished for a traveller to comment that the Finns were 'converting a heap of rocks into a beautiful city.'

The church of St Nicholas, now the Lutheran Cathedral, which was completed in 1852, dominates the Senate Square (Senaatintori), in which a statue of Alexander II, erected in 1863, overlooks the impressive buildings which occupy the remaining three sides. Following a disastrous fire in 1827 which damaged much of the centre of Turku including its ancient university, the national university was moved to Helsinki and renamed Tsar Alexander's University in 1828. The main buildings of the university occupy the western side of the square and face the Council of State building. In streets leading from Senate Square are the University Library, the Bank of Finland and other buildings of national importance. The centre of Helsinki is built on a peninsula, penetrated by arms of the sea which provide excellent anchorages for ships. Surrounding it are numerous islands, the largest of which are linked by causeways to the mainland; and as the city has grown these have been colonized by suburban settlements. Despite the congestion of a restricted site, the central area has a spacious air. There are several wide boulevards and open squares and some of the earliest municipal parks in northern Europe. Kaivopuisto (Brunnsparken), which occupies the southern tip of the peninsula overlooking Sveaborg (Suomenlinna) was originally developed as a spa in the 1830s, but became a park with formal gardens in the 1850s. Neither the Tsar nor the architect lived to see the completion of the original plan. Alexander died in 1825, Engel in 1840. Ehrenström was justified, however, in commenting in the early stages of the work that Helsinki would become 'one of the most illustrious memorials' to the reign of Alexander I.

Even before the decision had been taken to move the capital from Turku, some national institutions had been established in Helsinki – the Post Office in 1811 and the Board of Health in 1812. The Bank of Finland, one of the world's oldest central banks, moved from Turku to Helsinki in 1819.

4
The Finnish national awakening

The establishment of the Grand Duchy of Finland under the authority of the Russian Tsar came at a time when throughout Europe nations which had previously been submerged within the framework of large, multinational empires were awakening to the realization of their distinct cultural identity. The work of Vuk Karadžić among the south Slav peoples, within both the Habsburg Monarchy and the Ottoman Empire, had kindled the spark which awoke in the educated classes the realization that they were heirs to a tradition which had its roots amongst the ordinary people and owed nothing to their German, Hungarian and Turkish overlords. The language, the cultural traditions and the feeling of a distinct national identity owed much to the survival of oral traditions which had been passed on for centuries amongst people who had no written language. In the second half of the eighteenth century scholars such as Herder and the brothers Grimm and poets like Goethe and Schiller propagated the view that a nation must possess a language and a literature which was based on the culture of the ordinary people. From Greece to Finland and from Spain to Slovakia the peoples of Europe were encouraged to seek the origins of their national culture in the folk traditions of the peasantry. The spread of this concept and its translation into political terms owed much to the influence of Napoleonic France and to the ideas of Rousseau and the French Encyclopaedists, who helped to create the intellectual climate in which the French Revolution germinated.

In Finland H. G. Porthan, a contemporary of Herder, was the leading scholar who made the educated classes aware of the wealth of tradition which was embedded in the folk poetry of the Finns. Porthan died five years before the Declaration of Porvoo, but his ideas helped to shape the course of the Finnish national movement during the rest of the nineteenth century. Paradoxically, most of the historians and poets who contributed to the growing sense of Finnish national pride used their mother-tongue, Swedish – which was also the official language of the Grand Duchy. This phenomenon is not unknown in the nationalist literature of nineteenth-century Europe where, to obtain an audience amongst those who were able to influence events, writers used languages more widely known than those of the submerged nations whose vernaculars were only beginning to be established as literary languages. Thus, Grigor Prličev published his epic poem, the *Sirdar*, in Greek rather than in Macedonian, although the work is now regarded as the seminal work of the modern Macedonian national movement. Mickiewicz, Krasinski and Lelewel, who kept alive the flame of Polish nationalism after the failure of the 1830 insurrection, were equally at home in French as in their native Polish.

In Finland, the national poet J. L. Runeberg, who was born in 1804 – the year of Porthan's death – wrote his *Tales of Ensign Ståhl* (*Fänrik Ståls Sänger*) in Swedish, and even his *Vårt Land* (*Maamme*), which became the Finnish national anthem, was written in Swedish. Ensign Ståhl was one of the heroes in the fight against Russian occupation in 1808–9, and Runeberg's stories give a romanticized account of the exploits of the Finnish soldiers during those campaigns. Another who wrote in Swedish was Zachris Topelius (1818–98), whose *Tales of a Field Surgeon* (*Välskärin Kertomukset*) looked further back to the adventures of Finnish soldiers in the Swedish army during the Thirty Years War.

In the evolution of the Finish national movement the most important literary event in the early nineteenth century was the publication in 1835 of the first edition of Elias Lönnrot's *Kalevala*. Lönnrot was a doctor of medicine who had displayed an interest in folklore during his period as a student. In 1827 he submitted a dissertation on Väinämöinen, the folk hero of oral traditions, for his first degree at Turku University (*Åbo Akademi*), and later, for the degree of doctor of medicine, he wrote about folk medicine. Already before 1835 interest in Finnish oral traditions had led to the publication of some collections of folk poems, particularly a series of *Ancient Poems of the Finnish People* (*Suomen Kansan vanhoja runoja . . .*). Based partly on material collected in eastern Karelia by Zachris Topelius the elder (1781–1831), whose son was later to play a distinguished part in Finnish cultural life. When Lönnrot was forced to complete his studies in Helsinki, following the fire in Turku in 1827, he came into contact with a group of young intellectuals who shared his interest in Finnish folk traditions.

In 1831 this group established the Finnish Literature Society (*Suomalaisen Kirjallisuuden Seura*) and one of their first acts was to raise funds to finance journeys by Lönnrot into the remote regions of Karelia, where he collected the material which was later to be incorporated into *Kalevala*. There were four main areas which provided the raw material for Lönnrot's various compilations – Archangel Karelia, between the White Sea and the Russo-Finnish border, where Topelius the elder had worked; Olonets Karelia and Ladogan Karelia, further to the south; and Inkeri (*Ingria*), around the head of the Gulf of Finland. The survival of these oral traditions in the eastern borderlands of Finland (which had virtually died out in the more densely settled and culturally developed central areas) is a phenomenon which is well known to cultural geographers. It has been shown from numerous examples in different fields of study that cultural survivals frequently linger in areas peripheral to their original homelands long after they have been forgotten in the centres where they were first created. Thus, although the folk tales of the Finns may have been originally created in the more developed areas of southern Finland – where they survive only in 'fossil' form today as place names and fragmentary traditions – they were a living part of the culture in the peripheral regions, where they were discovered by men like Lönnrot. As Martti Haavio put it in 1935, the heroic runes of *Kalevala* 'were preserved in the periphery (Karelia) and forgotten at the centre.'

Lönnrot rearranged the material he had collected, even adding lines of his own, in order to shape it into a form which accorded with his own concept of what a national epic should be. The differences between the 1835 and the 1849 editions of *Kalevala* provide ample material for folklorists to speculate on the extent to which he imposed his own patterns of thought on the compilation. It is generally accepted that, out of over 20,000 lines, some 600 were composed by Lönnrot. The bulk of the work, however it may have been arranged, is thought to have come directly from the people.

The publication of *Kalevala* and of other collections in the 1840s stimulated a wave of activity by Finnish scholars, who laid before the public the evidence of a rich and authentic folk culture which was distinctly Finnish. Some investigated the links between Finnish traditions and those of other Finno-Ugrian speaking peoples. Finland's nearest neighbours, the Estonians, had oral poems which dealt with similar themes to those of *Kalevala* and these were collected under the title of *Kalevipoeg* (the son of Kalevala). The work of the Finnish scholars soon became known throughout Europe. Julius and Kaarle Krohn, who devised the so-called 'historical–geographical' method for sifting the many variants of a story in order to isolate the original elements from later accretions, made valuable contributions to the scientific study of folklore. Julius spoke Swedish, but he made a conscious decision to speak only Finnish with his family, and his son Kaarle was brought up as a Finnish speaker.

Whatever the interest of *Kalevala* might be to students of folklore and linguistics, there is no doubt that its greatest significance was in the inspiration which it gave to the movement for national independence. It gave the Finns a self-awareness which eventually made it possible to build a political movement for independence in the knowledge that, in the words of a Finnish historian writing in the 1890s (expanding on a well-known slogan of Snellman in the 1860s): 'Finland was an entity by itself which could no longer become Sweden and ought never to become Russian. In other words, we felt that we were Finns, members of the Finnish nation.'

Towards the end of the nineteenth century there was a flowering of Finnish art and music as well as of literature and many of the painters, composers and poets drew their inspiration from the folk traditions of which *Kalevala* was the most impressive embodiment. Akseli Gallen-Kallela's *Kalevala* inspired paintings, such as *Aino* (1891), *The forging of the Sampo* (1893), Lemminkäinen's *Mother* (1897) and Joukahainen's *Revenge* (1897) were created at the same time as his friend Sibelius was writing his Kullervo Symphony and his Lemminkäinen Suite, which were amongst the many compositions based on themes from *Kalevala*. In 1903 the poet Eino Leino published the first of his collection of poems *Helkavirsä*, which drew inspiration from the ballads and legends of the early Finns.

The language question

Herder and others held that a nation must have a common language as the badge of its distinct national identity. To the Finnish nationalists this posed a problem. Finland had two languages – Swedish and Finnish. In the early nineteenth century about 15 per cent of the population claimed Swedish as their mother tongue. Swedish was the language of the middle and upper classes, the administrators and most of those educated beyond the village school level. Many from the professional classes were able to speak Finnish as a second language because it was necessary for them to communicate with the 85 per cent of the population whose native tongue was Finnish. There were also Swedish speakers amongst the ordinary fishermen and farmers of the coastal areas of the south west and in Ostrobothnia. After 1809 Russian was only used in the office of the Governor-General and in communication with the Russian officials in St Petersburg. The Tsar had promised the Diet at Porvoo that the language situation would not be changed – which meant that Swedish rather than Russian would be the main language of the administration. Many of the Finnish-speaking folk could read and write, thanks to the efforts of the Lutheran parish clergy, but it was of little use for them in their dealings with authority, because official documents were written in Swedish.

In the early years of the Russian period a movement developed which drew its inspiration from the romantic nationalism which was gathering ground throughout Europe and which survived the overthrow of Napoleon and the re-establishment of the old order in Europe by the peacemakers at the Congress of Vienna. One of the earliest protagonists of this movement was Adolf Ivar Arvidsson, who laid great stress on the need for a uniform national language as the cement which would bind the nation together. 'When the language of its forefathers is lost, a nation, too, is lost . . . For language forms the spiritual, and land the material, boundaries of mankind; but the former is the stronger, because the spirit means more than the material.'

Arvidsson campaigned for the use of Finnish in secondary and higher education as being an essential step towards the achievement of linguistic unity. He started a Finnish language newspaper and circulated pamphlets preaching the doctrine of Finnish nationalism. Despite his opposition to the use of Swedish, he had a far greater respect for Swedish than for Russian culture. Eventually, when the authorities moved against him, closing his newspaper and dismissing him from his teaching post in Turku University, he emigrated to Sweden in 1823. Thereafter the Finnish language cause was taken up by others who were more skilful in their dealings with the Russian authorities. The Russians were not totally opposed to the spread of Finnish language and culture. They could see that, within limits, it could be a useful tool with which to drive a wedge between Sweden and Finland and so reconcile to their new status those Finns who still regretted the separation from Sweden.

The need for a Finnish grammar and for a modern Finnish literature was as important as the discovery of the ancient oral traditions. In 1818 Janko Juteini published a grammar book in Viipuri and during the next few decades, especially after the siting of the national university in Helsinki in 1828, a steady stream of books on the Finnish language appeared. A lectureship in Finnish was established in 1828 and in 1851 M. A. Castrén became the first professor of Finnish. Castrén was a philologist of international repute. He coordinated research amongst the peoples of Siberia and European Russia in order to establish the relationship within the group of Finno-Ugrian languages. 'Grammars are not my objectives', he wrote to J. V. Snellman in 1844, 'but without them I cannot reach my goal'. His goal was 'to prove to the people of Finland that we are not a nation isolated from the world and world history, but that we are related to at least one seventh of the people of the globe'. Castrén was writing at a time when the academic world accepted the theory that there was a mystical relationship between race and language.

In 1853 the German philologist Max Müller first used the Sanskrit word 'Aryan' to describe a group of inter-related Indo-European languages. He then made the scientifically untenable assumption that if two peoples spoke related languages, they must also be related by race. The term 'Aryan race' was taken up by writers in Britain, America, France and Germany, most of whom had no linguistic or ethnological training. Müller realized his mistake and attempted in 1888 to put the record straight.

> I have declared again and again that if I say Aryan . . . I mean simply those who speak an Aryan language . . . I commit myself to no anatomical characteristics . . . To me an ethnologist who speaks of Aryan race . . . is as great a sinner as a linguist who speaks of a dolicephalic dictionary or a brachycephalic grammar.

Müller's disclaimer came too late to be taken into account by those enthusiasts who wanted to use philology as a weapon in the struggle to prove their theories about the racial origins of the particular national group to which they belonged. In Castrén's case, this aim had been to prove the existence of a prehistoric Ural-Altaic community, from which the modern Finns had sprung. Another Finnish philologist who explored the linguistic connections between the various branches of the Finno-Ugrian linguistic family was P. A. Sjögren (1794–1855), who occupied the chair of philology at St Petersburg. The romantic theories of the philologists regarding the racial origins of the Finns and their movements across Eurasia in the dawn of history may be rejected by modern scholars, but their importance in the history of Finnish nationalism is that they provided another pillar – side by side with the folklore traditions of Kalevala – upon which the Finns could support their developing sense of national identity.

In the late nineteenth century, literature in Finnish began to make its impact. The older generation – men like J. L. Runeberg (1804–77) and Zachris Topelius (1818–98) – wrote mainly in Swedish, but in 1864 a young man from the parish of Nurmijärvi in southern Finland – a tailor's son from a poor village – won a state prize for his drama *Kullervo*, a tragedy based on themes from *Kalevala*. In his short life, Aleksis Kivi (1834–72) established both the Finnish drama and the Finnish novel. The production in 1864 of his short lyrical play, *Lea*, based on Biblical themes, is regarded as signalling the birth of the modern Finnish theatre; and his novel *The Seven Brothers*, published in 1870, is hailed as the first major novel in the Finnish language. Although *The Seven Brothers* made Kivi the most famous author in Finland, his genius was not recognized in his lifetime. His untimely death at the age of 38 years is thought to have been hastened by his bitter disappointment at the savage criticism which was poured on him by fashionable critics who accused him of dishonouring the author's trade by writing about coarse and unlettered peasants. Kivi died in poverty, disregarded by his contemporaries. However, editions of *The Seven Brothers* continue to be published over a century after his death and versions have appeared in all the major European languages and in Esperanto. The 1907 Finnish edition was illustrated by Akseli Gallen-Kallela, the greatest Finnish artist of his time.

In addition to literary works in Finnish, the end of the nineteenth century saw a profusion of newspapers and periodicals in Finnish at both national and local level. Some of these were of a literary nature or dealt with the domestic concerns of a rural community but, increasingly during the 1880s and 1890s, a highly political press developed. The press was subjected to censorship by the Russian authorities and the Governor-General was given wide powers under the Press Act. Whether or not these powers were used depended very much upon the political climate at any given time and upon the whim of the Governor-General. During the period in office of the relatively liberal F. L. Heiden (1881–97) there were few occasions when action was taken against newspapers under the censorship laws. In 1891 Heiden ordered the suppression of the Kuopio-based Finnish language paper, *Savo*, but it soon re-emerged under a different title. Although the laws were tightened in 1891, the press in Finland during most of the 1890s was freer than in other parts of the Russian Empire. The situation changed after the appointment of a new Governor-General, N. I. Bobrikov, in 1898. For the next few years a Russification drive resulted in the imposition of severe censorship under new regulations. In general the Swedish-language papers fared worse than those published in Finnish. Between 1899 and 1901, twenty-two papers were permanently suppressed. Forty-three others were suspended for varying periods. Licensing of new papers was also used as a weapon against the press. After 1903 Bobrikov found a new and more effective weapon than censorship: he acquired powers to exile to Siberia both editors and opposition politicians.

Between 1890 and 1905 there were more than eighty Finnish and more than fifty Swedish newspapers published in Finland. In Helsinki alone there were fifteen Swedish-language papers and seven written in Finnish; amongst provincial centres, Kuopio was the main centre for Finnish papers.

In 1900 an official Russian language paper, *Finlyandskaya Gazeta*, appeared and was intended by Bobrikov to be the model for a network of local papers published under the authority of Russian-appointed provincial governors. There was also a Finnish language version of the *Gazeta* – *Suomen Sanomat* – but this failed for lack of readers and the planned provincial newspapers were never started. *Finlyandskaya Gazeta*, propped up by state subsidies, limped along until it was finished by the revolution of 1917.

The Finnish language began to become accepted in the 1840s as a necessary medium for communication at certain levels of the administration. Civil servants were expected to have knowledge of Finnish as well as Swedish and the spread of bilingualism broke down some of the barriers between the two linguistic groups. In 1863 the liberal Tsar Alexander II decreed that Finnish should be an official language of government and should be available on an equal basis to Swedish to litigants in the courts. The language decree of 1863 was issued in response to a petition presented to the Tsar by J. V. Snellman (1806–81), who was a major figure in the movement to promote Finnish national interests, not only in matters of language and culture but also in the sphere of politics, economics and administration. Snellman played a major role in the convening of the Diet of 1863, the first to be held since 1809. As a young man Snellman had been a student in Turku at the time of the fire in 1827. When the university was re-established in Helsinki in 1828 he moved there to complete his studies, which he accomplished in 1831. Between 1835 and 1839 he held the post of lecturer in philosophy, but his views on academic freedom offended the authorities and he was forced to resign. He went to Sweden and then to Germany between 1839 and 1842. Before leaving Finland he had already absorbed many of the ideas of the romantic nationalist movement which were then in full flower in universities like Heidelburg, Jena, Nuremburg and Berlin – in all of which Georg Friedrich Hegel (1770–1831) had held the chair of philosophy. Snellman was already familiar with Hegel's writings – especially his *Philosophy of Right* (1821). Hegel's thought was still the dominant influence in German universities at the time of Snellman's sojourn, and his *Theory of the State,* published in 1842, was inspired by Hegelian concepts.

When Snellman returned to Finland in the autumn of 1842 he was unable to resume his university career and he took a post as headmaster of a boys' school in Kuopio, where he remained for seven years. Whilst in Kuopio he founded two newspapers, one in the Finnish language – the *Farmer's Friend* (*Maamiehen Ystävä*) and one written in Swedish – *Saima.* The former provided practical advice for farmers and was non-political. *Saima* became a highly political mouthpiece for Snellman's nationalist philosophy and soon acquired national status amongst the educated classes throughout Finland. Inevitably, it attracted the attention of the censor and was closed in 1846, but it was almost immediately succeeded by a monthly literary review which continued to carry Snellman's views, although in a less overtly political manner. Returning to Helsinki in 1849, he was soon involved in the political life of the capital and in the changed atmosphere of the 1850s he was able to secure a post as professor in 1852.

Alexander II came to the throne in 1855, whilst the Crimean War was in its final stages. During the first decade of his reign he instituted a series of reforms, the most far reaching of which was the emancipation of the serfs in 1861. This act did not, of course, have a direct bearing on Finland, where serfdom had long since disappeared. However, the generally more relaxed atmosphere did encourage the reformers in Finland to press for further concessions from the Tsar. Snellman's efforts in the late 1850s were directed to the spread of Finnish throughout the educational system. He believed that the strength of a nation lay not only in its material strength: 'Education is also power . . . not the least because it makes a nation an integral part of the civilized . . . world.'

The work begun in the 1850s by Snellman and others bore fruit during the later decades of the nineteenth century. The spread of Finnish secondary schools increased to the extent that in 1880 less than one third of the 3,500 grammar schools were Finnish speaking, whilst twenty years later almost two thirds of 8,600 schools were classed as Finnish. The increase in Finnish-speaking students in higher education, in commercial and technical colleges and in the University of Helsinki was a reflection of the growing numbers of the educated classes who used Finnish as their mother tongue. In 1870 only 8 per cent of students admitted to the university were enrolled as Finnish speakers. In 1900 the proportion had risen to 56 per cent. Finnish teachers were able to train at a college established in Jyväskylä in 1863 – although this was not an exclusively Finnish institution. In 1862 the historian Yrjö Yrjö-Koskinen (also known as G. Z. Forsman) presented his professorial dissertation in Finnish and a few years later he published the first major history of Finland (*Suomen Kansan Historia*), written from the nationalist standpoint in the Finnish language. Unlike many of the advocates of Finnish from Arvidsson to Snellman, Yrjö-Koskinen wrote and spoke in Finnish, although he knew Swedish. Most of the early leaders of the movement to promote the Finnish language found it easier to use Swedish.

This is not to say, however, that they subscribed in any way to the views of an extremist group of Swedish speakers, led by August Sohlman (1824–74) and Axel Olof Freudenthal (1836–1911), who developed theories about the racial superiority of the Swedes and the inadequacy of the Finnish language as a medium of expression for a civilized nation. Some Swedish speakers were attracted to the idea of 'Scandinavianism' – the creation of a common Nordic community embracing Noway, Sweden, Denmark and Finland. If Finland were to participate in such a venture, the link with Russia must be broken. It is not surprising that the Russian authorities in Finland reacted strongly against any manifestations of 'Scandinavianism'. In 1843 a party of students from Helsinki participated in the annual summer meeting of Scandinavian students at Uppsala, and all were suspended from the university when they returned home.

On the whole, however, the Finns were less enthusiastic about becoming involved in a Scandinavian union than were the Swedes and the Danes. Bishop Gruntvig in Denmark was one of the most enthusiastic supporters of the idea and spoke warmly about the revival of the common Nordic past. In 1845 a gathering of Scandinavian students in Copenhagen openly pledged loyalty to 'our great common fatherhood,' but there is no evidence that any Finns were present. The majority of those Finns who wanted to break with Russia – whether Swedish or Finnish speakers – saw independence rather than a merger with a Scandinavian superstate as their goal. The extremism of the so-called Svecomen was in part the reaction of a privileged minority to the advancing cause of the majority of Finnish speakers. The leading figures in the Swedish movement were aristocrats, such as Baron von Born and Baron Wrede, and they appeared to the more concerned with the preservation of the position of Swedish speakers in the upper echelons of society than in championing the cause of the Swedish-speaking farmers and fisherfolk of Ostrobothnia and the coastal areas, where they formed a majority amongst the ordinary people in many communities.

Snellman became a Senator in 1863 but was forced to resign in 1868 after a dispute with the Governor-General. The Finnish nationalist cause suffered an eclipse during the next decade. It revived again in 1882, a year after Snellman's death, when Yrjö-Koskinen took his seat on the Senate. Snellman's achievement was not only in the field of politics. He was a major figure in the establishment of a Finnish currency and in the strengthening of the power of the Bank of Finland, so that the Finnish economy was able to develop in the late nineteenth century in virtual independence of Russia. His work in this field was as great a contribution to the independence movement as were his activities in promoting the Finnish language and in establishing the Diet as a body which could represent Finnish political opinion. In 1868 the bank was placed under the authority of the Diet and when a more democratic parliament, the *Eduskunta,* was formed in 1906, this supervisory function was transferred to it.

The constitution of independent Finland passed in 1919 contains a clause (Article 73) which reaffirms this principle: 'The Bank of Finland is under the guarantee and care of the Eduskunta, and under the surveillance of Supervisors whom the Eduskunta appoints.' The degree of autonomy from the government which this relationship with parliament ensures is an important aspect of present-day Finnish economic policy. It stems directly from Snellman's reforms of 1868. Snellman also helped to ensure a unique position within the Tsarist economy for the Finnish unit of currency, the *markka*. The first step was to weaken the link between the markka and the paper rouble. When the markka was first issued it was tied to the rouble, which was then linked to a silver standard. The strain on the Russian currency during the Crimean War forced the Russians to abandon the link between the rouble and silver. Wartime inflation devalued the paper rouble and had serious effects on the Finnish economy. By re-establishing the link between the markka and the silver standard, Snellman was able to stabilize the Finnish currency and insulate it from fluctuation in the value of the paper rouble. In 1878 Finland went on to the international gold standard and in 1886 won the right to issue its own bank notes. These developments enabled Finland to achieve a degree of financial autonomy.

5
The Finnish economy in the nineteenth century

During the first half-century of Russian rule the Finnish economy changed little from the position which the Tsars had inherited from the Swedes. The majority of the population depended for their livelihood upon fishing and farming, hunting and trapping, except in some areas where forest-based industries based on the export of timber and tar provided a supplementary income. The import into Britain of what was known as 'naval stores' included spars and planking for ships and 'Stockholm tar' for caulking. Until the reforms of the 1760s these products had to be exported through Stockholm as the staple port, but thereafter they could be sent directly from Finland to the outside world.

Iron working had a long history, but the iron forges and associated workshops were on a small scale, often organized in paternalistic communities known as *ruukit*, such as that which was established at Tammisaari (Ekenäs) on the southwest coast. In a typical ruukki the iron master was the overlord of a community of craftsmen and their families. Charcoal was the main fuel and the ores often came from nodules of bog iron recovered from lake beds and marshes. In 1815 there were only 600 workers employed in metal working and both the iron and non-ferrous metal industries had only local importance. There was some expansion in the middle of the century, because the demand for metal goods increased in Russia, and by 1870 the number of metal workers had increased to over 3,000.

The textile industry, which expanded in the 1820s, owed its growth to the initiative of a Quaker engineer from Glasgow, James Finlayson. Finlayson had worked for twenty years in the Kolpino workshops near St Petersburg and it is said that he made the acquaintance of the Tsar during his stay in Russia. He settled in Tampere, then little more than a village with about 1,000 inhabitants, in 1820. In 1821 he persuaded Alexander I to grant Tampere the right to import raw materials and machinery free of duty. Without this encouragement it is doubtful whether this inland centre over 100 kilometres from Pori, the nearest seaport, could have developed into a thriving industrial city. In 1828, after experimenting with the manufacture of woollen cloth, Finlayson opened a cotton factory which by 1845 was employing over 500 workers. The raw cotton was, of course, imported, but until the end of the century the exemption from payment of duties which Alexander granted to Tampere in 1821 was honoured by subsequent Russian governments. The greatest asset which the site at Tampere initially possessed was an abundant and reliable source of water power. The works were located on a stream which connects two lakes, Näsijärvi and Pyhäjärvi, between which there is a fall in level of 20 metres, thus giving a sufficient head of water to turn the machinery. Later in the century steam power was installed, but with the development of hydro-electricity Tampere was again able to provide a cheap source of power. Finlayson's was the first firm in Scandinavia to light its factory by electricity when Carl von Nottbeck, the son of the then owner, returned from studying in America under the guidance of Thomas Alva Edison. The lights were first switched on in 1882 but it was not until the twentieth century that electricity was used as the motive power for driving the machinery.

Finlayson returned to Scotland in 1838, having sold out to two businessmen of German origin living in St Petersburg. They increased the capital of the firm, built a new factory – the largest in Finland – and soon captured a large share of the Russian market for machine-woven cotton cloth. Other textile industries were established in Finland during the mid nineteenth century and by the 1860s textile manufacturing had become the largest source of industrial employment in Finland. Over 4,000 were employed in cotton factories and a further 1,000 were engaged in the woollen and linen industries. (These figures exclude, of course, hand spinning and weaving for domestic use.)

Despite the early importance of textiles and the survival of metal-working industries from the Swedish times, the driving force which propelled Finland towards industrialization was generated by the development of its most abundant natural resource – the forests. Most Finnish farmers had access to a few acres of growing timber and in the north there were vast tracts of state-owned forests. At the time of independence it was estimated that 37 per cent of all forest land was publicly owned – either by the state, the parish government or the church. The state ownership of forests dates back to 1542, when Gustavus Vasa decreed that all lands not then allocated to private owners should pass into the royal domain. There were further acquisitions by the Swedish crown at the time of the Great Partition (*Isojako*) of the eighteenth century. Until the second half of the century, forest-based activities were primarily for local use – for fuel, building materials, fencing and so forth – and the export trade in such commodities as tar played only a small part in the national economy.

Technological changes in Western Europe reduced the demand for tar and charcoal but simultaneously produced new demands for forest products. At a time when Finland began to import coal and coal tar from Britain, a return traffic developed in pit props and sawn timber. Hand sawing gave way to mechanization, with both water and steam power being used. Joint stock companies, often employing foreign capital (usually British) were formed to exploit the forest resources for the export trade. In the late nineteenth century about 7 per cent of the forest area was owned by timber, pulp and paper companies, who worked the more accessible areas of forest within reach of the coast. The internal waterway system was improved by the cutting of canals, linking the long, finger-like lakes which stretched for hundreds of miles into the interior of the Lake Plateau. The Saimaa Canal, opened in 1856, connected the 240 kilometre long Lake Saimaa system with the port of Viipuri, thus providing a water route which penetrated deep into the heart of eastern Finland.

Sea-going ships could sail from Kuopio to the Gulf of Finland and beyond to the ports of northern Europe. The first steam-powered ship to operate in Finland was the tug *Ilmarinen*, which went into service on Lake Saimaa in 1833. In 1856 the steamship *Suomi* began to play the waters of Lake Päijänne and in 1857 the *Valamo* provided a steamer service between Lake Ladoga and St Petersburg. By 1875 there were forty-five steamers operating on the inland waterways of Finland: some were tugs, used to haul rafts of logs to sawmills situated near waterfalls and others were general carriers of goods and passengers.

The construction of railways, which began in 1862 with the opening of the Helsinki–Hämeenlinna line, provided an additional means of access into the interior. By the end of the century every major seaport was served by railways and the whole system was joined to the Russian network by a line built in 1870, from Riihimäki on the Helsinki–Hämeenlinna line to St Petersburg. The railways operated – and still do so today – on the Russian broad gauge of five feet. From the beginning they were state owned. In a country as sparsely populated as Finland it is unlikely that the traffic would have been sufficient to provide a profit for private entrepreneurs, yet without the railways the economic development of the country would have been held back.

With a rail density of only 1.8 kilometres per 100 square kilometres of its area, Finland records the lowest figure in Europe after Norway, but in relation to its population it has 12.8 kilometres per 1,000 inhabitants – a higher figure than any other European country except Sweden. (The comparable figures for Britain are 7.7 kilometres per 100 square kilometres and 3.4 kilometres per 1,000 inhabitants.) For example, Finnish railways traverse long distances through virtually uninhabited country in order to link important inland centres of economic activity with seaports. The principal goods carried, as has always been the case, are bulk cargoes of metal ores, timber, wood pulp, paper and raw materials. In 1981 these commodities amounted to over 70 per cent of the freight carried. Most of the railways were built during the last three decades of the nineteenth century and virtually no new lines have been constructed since independence was achieved. The period of railway building coincided with the expansion of the economy, and without the railways this economic growth would not have been possible.

The boom in the demand for forest products transformed the Finnish economy. It occurred after a period of privation and difficulty in the 1850s and 1860s. The Crimean War (1853–56) created some disruption to the Finnish economy. Trade links with Sweden and Britain were interrupted. British warships bombarded Finnish coastal towns and stocks of pitch and tar were destroyed. The damage inflicted by these events was small, however, compared with the consequences of the disastrous famines of 1862 and 1867, which caused widespread distress in rural areas. The whole decade was known as the 'hungry sixties' and, as in Ireland in the 'hungry forties', large numbers of poor farmers and landless peasants emigrated in order to escape from the misery which followed the failure of crops. The worst hit areas were Ostrobothnia and Northern Satakunta, and it was from there that the first wave of Finnish migrants to America came. Hunger was not the only force which impelled them to cross the Atlantic. There was also a belief that life in America and Canada was freer than in Finland. Recruiting agents began to operate in Finland in the 1860s, often luring poor Finns to emigrate on the promise of unlimited opportunities and untold wealth awaiting them in the New World. Letters home from those who had prospered in their new country added to the illusions of the starving Finns at home. In one such letter, sent in 1866 to a relative in Ii, a small town on the Bothnian coast between Oulu and Kemi, a recent arrival stated that 'in America even the grain grows up in a week . . . and the supply of red wine flowing from between cracks in the cliffs never became exhausted, not even by drinking it'. Zachris Topelius, then a professor of history in Helsinki, told the students in 1867, 'Nature seems to cry out to our people "Emigrate or die"!' Between 1883 and 1917 at least 300,000 Finns (out of a total population of between two million in 1881 and three million in 1921) left for the United States. The total number of migrants was much larger: others went to Russia, Sweden and elsewhere.

A minority of those who stayed at home prospered as the Finnish economy began to develop. One Finnish writer, describing the lifestyle of the *nouveau riche* in 'the flush and boisterous logging years', spoke of the time 'when the horses of the lumber barons drank champagne and the nabobs themselves lit their cigars with banknotes'. The first wave of prosperity came with the demand in western Europe – and especially Britain – for sawn timber and pit props from the coniferous forests and beech wood for the bobbins and reels used in the textile industry. Soon, however, a new forest product was in demand – paper. The market for paper grew rapidly as mass circulation newspapers were established in western Europe around the turn of the century, but even before then the Russian market for Finnish pulp and paper was already creating a demand which Finnish manufacturers were eager to satisfy. Until 1917 Russia was the biggest customer for Finnish paper products.

For a time in the 1870s and 1880s the Finnish metal-working industries were able to expand on the basis of exports to Russia. Towards the end of the century the establishment of a modern Russian iron and steel industry, based on the abundant ores of Krivoi Rog and supplied with foreign capital and technical expertise, soon ousted the older and less efficient Finnish manufacturers from the Russian market. The Finnish metal-working industries had a brief revival during the First World War, when they supplied the Russian armed forces with essential war materials, but after independence they were forced to reorganize on the basis of a restricted home market.

Although industrialization began in Finland during the nineteenth century, agriculture remained the principal occupation of the majority of the population. At the time of independence two thirds of the three million Finns lived mainly from farming. Feudalism had been abolished in the greater part of Finland before 1809, although traces survived in the areas of 'Old Finland' which Alexander I restored to the Grand Duchy in 1812. The land reforms which affected Russia between the emancipation of the serfs in 1861 and the revolution of 1905 (and which provided the material for Gorkii's novel *The Artamonovs*) had little direct bearing on the situation in Finland. The Finnish equivalent to Gorkii's novel is F. E. Sillanpää's *Meek Heritage* (*Hurskas Kurjuus*), which describes the life of a poor Finnish 'crofter', Juha Toivola, from his birth in 1857 to his death during the civil war of 1918. Despite the superficial differences, however, there is much in common in the lifestyle of the liberated serfs described in Gorkii's work and that of Juha Toivola and his circle – the landless peasants and small tenant farmers of southern Finland during the same period. At the turn of the century about a third of the farm land of Finland was under owner occupiers, much of the rest being farmed by *torpparit*, or tenant farmers. There was also a large class of landless labourers, the *mäkitupalaiset*, who hired their labour to the more prosperous farmers or, like many rural dwellers, worked during the winter in the forests whether or not they owned land.

The changes which occurred in Finnish agriculture during the late nineteenth century tended to benefit the yeoman farmers and the wealthier tenants at the expense of the poorer tenants and the mäkitupalaiset. Alexandra Kollontai, who was half Finnish, may have exaggerated when she wrote in 1903 of the revolutionary potential of the 900,000 landless peasants in Finland, but the events of 1917 and 1918 suggested that there were a large number of poor Finnish peasants who were prepared to resort to desperate measures against the richer farmers in order to wreak vengeance upon those who had oppressed them. The land reforms and the timber boom of the late nineteenth century tended to benefit those who owned farm and forest land at the expense of their landless neighbours. The consolidation of arable strips into larger fields, the introduction of new machinery, the establishment of co-operative dairies and the provision of credit facilities all helped to widen the gulf between the haves and the have nots. Finland was moving from a subsistence agriculture, based on self-sufficient rural communities, into a new era in which specialization for the urban markets of Finland and St Petersburg was to become increasingly important. In the 1850s Finland was virtually self-sufficient in foodstuffs in the better years. When the crops failed, as in the 1860s, famine was inevitable. At the beginning of the First World War self-sufficiency in food was at the level of about 60 per cent.

Finland had become an exporter of dairy produce – first to Russia then after 1900 to Germany and Britain – and an importer of food grains, mainly from Russia. In 1913 the production of wheat, rye and barley was at or below the level of 1880. Amongst the cereals only oats had increased in output, from 7.9 million bushels in 1880 to 22 million in 1913. The oats were used to feed the growing herds of cattle, there to provide the milk, butter, cheese and meat which began to play an increasing part in Finnish exports.

Half-hearted efforts were made to reform land ownership during the early years of the twentieth century in order to alleviate the lot of the poorer rural dwellers, but no serious advance was made until after independence. The number of *torpparit* and *mäkitupalaiset* actually increased, because the total population grew – from 1.76 million in 1870 to 3 million in 1913. The numbers in rural areas increased during the same period from 1.5 million to 2.5 million. This potentially explosive situation was defused, however, by the mass emigration of the period.

6

The political development of Finland, 1863–1917

The convening of the Finnish Diet in 1863, after a break of over fifty years, marked the beginning of a new era in Finnish political life. The Language Decrees of 1863 and 1865, described during a meeting of the Diet in 1877 as 'a sort of Magna Carta for the Finnish-speaking part of the nation', took over twenty years to be implemented, but progress was made, however slow. It would have been much slower if the authorities had not been constantly prodded by the Diet. The Diet Act of 1869 laid down that the Diet should be summoned at least every five years, and in fact it was summoned more frequently. In 1879 the electoral laws were relaxed and the franchise in the towns was widened. Legislation on economic and commercial questions and on education was enacted during the 1870s and 1880s. Although the Tsar still had the power to reject legislation passed by the Finnish Diet, in practice the degree of self-government increased at both national and local level within the Grand Duchy.

The gradual liberalization of the system gave an opportunity for political parties to develop. The language issue was foremost in the early period, with the Finnish nationalists – the so-called Fennomen, led by Yrjö-Koskinen (also known as Forsman) opposing the Swedish language supporters – the Svecomen. These labels were attached to groups of people who generally took up similar positions on certain political issues, but there were at this time no political parties in the modern sense. The pattern began to change in the 1870s, when Professor Leo Mechelin (1839–1914) attempted to form a Liberal Party (which stood outside the language dispute) on a programme which was *laissez faire* in economic policy and constitutional where the rights of the Grand Duchy were concerned. Snellman, almost at the end of his life – he died in 1881 – denounced the new party, stating that 'true liberalism is dedication to the task of liberating the majority from the tutelage and linguistic tyranny of the minority.'

Mechelin became a member of the Senate in 1882, at the same time as Yrjö-Koskinen took his seat. Mechelin's attempt to form a strong Liberal Party foundered and his group drifted towards the Svecomen. The Fennomen split into two groups – the Young Finns, who were more radical in their economic policies than the other group, the conservative Old Finns, and less willing to compromise on the language question. In 1889 the Young Finns founded a newspaper in order to propagate their ideas. This was *Päivälehti,* which later became *Helsingin Sanomat,* the leading Finnish-language newspaper of the present time. In 1894 they formally instituted a new party dedicated to the cause of the Finnish language and also to a widening of the franchise and an improvement in the social conditions of the rural poor. The social reform aspects of the programme took second place to the fight for Finland's autonomy, especially after the Russification programme – initiated in the last years of the reign of Alexander III (1881–94) and intensified under Nicholas II (1894–1917) – began to gather momentum. They were able to form a constitutional front with which to confront the Russians and also to oppose more conservative Old Finns, who believed in a more flexible policy which involved co-operation rather than confrontation with the Russian authorities. The Old Finns became known as the Compliants, as opposed to the Constitutionalists.

Russification

The toleration of Finland's special status within the Tsarist Empire, which had existed from 1809 until the accession of Tsar Alexander III in 1881, began to crumble during the 1880s. Many leading Finns had assumed that the promises made at Porvoo and renewed by each succeeding Tsar formed a solid foundation for Finnish autonomy. Although Alexander III made the traditional promises and even reaffirmed them in 1891, he was in fact suspicious of Finnish nationalist aspirations. He came under increasing pressure from

Russian nationalists and pan-Slavists – especially as Russian expansionist aims in the Balkans were thwarted by countervailing pressures from the rising power of Bismark's German Empire – as well as from the more traditional opponents of Austria–Hungary and Britain. Russian fears of Finnish separatism were increased by signs of the growth of German influence in the Baltic provinces of Russia, where German commercial and cultural influences dated back to mediaeval times. There were also links between Finland and Germany, Sweden and Britain which could create doubts about the loyalty of the Finns in the minds of suspicious Russian nationalists. Further evidence which the Russians could adduce to justify their concern about Finland arose from the attitude of some Finnish nationalists to Russia's involvement with Britain in Afghanistan in the 1870s and 1880s. There was a strong feeling that Finland should remain neutral in any conflicts in which Russia might become involved, if the struggle for influence on the North West Frontier should escalate into open war between Britain and Russia. This was partly coloured by the Finnish desire to protect their maritime trade, which was becoming an increasingly important element in the developing Finnish economy.

Alexander has been described as 'a foolish narrow-minded man', who wished 'to return to the rigorous absolutism of Nicholas I, and to maintain it by a reactionary policy, based on police rule'. He lacked self-reliance and leaned heavily on the advice of his former tutor, Konstantin Pobedonostsev (1827–1907), who advocated a policy based on Autocracy, Orthodoxy and Nationalism. He did not regard the promises made by the Tsars to the Finns as binding constitutional guarantees. They were concessions made by absolute rulers whose powers could not be trammelled by the resolutions of so-called representative assemblies ('the great lie of our time'), which could be withdrawn at the will of the Tsar. 'What is this freedom by which so many minds are agitated?' wrote Pobedonostsev, 'it leads the people so often to misfortune.'

The full force of russification did not strike Finland until after Alexander's death in 1894, although there were signs of the growing constitutional battle in 1890. In that year Alexander issued an imperial decree, anulling legislation reforming the criminal law which had been passed by the Diet and approved by the Tsar. The reason given for the reversal of policy was the 'separatist' character of some of the provisions of the new laws. Shortly afterwards another imperial decree placed the Finnish Post Office under direct Russian rule, without any attempt to discuss the issue with the Finnish Diet. The Post Office had been established in 1811 and had acquired the right to issue its own postage stamps, a right which continued for ten years after the promulgation of the 'Post Office Manifesto' of 1890.

Pobedonostsev's influence continued under the reign of Nicholas II, at least until he retired from the post of Procurator of the Holy Synod – a kind of lay director of the Orthodox Church – a position of great power which he held from 1880 until his resignation at the time of the revolution of 1905. Nicholas was a weak man, easily influenced by his advisers, and under his rule russification gathered momentum in Poland, the Baltic provinces and Finland. In 1898 he appointed General Nikolai Bobrikov (1839–1904) as Governor-General of Finland and a programme of systematic russification was launched. One of the first acts was the issuing on 15 February 1899 of the so-called February Manifesto. This placed most of Finnish legislation under the direct surveillance of the Russian government.

> While maintaining in full force the prevailing statutes concerning the promulgation of local laws which relate exclusively to the internal affairs of Finland, We have found it necessary to reserve to Ourselves the final decision as to which laws come within the scope of general Imperial legislation.

Opinion in Finland was divided as to the best method of confronting this new situation, which was seen by some as an Imperial coup d'état which threatened all the hard won gains of the Finns acquired during the previous century. The mainly Swedish-speaking Liberals (led by Mechelin) and the Young Finns formed an opposition which acquired the label 'Constitutionalist'. The Old Finns, who held on to their seats in the Senate when the Constitutionalists resigned, believed in a policy of compromise and negotiation, fearing that confrontation would destroy any influence which Finns might have with the Russian authorities, and would take the government of Finland entirely out of Finnish hands. They were called the Compliants. A third group, known as the Activists, believed in direct action against Tsarism by means of strikes and even military insurgency, a policy which went far beyond the cautious advocacy of passive resistance which was urged by the Constitutionalists.

The Finnish Labour Party, founded in 1899 and renamed the Social Democratic Party in 1903, was split. One group, led by Yrjö Mäkelin of Tampere, favoured co-operation with the Constitutionalists and in the elections for the Diet in 1904 three of its members were elected on a joint ticket with the Constitutionalists. They were the first socialists to serve on a parliamentary body within the Tsarist Empire. The Helsinki section of the Social Democrats, led by Edvard Valpas, refused to cooperate with the bourgeois parties. Accusations that they were in collusion with the Old Finns, or Compliants, were based on the common opposition of the two groups to the Swedish-speaking minority, but subsequent events showed that such charges were unfounded.

Further russification came in 1901 with the decision that Finnish conscripts, who since 1878 had served in a separate Finnish defence force of some 6,000 men, should be placed under Russian officers and that their NCOs should be required to speak Russian. Finnish soldiers, as subjects of the Tsar, had always been eligible for service as volunteers in the Russian army. Some had fought in the Crimean War, in Poland and in the Russo-Turkish War of 1877–78, as a monument in the army headquarters in Helsinki commemorates. One of the most famous Finnish soldiers in the Russian army was C. G. E. Mannerheim, who volunteered in 1887 at the age of 20 years, rose to the rank of Lt. General; becoming Regent of Finland in 1918, Marshal of Finland in 1942 and President of the Republic in 1944.

The conscripts who were affected by the decree of 1901 were, of course, in a different category from regulars like Mannerheim. They served on the territory of Finland, in Finnish units, under Finnish officers. One reaction of the Finns both to the February Manifesto and to the conscription decree of 1901 was to raise petitions to present to the Tsar. The first, signed by over half a million Finns – out of a total adult population of 1.5 million – was taken to St Petersburg by a deputation of 500 representatives. The Tsar refused to see them. The petition against the Conscription Act, which also received half a million signatures, was likewise rejected. Support was organized outside Finland.

In June 1899 a thousand public figures in western Europe signed a petition to the Tsar. They included Emile Zola, Anatole France, Henrik Ibsen, Herbert Spencer and Florence Nightingale. The delegation which went to Russia to present it was also refused an audience with Nicholas II, but on their return home via Finland they were received with enthusiasm by the grateful Finns.

After the rejection of the 1901 petition the passive resistance movement in Finland gained momentum. Several of the Constitutionalists were forced to flee abroad. Young men were urged not to register for the call-up, and many thousands failed to respond to the notices for the 1902 draft. Some diplomatically removed themselves to Sweden or went into hiding. There had always been a selective draft, because the numbers in the relevant age group were far too large for the needs of the Finnish defence force. Taken aback by the domestic and international reaction to its arbitrary decrees, the Russian government attempted to conciliate the Finns by suggesting that only 1 per cent of those eligible would be called, the choice to be made by the drawing of lots. More than half of those summoned refused to report and after further attempts the authorities gave up. Finland's requirement for military service was commuted to a nominal monetary payment, and the Finnish army was disbanded. This gave rise to the curious situation that at the time of the First World War, the Russian Revolutions of 1917 and the declaration of independence and the subsequent civil war, there was no Finnish army. Its place was taken in 1917–18 by Red Guards – raised by the labour movement; and a White Army – composed of Finnish youths (some of whom had been trained in Germany), a collection of volunteers from Finland and Sweden and Finnish defectors from the Tsar's regular army.

The situation in Finland changed dramatically in 1904. Without the formality of a declaration of war, the Japanese attacked the Russian fleet at Port Arthur on 8 February and proceeded to inflict heavy defeats on the Russian forces in Manchuria. The shock to the Tsarist system led to a wave of strikes throughout Russia. In July the Minister of the Interior, Plehve, was assassinated. A strike at the Putilov engineering works in St Petersburg led to 'Bloody Sunday', 22 January 1905, when Father Gapon, an Orthodox priest, led a procession of workers and their families, carrying a petition asking the Tsar to summon a Constitutional Assembly and grant various modest reforms. Troops guarding the Winter Palace in St Petersburg opened fire, and hundreds were killed.

Meanwhile, in Finland, the hated Bobrikov was assassinated in Helsinki on 16 June 1904 by Eugen Schauman, a young Finn acting on his own. The assassin immediately committed suicide after the shooting, thus saving the Russians the embarassment of a trial. The Russian authorities did not make the mistake of increasing the repression of the Finns. They appointed Prince Obolensky as Bobrikov's successor. Although accepting the general policy of russification, he behaved in a more conciliatory manner. Elections for a new Diet were permitted and some of the Constitutionalists who had fled abroad in 1901 were able to return and to take their seats. The Compliants were heavily defeated and the new assembly became a centre of resistance to Russian rule. In September 1905, assisted by the efforts of President Theodore Roosevelt, Russia and Japan signed the Peace of Portsmouth (New Hampshire) and formally ended the state of war between them.

Tsarist Russia not only sustained material and territorial losses but also suffered a heavy blow to its standing, both internationally and at home. Already reeling from the effects of the revolutionary ferment within its own borders, the government was in no position to resist the demands of the Finns. In a declaration on 30 October 1905 the Tsar conceded a Duma, or parliament, to his Russian subjects. The following day a general strike was called in Finland.

Although the leading members of the strike movement were members of the Social Democratic Party, they were supported by members of the bourgeois parties and the Tsar found it impossible to resist the demands of a united Finnish opposition. He agreed on 4 November 1905 to sign the November Manifesto, which cancelled many of the decrees issued under the authority of the February Manifesto of 1899. A new Senate was invited to submit the draft of a bill which would establish a parliament elected by universal suffrage, with equal voting rights for men and women and with guarantees of civil liberty. The dominant figure of the Senate which took office 1 December 1905 was Leo Mechelin, one of the Constitutionalists who had returned from exile in 1904 to take his seat in the Diet. The 'Mechelin Senate' completed its work within a few months and on 29 May 1906 the Diet passed laws which established a 200-member, unicameral parliament – the *Eduskunta* – which was to be elected by universal male and female suffrage. In the first elections under the new system, held in 1907, 890,000 votes were cast. The largest party, the Social Democrats, gained 37 per cent of the popular vote and received 80 of the 200 seats. The next largest party, the *Suomalainen Puolue* (Old Finns) had 27 per cent of the vote and 59 seats. The Liberals (Young Finns) obtained only 26 seats, two more than the *Svenska Folkpartiet* (Swedish People's Party), and the *Maalaisliitto* (Agrarian Union) gained only 9 seats.

The relatively good showing of the Old Finns may seem surprising in view of their collaborationist attitude to the Russian authorities. It was one of their number, Professor Danielson-Kalmari, who had spoken in 1901 of the need to preserve a bridge across which the Tsar and the Finnish nation 'can once more find each other', and another, E. Soisalon-Soininen, who had served the Tsar as Attorney-General for Finland in 1904–5, until he was murdered by a Finnish patriot. Another, Juho Kusti Paasikivi, served as Paymaster-General after 1903. He was elected to the Eduskunta in 1907 and became President of the Republic in 1946. The explanation may lie in the consistency of the Old Finns in opposing the Swedish language minority, and also in the fears of many conservative-minded Finns in the face of the rising power of the labour movement. The Young Finns were suspect in the eyes of many Finnish nationalists because of their willingness to collaborate with the Swedes in the struggle against the Russians.

The speed with which Finland acquired a range of political parties almost overnight, most of which have survived in some form up to the present time, is a remarkable tribute to the political maturity of the nation. During the years of preparation, when they struggled to achieve some form of modern representative democracy, the foundations for a new political system were being laid. The dramatic events of 1904 and 1905 released them from the shackles of a system which had been imposed on them by their Russian masters, and whose roots went back to mediaeval Sweden. From labouring under one of the most archaic systems of government in contemporary Europe they were suddenly launched into a parliamentary system which had features in advance of some of the long-established democracies of western Europe – a single chamber parliament, equal voting rights for men and women and a recognition of civil liberties. As long as they were tied to Tsarist Russia these democratic rights were liable to be taken from them and it was not until full independence was achieved that the system was secure.

The Old Finns became the Finnish Party (*Suomalainen Puolue*) and were eventually transformed into today's National Coalition Party (*Kansallinen Kokoomus*), of whom the leader, Harry Holkeri, became Prime Minister in 1987. They are the nearest equivalent in the west European political spectrum to the Conservatives, and their greatest figure – the Churchill of Finland – was J. K. Paasikivi.

The Young Finns became the Liberals and managed to maintain their position in the Eduskunta until 1983, but they are no longer represented. The Swedish Peoples Party is the only party surviving today which bases its appeal on the representation of the interests of a linguistic group. It therefore covers a wide political spectrum, from conservative to far left, although its main platform is within the western liberal tradition.

The Agrarian Union (*Maalaisliitto*) changed its name in 1965 to that to the Centre Party. Its support steadily increased after independence. In 1907 it secured 51,000 votes and 9 seats. Today it can command half a million votes and is one of the three major political parties.

The Social Democratic Party, which emerged as the largest single party in 1907, has maintained that position in almost every parliament since, despite splits and defections; and the growth has occurred of a far left group, the Finnish People's Democratic League (SKDL), in the first three decades after the Second World War. The Social Democrats are the only party to have obtained more than half the seats in the Eduskunta – in 1916 they won 103 of the 200 seats. It is difficult for one party to gain an absolute majority because the method of election is by a system of proportional representation.

The success of the Social Democrats in 1907 depended upon their appeal to the rural electorate. There were few industrial workers in 1907, but many poor farmers and landless peasants were living in the countryside. The activity of the Social Democrats in the early years of the century, especially in their fight against the Bobrikov regime, drew support from many strata of society. Amongst the leaders there were several who had started their political life as supporters of the Old Finns in the 1890s – including Otto Ville Kuusinen, who later became a member of the Secretariat of the Comintern. There was a radical element in the domestic programme of the Old Finns which appealed to rebellious spirits, but this soon became overlain by Finnish nationalism and by hostility to the Swedish-speaking elements in Finnish society. This led them into collaboration with the Russian authorities. As one speaker ironically alleged during the first phase of russification in the 1890s, the Old Finns would sell 'our country's most cherished rights, provided that the deed of sale is drawn up in Finnish.' The drift into right-wing nationalism of the Old Finns lost them the support of the younger radicals, and several crossed over to the new Social Democratic Party. One of the few who crossed from the Young Finns to the Social Democrats was Yrjö Sirola, who was later the Director of the Finnish Section of the Lenin School when he died in Moscow in 1936.

Some of those elected as Social Democrat members of the Eduskunta in 1907 were Marxists, young intellectuals who had been influenced by the ferment of revolutionary ideas which was then disturbing the academic community in Russia and the Russian émigré communities in western Europe. Personalities like Plekhanov, Martov, Trotsky, Lenin, and Vera Zasulich were conducting polemical debates in journals and in clandestine assemblies – some of which were held in the relatively freer atmosphere of Finland. At the Second Congress of the Russian Social Democrats, held in Brussels and London in 1903, the fateful division occurred between the Bolsheviks and the Mensheviks. These debates had their effect upon the Finnish Social Democrats, but the divisions did not come to the surface until later. In 1907 the main issues concerned the relations between the Finns and the Russians, and the Social Democrats enjoyed a wider degree of popularity as the protagonists of the rights of the mass of the Finnish people.

The November Manifesto of 1905, which formed the basis for the new electoral law, was derived from ideas promoted by a group of Social Democrats – the so-called November Socialists. They included Yrjö Sirola, who described himself as 'a product of a parsonage' and who later became a leading member of the Finnish Communist Party; Kullervo Manner (1880–1937), who was briefly Prime Minister of the 'Red' government of 1918 and who met his death during Stalin's purges in Russia in 1937; Otto Ville Kuusinen, the founder of the Finnish Communist Party, who achieved high office in the Soviet Union under Stalin and survived to die in his bed at the age of 83 in 1974; Edvard Gylling (1881–1938), who became Prime Minister of Soviet Karelia and was purged by Stalin in 1938; and two who remained in Finland to struggle for their differing concepts of socialism – Karl Wiik (1883–1946) on the left and Väinö Tanner (1881–1966) on the right wing. These mainly intellectual leaders, however important in the later history of the Finnish Left, were in a minority amongst the eighty Social Democrats elected to the Eduskunta in 1907.

Oskari Tokoi, one of the deputies elected to represent a farming constituency in Ostrobothnia, wrote in his memoirs: 'Almost all its members [i.e. the Social Democratic Party] came from the labouring classes; and as farmers, chiefly from tenant families. Only one man among them had a doctor of philosophy degree, another was a master of arts. Six had studied a semester or two at the university; and there were seven grammar school teachers.'

The hopes of reform being achieved through parliamentary means were soon shown to be illusory. In Russia the Tsar recovered his equilibrium after the traumas of 1905 and 1906. In June 1907 the second Duma, which had proved to be as radical in its demands as the first, was dissolved and a third Duma, elected on a restrictive franchise in November 1907 and with even more limited powers than its predecessors, became the servant of a conservative, nationalist and reactionary regime. In Finland, the radical Eduskunta found its powers constrained both by the Finnish government (the old Senate remained as the government of Finland) and by the Tsarist government in St Petersburg. One of its first acts was to pass a law prohibiting the sale of alcohol. The Senate did not even submit this to the Tsar for ratification. The 1909 Eduskunta passed a similar law and this was sent to St Petersburg in 1917. A series of reactionary Governors-General were sent to Helsinki to represent the Tsar and the programme of russification was resumed with an intensity comparable with that pursued by Bobrikov in the first years of the century.

The Eduskunta was frequently dissolved – twice in 1910 – because the Governor-General objected to some aspect of its activities. On the first occasion in 1910 the dissolution occurred on the first day because the Speaker, Pehr Ervind Svinhufvud (1861–1944), criticized the Tsar in his opening speech. At each of the six elections between 1907 and 1916 the Social Democrats increased their majority, their representation rising from 80 in 1907 to 103 in 1916. Over the same period the Agrarians increased their number of seats from 9 to 19, the Finnish Party declined from 59 to 33, and the numbers of members of the two other major parties, the Swedes and the Liberals, remained virtually the same. In 1909 the last representatives of the Finnish Party resigned from the Senate in protest against the new round of russification measures. This produced a confrontation between the Finnish constitutional politicians, pledged to passive resistance against the alleged illegalities, and the Russian government, working through a collaborationist Senate of officers and bureaucrats. But after 1906 the Russians had tightened their grip by a series of measures to ensure they would not again lose control in Finland, as had happened temporarily in 1905. By 1914 the signs were that the Russians were winning the prolonged war of attrition, and voices were again raised in the Finnish Party in favour of resuming dialogue with the regime.

There were some on the left who saw no future in the state parliamentary game. They found themselves in sympathy with the various groups of Russian revolutionaries who were preparing to overthrow the Tsarist system by force, if this objective could not be achieved through parliamentary means. One of the leading activists in Finland was the colourful adventurer, Konni Zilliacus (1855–1924), a Swedish-speaking lawyer who had learned to be a journalist during his travels in the Americas, Japan, Egypt, France and England in the 1890s. (His son, Konni, who later became a Labour M.P. in

Britain, was born in Japan in 1894, where Zilliacus and his American wife were then living.) Zilliacus settled in Stockholm for a time and smuggled across the Gulf of Bothnia both his own anti-Russian paper, *Fria Ord*, and several tons of underground literature for the Russian revolutionaries in St Petersburg. Zilliacus was not interested in the niceties of revolutionary politics and did not discriminate between Social Revolutionaries, Bolsheviks, Mensheviks or any other anti-Tsarist groups. He seemed to operate on the assumption that whoever was an enemy of the Tsar was his friend. He was even prepared to collaborate with Akashi Motojiro, the Japanese Military Attaché in St Petersburg until the outbreak of the Russo-Japanese War in 1904 and in smuggling arms through Finland to the revolutionaries in Russia. The voyage of the *John Grafton*, which sailed from London to Kemi in 1905 and was eventually blown up off Pietarsaari, is one of the more bizarre episodes in the history of the 'Northern Underground', which linked the Scandinavian left with the Russian Revolution. Even Father Gapon, the figurehead in the 'Bloody Sunday' demonstration in January 1905 appears in a minor role – he had been smuggled out of Russia by the Social Revolutionary Pinchas Rutenberg and was living in the Charing Cross Hotel!

More orthodox contacts were maintained by the austere Karl Wiik, to whom the extravagant antics of Zilliacus were anathema. Wiik was one of those rare left-wing socialists who were later repelled by the authoritarianism of the Bolsheviks in power, but who were not driven into the camp of the anti-socialists. In the period between 1905 and 1917 Wiik, together with Zilliacus and other members of the Finnish left, rendered invaluable service to the Russian revolution by offering sanctuary and a base from which the anti-Tsarists could recuperate before they resumed the journey which culminated in Lenin's arrival at the Finland Station in November 1917 to overthrow the Kerensky government. Although he had returned to Petrograd from Switzerland on 16 April, he had been forced into hiding in Finland, along with other prominent Bolsheviks in the summer of 1917. The Russian poet Osip Mandelstam, writing in 1925, said that before 1917 Petersburg 'breathed through Finland . . . one travelled there to think out what one could not think out in Petersburg'.

The First World War

Germany declared war on Russia 1 August 1914, four days after Germany's ally, Austria–Hungary, had attacked Serbia. Within the next few days Belgium, France, the British Empire and Japan became involved; and eventually Turkey, Bulgaria, Romania, Italy and USA were drawn into what was then known as the Great War and later as the First World War. In many respects it was a European civil war and when it ended in November 1918 the political map of Europe had been transformed. The peacemakers at Versailles ratified many of the *faits accomplis* which were presented to them or made minor alterations where it lay within their power to do so.

When Finland's Grand Duke, Tsar Nicholas, became a belligerent, the Grand Duchy had to follow. Finland had no army of its own, but many Finns served as volunteers in the Russian army at all levels from private soldier to senior staff officer. The main impact of the war on Finland was in the economic sphere. The demands of the Russian war machine and the disruption of foreign trade caused by the war distorted the Finnish economy. The forest-based industries, whose export markets were in Britain and western Europe, suffered badly. In pre-war days 70 per cent of Finland's total exports were in timber, pulp and paper, and 34,000 workers were directly involved in the cutting and processing of forest products. Half this work force was laid off in the first year of the war, the redundancies amounting to 30 per cent of the total industrial workers in Finland. Pulp and paper production suffered less than sawn timber as the Russian market still had the capacity to absorb Finnish paper exports until 1917, when the March Revolution and the subsequent turmoil in Russia threw the economy into chaos. The war caused a considerable loss of employment in the forest-based industries but gave a boost to the metal-working industries, textiles and chemicals. Many small metal-working establishments were started to satisfy the demands of the Russian war effort. Finland's iron ore production was only 4,000 tonnes in 1916, but in the same year Finland exported to Russia 8,500 tonnes of iron and steel and 5,000 tonnes of machinery. To produce this amount of metal goods for export required the importation of iron ore, scrap and pig iron, most of which could be obtained in Sweden. In 1916 Finland imported 8,000 tonnes of ore and 16,000 tonnes of pig iron.

Some branches of agriculture also benefited from the war. Dairy produce and meat could easily be sold in Russia and where possible farmers shifted from crop farming to animal husbandry. Grain for both animal feed and human consumption was imported from Russia and the dependence of Finland upon Russian grain created serious problems in 1917, when the trade was interrupted by revolution and civil war. Whilst the going was good, there were rich pickings to be made by some Finnish war profiteers in industry, commerce and agriculture. The arrogant affluence of the few contrasted with the poverty of the masses, especially in the rural areas out of reach of the lucrative food markets of St Petersburg.

In 1916 thousands of young men were drafted by the Russians to strengthen the military defences around the coasts, especially in the Helsinki area. While the war lasted they received good wages, but when the work ceased in 1917 an army of unemployed and angry workers provided a reservoir of potential revolutionaries. Long before 1917 unrest had been growing. Crisis point was reached in the summer of 1917, following the 'March Revolution' which overthrew the Tsar and brought to power a liberal Provisional Government under Prince Lvov. In Finland F. A. von Seyn, the much-disliked Russian Governor-General, was replaced by the liberal-minded Mikhail Stakhovich, and many political deportees were allowed to return from exile and to resume their activities. One of the most prominent of these was Pehr Evind Svinhufvud, who had been Speaker of the Eduskunta from 1907 to 1912. He had been exiled to Siberia in 1914, but returned in triumph to Helsinki in 1917 in time to play his part in the dramatic events which led to the declaration of independence on 6 December 1917.

On 20 March the Russian Provisional Government proclaimed the restoration of Finland's constitutional rights. The elections for the Eduskunta in 1916 had returned 103 Social Democrats, the largest majority ever received by a single party. However, the parliament did not meet until March 1917, when it proceeded to appoint a coalition government headed by Oskari Tokoi. Tokoi thus became the first socialist in the world to be Prime Minister of a democratically elected government. The new cabinet took office on 27 March 1917 and was immediately faced with serious problems both internally and in its relations with the new regime in Russia. The internal problems centred on the maintenance of law and order and the securing of adequate supplies of food. The cabinet, which was equally divided between the socialists and the non-socialists, found it impossible to agree on the measures to be taken to provide adequate policing arrangements. In some towns workers' militias had been formed and these were soon confronted by civil guards, recruited by the bourgeoisie and often receiving support from Germany. In 1914 many young Finns had gone secretly to Germany, where they had been organized into a Prussian Jäger (light infantry) battalion. The workers' militias evolved into the Red Guards (*Punakaarti*) and the civil guards into a Security Corps (*Suojeluskunta*). The divided government could do little to stop this polarization of the community into two paramilitary formations.

The problem of relations with Russia reached a crisis in July 1917. On 18 July the Eduskunta passed by 136 votes to 55 an Enabling Act which unilaterally proclaimed the independence of Finland in all matters except foreign affairs and defence. They were sustained in this attitude by a resolution of the All-Russian Congress of Workers and Soldiers' Deputies, meeting a month earlier, which had called for full internal independence for Finland. Before this, in April, during a visit to Helsinki, Alexandra Kollontai had urged the Finns to seek independence. Tokoi's speech to the Diet in April had echoed this sentiment.

The Enabling Act implied that the Eduskunta and the Finnish Cabinet (i.e., the Senate) could act without the approval of the Governor-General or, above him, of the Russian government. On the other hand, Kerensky and the members of his Provisional Government took the view that, when the Tsar abdicated, his powers as Grand Duke of Finland passed to them. They therefore had the power to dissolve the Eduskunta and call for new elections. Accordingly they issued a manifesto, ordering the dissolution of the Eduskunta and the calling of a general election at the beginning of October. The Finnish Cabinet had to decide whether to accept the orders of the Eduskunta or of the Provisional Government. The vote in the

Cabinet was evenly balanced, but the presence of Governor-General Stakhovich decided the issue. Normally the Governor-General did not attend cabinet meetings – a tradition which went back to the old Senate, established in 1809, but under pressure from Kerensky Stakhovich broke with tradition, exercised his legal right to attend and cast his vote in favour of the manifesto.

There have been suggestions that Russia's allies, Britain and France, exercised some pressure. The Provisional Government had just launched its last offensive against the Germans. Their allies hoped that the declaration of 20 March would be sufficient to persuade the Finns to support wholeheartedly the Russian war effort, and that the issue of Finnish independence would be allowed to recede until after the war. There is also evidence that some members of the anti-socialist parties in the Finnish government wanted Kerensky to call new elections, so that they would have an opportunity to reverse the socialist majority in the Eduskunta. This they achieved. At the election held in October 1917 the Social Democrats lost their overall majority, although still remaining the largest single party, with 92 seats. The main beneficiaries were the Agrarians, whose representation rose from 19 to 26 seats, the other parties remaining at roughly the same strength as in 1916. Despite this apparent setback, it should be noted that the Social Democrats polled 45 per cent of the total poll, compared with 47 per cent in 1916, and that the size of their vote – 445,000 – was not again equalled by them until the mid 1930s.

The Social Democrats were bitterly divided amongst themselves. Lacking a united voice, they were unable to respond adequately to the rapidly changing events during the last months of 1917. When Lenin came to power in November 1917 he had already expressed himself in favour of Finnish independence, although he hoped that once given the right to secede from Russia, a Finnish workers' state would wish to remain in some form of association with a Russian socialist republic. He felt, however, that the Finns must settle their own affairs. He had urgent matters nearer home and was in no position to take responsibility for Finland.

The situation in Finland was rapidly getting out of hand. The Red Guards and the Civil Guards were squaring up for a fight. There were gangs of unemployed workers, starving peasants and ill-disciplined

Russian soldiers committing acts of violence in all parts of the country. Many Social Democrats did not accept the right of the Provisional Government to dissolve the Eduskunta and would not accept the government based on the 1917 elections. They attempted to influence events by means of extra-parliamentary activities. A Central Revolutionary Council, formed on 8 November brought the executives of the Social Democratic Party and the Trade Union Federation together. The Trade Unions had increased their membership to over 160,000 and many of their members had become disillusioned with the slow and ineffective processes of change which could be wrought by parliamentary means. On 14 November the Revolutionary Council called a general strike, but in the words of Oskari Tokoi, 'what ensued was more than a strike; it was rebellion and revolution'. Armed Red Guards took the law into their own hands in some towns. In the ensuing violence there were instances of pillage and twenty-two opponents of the Red Guard were murdered. This alarmed and outraged the community, including a majority of the Social Democrats. The Eduskunta, in the absence of any clear lines of authority from Russia, assumed *de facto* independence and took decisions regarding the reform of local government and the reduction of working hours, which placated the strikers. The strike was called off but the revolutionary ferment continued. A government was voted in by the Eduskunta which was headed by the ultraconservative champion of Finnish rights, P. E. Svinhaufvud. On 6 December he presented to the Eduskunta a formal declaration of independence, which had been drafted by the liberal-minded constitutional lawyer, K. J. Ståhlberg (1865–1952).

7
Independent Finland

The declaration of independence was accepted by Lenin, who met Svinhufvud in Petrograd 31 December 1917 and told him that the Bolsheviks would recognize the right-wing government in Helsinki. Sweden, Denmark, Norway, France, Germany and Austria–Hungary soon followed, but Britain and the United States waited until 1920 before they accepted Finnish independence *de jure*, although *de facto* recognition was accorded by Britain in 1918.

One of the factors which delayed full British recognition was the equivocal relationship of the new Finnish government to Germany. Another was the continued presence of 40,000 Russian troops on Finnish soil. There was a link between these two items. The Bolsheviks feared that Finland might be used by Germany as a springboard for an attack on Petrograd, and justified their failure to evacuate their troops and the naval garrison at Helsinki on these grounds.

In January 1918 the civil war which had been looming for several months finally broke out. Both sides had been preparing for it for some time. The Svinhufvud government requested the Germans on 19 January to return the Jäger battalion and all its equipment to Finland as soon as possible. On 24 January the government demanded the removal of Russian troops and requested help from those countries which had recognized Finland's independence – which included Germany. General Mannerheim, who had left the service of the Russian army on the abdication of the Tsar, was put in charge of a Military Committee and charged with the responsibility of establishing a military headquarters in Vaasa, out of reach of the Red Guards, who were in virtual control of Helsinki and Tampere. He left Helsinki for Vaasa on 18 January. On 25 January the government officially constituted the Civil Guards as being the state force responsible for the maintenance of law and order.

The civil war began on the night of 27/28 January. The Red Guards formally took control of Helsinki and established a revolutionary government, the Peoples' Commission (*Kansanvaltuuskunta*). The same night Mannerheim ordered the Civil Guards in Vaasa to disarm the Russian troops. In his memoirs Oskari Tokoi gives an account of the confusion and lack of clear objectives which undermined the possibilities of success for the revolutionaries. On the morning of 28 January he wrote:

> I went to my office at the Finnish Federation of Labour. My secretary showed up, waving a printed handbill . . . announcing that the revolution had begun . . . The workers, it stated, had already taken the government into their own hands . . . I had known nothing of these developments, for I was not a member of the Revolution Committee, but I hurried to the committee headquarters. There I found an indescribable confusion.

The revolutionary government, led by Kullervo Manner, former Speaker of the Eduskunta, appointed Tokoi as Minister of Food. There had been a poor harvest in 1917 and the upheavals in Russia and Finland during the winter had badly disrupted food supplies. Many Finns faced starvation. Although aid committees had been set up in Sweden, Britain and the United States to send food to Finland, it was unlikely that they would be willing to send it for distribution either by a Red Government, or by a White Government which appeared to be in alliance with Germany.

At the beginning of February the country was divided between the area in the south controlled by the Red government in Helsinki and the area to the north where the Svinhufvud government, backed by Mannerheim's Civil (or White) Guards held sway. The dividing line ran north of Pori, Tampere, Lahti, Lappeenranta and Viipuri, so that all these major urban centres, together with Turku and Helsinki, were in the Red zone. The Whites were better equipped, better organized and more united than the Reds. They also received a great boost to their strength from the arrival on 25 February of the Finnish Jäger battalion. In March German naval forces landed on the

Åland Islands and on 3 April a German expeditionary force under General Rüdiger von der Goltz landed at Hanko, on the south-west coast, and advanced on Helsinki. A few days later a force of 2,500 German troops landed at Loviisa, on the coast east of Helsinki, and thrust northward to cut the railway line to Petrograd. By this time Mannerheim had taken Tampere and the resistance of the Reds was crumbling. Helsinki fell to von der Goltz on 13 April. Two weeks later the leaders of the Red Guards and several members of the revolutionary government fled to Russia. The end of the Civil War was celebrated on 16 May when Mannerheim rode at the head of a victory parade in Helsinki.

There followed a period of bloody reprisals, when the victorious Whites exacted a terrible vengeance on their defeated enemies. It is probable that some 5,500 men on each side were killed in battles during the Civil War, and in addition, about 2,000 Reds were executed during the war by agents of the Vaasa government. Urho Kekkonen, who later became President of Finland, was a young officer aged 18 in the White Guard during the Civil War. In later life he described how he was haunted by the memory of his action in 1918 of ordering the execution of three Red prisoners who had been captured by his men. Even worse were the killings and the deaths from starvation and neglect which occurred during 1918 and 1919 in the prison camps, where captured Reds and their families were incarcerated. Some 90,000 Red prisoners were held pending trial by special courts. It has been estimated that 9,500 died in the camps, one of the most notorious of which was on the island fortress of Suomenlinna, in Helsinki harbour. Of 403 death sentences passed by lower courts, 125 were eventually carried out. By April 1919 the numbers held had been reduced to 6,000. As memories of the terrible events of January to May 1918 faded, more and more sentences were commuted. The newly elected President, K. J. Ståhlberg, who held office from 1919 to 1925, used his prerogative to pardon hundreds of convicted Reds. By 1924 the problem of political prisoners had been eliminated, but the bitterness lingered on to taint the political life of Finland for another generation.

Finnish nationalist historians see the events of 1918 not as a civil war, but as part of a war for independence. They draw attention to the help given to the Reds by the Russians and stress the fact that the Red leaders who took refuge in Russia founded the Finnish Communist Party in Moscow and remained as tools of the Comintern until they were either wiped out in Stalin's purges or, like O. V. Kuusinen, appeared in 1939 as members of the 'Democratic Government of Finland' which was to rule the country when the Red Army won the war. The reality was that both sides had employed foreign military advisers to help organize their armies, had received some military support from foreign troops and had obtained most of their weapons from foreign sources, the Whites from Sweden and Germany and the Reds from the Bolsheviks. But most of the actual combat consisted of Finns fighting Finns – a civil war by any normal definition.

The Eduskunta met in Helsinki on 18 May, two days after Mannerheim's victory parade, but it was a rump parliament from which all but two members of the largest party, the Social Democrats, were excluded. Svinhufvud was accorded the title of Regent and given the powers previously vested in the Tsar as Grand Duke of Finland and wielded in practice by the Governor-General. The Vice-President of the Senate – the Prime Minister – was J. K. Paasikivi, the conservative banker who had been prominent during the first decade of the century as a Compliant and who believed that Finland should find a *modus vivendi* in its relations with Russia.

One of the first issues to be decided was the basic form of the constitution. Was Finland to be a republic or a monarchy? Although in 1917 Svinhufvud had originally favoured a republic, in the changing circumstances of May 1918 and still expecting a German victory in the Great War, he supported the idea of a monarchy headed by Prince Friedrich Karl of Hesse. Paasikivi threw his weight behind Svinhufvud. A coalition of former Old Finns and Young Finns, together with most of the Swedes, were able to muster 58 votes in favour, whilst the opposition, led by the Agrarians, could only attract 44 votes against the proposal. Before any practical steps could be taken to introduce a monarchy, Germany had been defeated and the Prince of Hesse made it known that he could not accept the proffered crown. This refusal coincided with the withdrawal from Finland of the last German troops there and both Svinhufvud and

Paasikivi resigned office as their policy collapsed. C. G. Mannerheim was invited to succeed Svinhufvud as head of state by a vote of the Eduskunta, whose powers in this matter derived from those granted to the old Diet of the Four Estates by King Gustav III of Sweden in 1772. When the call came Mannerheim was in Britain where he was engaged on an unofficial mission to undo the damage which had been caused to relations with Finland by the pro-German orientation of Svinhufvud and Paasikivi. Mannerheim was, perhaps, the only Finn who could accomplish this task. His military prowess and his anti-Bolshevism were well known but, which was even more important, he had resigned his post as head of the Finnish Army at the end of May in protest agàinst the undue influence of Germany in Finnish military affairs.

At the time when he became Regent the British, French and other allies were engaged in the futile attempt to overthrow Lenin's regime in Russia. The anti-Bolshevik forces were themselves disunited and the allies were uncertain about their ultimate objectives. Mannerheim and many others in Finland hoped that they could detach from Russia the border regions of Karelia which were inhabited by Finnish-speaking peoples. The concept of Greater Finland had considerable appeal and generated some wildly romantic notions about the destiny of the Finns as the defenders of civilization against the godless hordes of Russia. Unfortunately the Russian anti-Bolsheviks – men like Kolchak, Denikin and Yudenich – were not prepared to accept the loss of territory by 'Mother Russia', even if it was inhabited by non-Russians.

By 1920 the White forces in Russia had been reduced to a few marauding bands and Trotsky's Red Army had successfully defended the new socialist state against both domestic insurgents and foreign invaders. It was time for Finland to make its peace. This was achieved by the Treaty of Tartu (Dorpat), signed 14 October 1920 after four months of negotiation. Apart from ending the state of war, the treaty provided for the transfer to Finland of the ice-free port of Petsamo and part of the adjacent Fisherman's Peninsula (Kalastajasaarento) on the Arctic coast of Lapland. The area had been promised to Finland by Tsar Alexander II in 1864, in exchange for two districts in the Karelian Isthmus which Finland had ceded to Russia, but the

Russians had not kept their side of the bargain. It was left to the Bolsheviks at Tartu to honour the Tsar's promises.

The most important internal development in Finland during Mannerheim'a regency was the drawing up of the republican constitution under which Finland is still governed. The main architect of the new constitution was Professor K. J. Ståhlberg, who was elected as the first President of the Republic on 25 July 1919, defeating Mannerheim, who was the candidate of the right. The President was chosen by the Eduskunta which had been elected in March 1919, 143 members voting for Ståhlberg against only 50 for Mannerheim.

One of the most remarkable features of the 1919 election was that the Social Democrats, who a few months earlier had been excluded from the vital 1918 session of the Eduskunta which voted for a monarchy, were able to return to parliament and again to become the largest single party, with 80 seats. Now led by Väinö Tanner, and supported by the moderates who believed in a parliamentary rather than a revolutionary road to socialism, the party showed that it could still command the allegiance of the majority of Finnish workers. It was their votes which decided the issue between Mannerheim and Ståhlberg. The result of the elections also revealed a realignment of political forces on the centre and the right. The Agrarians became the second largest party, increasing their representation from 26 to 42 seats. The Old and Young Finn factions disappeared as two new political groupings emerged, the National Coalition Party (*Kansallinen Kokoomus*) and the Progressive Party. The National Coalition represented the conservative, monarchist elements of the Old Finn Party, represented by men like Paasikivi, whilst Ståhlberg was the leading figure in the more liberal, republican-minded Progressive Party until his election to the Presidency took him out of party politics.

The new constitution retained the unicameral legislature of 200 members which had replaced the old Diet under the 1907 electoral law. The same universal franchise under a system of proportional representation also remained. The Senate was changed into a modern executive government, nominated by the President, but requiring a vote of confidence from the Eduskunta to assume office. The powers previously exercised by the Grand Duke and his representatives – and more recently entrusted to the Regent – were transferred

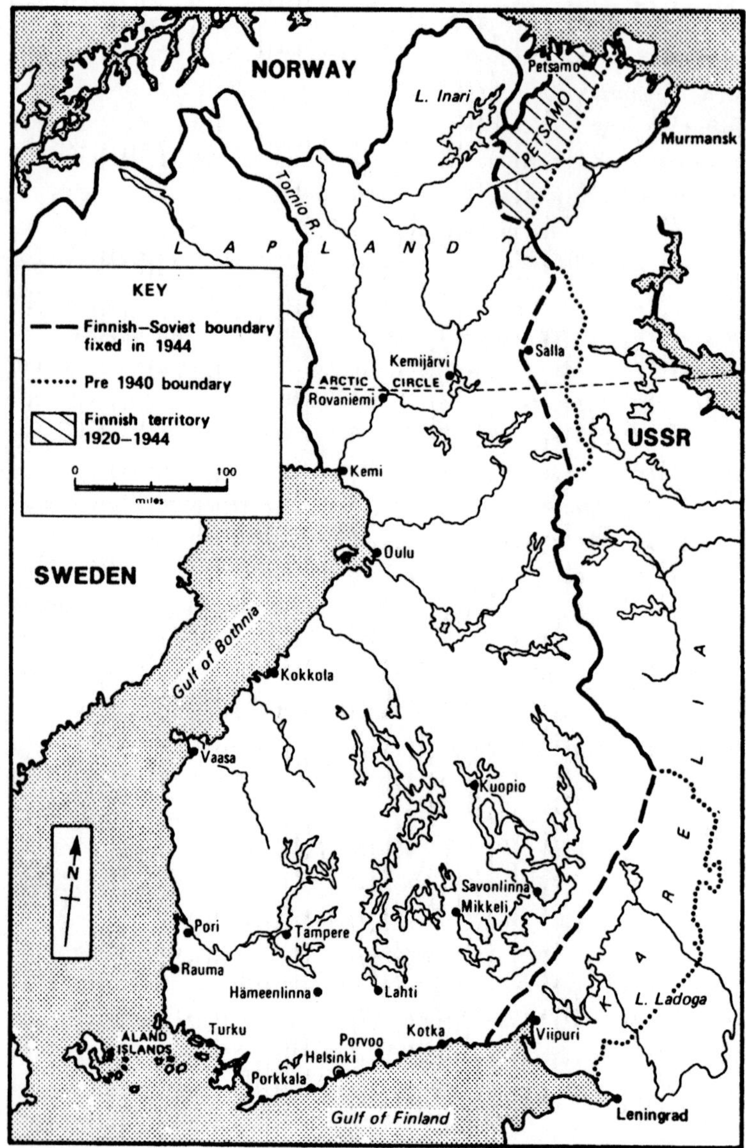

Map 2 Finland: twentieth-century boundaries and major towns

to the newly created office of President of the Republic. The President is normally chosen for a six-year term by an electoral college, but in exceptional circumstances the Eduskunta could choose the next President – as happened, for example, in March 1946 when Paasikivi replaced Mannerheim, who had resigned in mid-term; and in 1973 when Kekkonen's term in office was renewed by vote of the Eduskunta.

The powers of the President are far greater than those available to many other heads of state, whether in constitutional monarchies or democratic republics. The President has the right to summon and dissolve parliament and can initiate legislation. He has the power to veto bills, but the Eduskunta can override the Presidential veto after an appeal to the country in a new election. In foreign policy the President has wide powers in the handling of Finland's relations with other countries, although in matters of peace and war the Eduskunta's approval must be sought. The President is also Commander-in-Chief of the armed forces, although in time of war these powers are normally delegated to the most senior army officer. He has wide powers of patronage in public appointments and considerable informal influence in social, cultural and political life. Since the Second World War the powers of the President have increased both formally and informally, especially during the incumbency of Presidents Paasikivi and Kekkonen, who between them were in office from 1946 to 1981.

Political life in Finland, 1919–1939

During the first decade of independence there were five major parties which participated at various times in government. Because of the system of proportional representation, governments were normally coalitions in which either the Progressives, the Conservatives or the Agrarians occupied the premiership, with support from time to time by the Swedish People's Party. The exception to this rule was the short-lived minority government headed by the Social Democrat leader, Väinö Tanner, which held office between December 1926 and December 1927. The fact that the Social Democrats, albeit led by the right-wing Tanner, could form a government so soon after the Civil War of 1918 is a tribute to the growing political maturity of the

Finnish people and to the efforts at reconciliation made by the first two Presidents of the Republic – Ståhlberg, from 1919 to 1925 and L. K. Relander (1883–1942) who held office between 1925 and 1931; and by Tanner and the moderate Social Democrats. Equally remarkable was the emergence of the large communist front organization, the Finnish Socialist Labour Party. This body was formed in 1920 and began to produce a daily newspaper, *Suomen Työmies* (*Finnish Worker*) in Helsinki in the autumn of that year.

Already in May the Communists had captured the Federation of Trade Unions. The official Communist Party, founded by Kuusinen and others in Moscow in 1918, was illegal in Finland. It operated in Finland through various front organizations which were manipulated by the exiled leaders in Stockholm and Moscow. The main representative in Finland was Arvo Tuominen (1894–1981), who had been given the nickname 'Poika' (Boy) by Lenin because of his youth. Tuominen became editor of *Suomen Työmies*, secretary of the Socialist Labour Party and vice-chairman of the Trade Union Federation. In 1922 Tuominen was arrested for expressing openly pro-Soviet views and served four years in prison. After his release in 1926 he became secretary of the Trade Union Federation and was entrusted by the leadership of the Moscow-run international union organization, the Profintern, with the task of obstructing and undermining the Tanner government. Writing afterwards about his reimprisonment in 1928, again for pro-Soviet activities, he said; 'For the most part the charges were . . . true, for I had tried my best to instil communist order in Finland.'

In the elections of 1922 the communist front organization received 128,000 votes and 27 seats. It is perhaps significant that, at the same election, the number of seats held by the Social Democrats dropped from 80 to 53 – a fall of exactly 27 seats. The left-wing front managed to win almost the same number of votes in the 1929 elections, but in 1930 it was suppressed and did not re-emerge until 1945 in the form of the Finnish People's Democratic League (SKDL), in open electoral alliance with the legalized Communist Party.

The sharp turn to the right which occurred at the end of 1929 can be explained partly as a reaction to the increase in communist activity, especially through the youth organization which was controlled by communists. The world economic crisis, the impact of which on Finnish exports of timber and farm produce began to be noticed in 1929, provided a reason for protest demonstrations against the system. At this point the Soviet Union decided to enter into world markets with exports of grain, timber and other commodities, at prices which gave rise to accusations of dumping. By the end of 1930 export prices of Finnish farm produce stood at only 64 per cent of their 1928 level and the rapid growth of the timber industry in the mid 1920s came to an abrupt halt in 1928. The growing militancy of the young workers in the face of these indications of economic distress provoked an even more violent reaction from the right wing. The flashpoint came on 23 November 1929 when 400 red-shirted members of the Young Workers Educational Association held a rally in the market town of Lapua, in the farming region of Ostrobothnia. The rally was broken up by force – whether by the spontaneous action of outraged local inhabitants or as part of an organized right-wing backlash against the left is not certain. Soon, however, a Lapua Movement had sprung up. 'Farmers, clergymen, academicians, industrialists, military leaders and territorial expansionists of all occupations united in a movement which formally announced its goal to be the extinction of Communism in Finland.'

It soon became apparent that right-wing extremists with leanings towards fascism were in command of the Lapua Movement and that their target was not communism but Finnish democracy. Many of those originally attached to the Lapua Movement recoiled from its excesses. One of these was General Mannerheim, who wrote to his brother Johan at the end of 1929:

> A remarkable feature of the movement is the strong contribution made by the pietists, those devout men who went off to the War of Independence singing hymns and who now regard bolshevism with its anti religious struggle as a manifestation of the Devil on earth. One cannot know the Ostrobothnians and their deep rooted democratic attitude and consider this movement as anti democratic.

He changed his view when Lapua extremists kidnapped Professor and Mrs Ståhlberg and beat up Väinö Hakkila, the Social Democratic Deputy Speaker of the Eduskunta.

The government led by the Agrarian leader Kyösti Kallio (1873–1940) was replaced after the elections of October 1930 by a more right-wing administration led by Svinhufvud. The government appeared to be unable or unwilling to curb the excesses of right-wing gangs who beat up suspected communists or even carried them to the Soviet border and pushed them over into the arms of Stalin's frontier guards. Under pressure from the far right laws were passed which outlawed all manifestations of communism and gave powers to the government to suppress anti-democratic movements. The communist front organizations were unable to participate in the 1930 elections and a purge was carried out in trade unions, sports clubs and youth organizations which were suspected of being infiltrated by communists.

In February 1932 a group of 500 armed supporters of the Lapua movement gathered at Mäntsälä, on the main road between Helsinki and Lahti. They demanded the suppression of the Social Democratic Party and attempted to force upon the government their so-called *Lapuan laki* (the law of Lapua), which they claimed to be higher than the written laws of parliament. President Svinhufvud acted promptly to suppress the incipient counter-revolution and used the laws intended to be used against the left in order to suppress the anti-democratic right. The movement regrouped under the banner of the Peoples Patriotic League (IKL), an ultra-nationalist body whose newspapers lauded the achievements of Hitler and Mussolini. The IKL contested the elections of 1933 and gained 14 seats at the expense of the Conservatives with whom they collaborated. They retained this number in 1936 when they fought independently, but dropped to 8 in 1939. The party was dissolved in 1944, under legislation outlawing fascism.

The mainstream of Finnish political life was not unaffected by the activities of the right and left-wing extremists, but although bruised and battered, it weathered the storms of the 1930s. In 1936 the Social Democrats under Tanner won 83 seats and were able to join a government in alliance with the Agrarians – the so-called red-green coalition. The Prime Minister, A. K. Cajander (1879–1943) was one of the two Progressive Party members of the coalition. Tanner became Minister of Finance in March 1937. This government remained in office until December 1939, after the outbreak of the Winter War. It was important for Finland to have a broadly based government during the period in which the international situation deteriorated and Europe drifted into a war into which Finland was reluctantly dragged on 30 November 1939.

Economic and social conditions in the inter-war period

In 1918 Finland was still primarily an agrarian country with two thirds of the working population engaged in farming. Almost half of the GNP was derived from agriculture and most non-agricultural activities concerned the processing of timber, the making of pulp and the extraction of raw materials. Manufacturing was mainly for the home market and was on a small scale.

The independent government which came into office in 1918 after the chaos and disruption of the Civil War was faced with formidable economic problems. The bad harvest of 1917, the loss of grain imports from Russia and the upheaval caused by months of fighting led to serious food shortages. These could not be easily overcome by the importation of food from overseas. Apart from the lack of foreign currency, the continuation of the war in Europe and the reluctance of Britain and the United States to send food aid forced Finland to rely on what limited supplies could be sent across the Baltic by Germany and Sweden. Industry was also badly hit. The Russian market had disappeared in 1917 and no alternative outlets could be found. Imports of essential fuel and raw materials dried up. Industrial employment fell by over 25 per cent during 1918 and continued to fall during the next year. Before the revolution Russia had taken three quarters of Finland's exports and supplied two thirds of its imports.

The development of the Finnish economy between the wars falls into four phases. In the early years, from 1918 to 1922, the emphasis was upon survival and reconstruction. Once the German connection was broken in December 1918 it became possible for food aid to be sent under the scheme organized by Herbert Hoover. This source saved thousands of Finns from starvation. The phrase *elää hooverille* (to live by Hoover) became the Finnish equivalent of 'living off the parish'. Gradually, life began to return to normal. European markets started to revive and the demand for Finnish timber products grew as post-war reconstruction in western Europe gathered momentum. By 1922 industrial production was back to pre-war levels and agriculture had recovered from the dislocation of war and revolution. The second phase, from 1922 to 1927, was a period of economic growth. There was an export-led boom in forest products which provided much-needed foreign currency. Industrial production grew in value by 50 per cent and there was a growth in industrial investment which laid the foundations for new industries. Some of these were state financed and many were protected by tariffs to shield them from foreign competition during the formative years. Changes in land tenure, the growth of co-operatives and the encouragement of technical improvements in agriculture helped towards the goal of self-sufficiency in agriculture.

The third phase was one of adjustment to the effects of the world economic slump. Finland suffered less than did some of the more industrially developed nations of western Europe. Paper production actually increased during the depression, although the fall in world prices meant that income from the sale of paper products fell and painful reorganization had to be introduced to keep the industry afloat. Despite government assistance many farmers were forced into bankruptcy.

The final phase lasted from 1933 until the outbreak of the Winter War in 1939. Finland emerged from the depression with its basic economy in a condition which enabled it to expand and to develop new industries. By 1939, 21 per cent of GNP was derived from metal-working industries, compared with only 15 per cent in 1924. The industrial work force had doubled and the proportion of the population dependent upon agriculture had fallen from two thirds in 1920 to one half in 1939. Although Finland in 1939 was much poorer than its Scandinavian neighbours, it was advancing faster than Sweden – from a much lower starting point – and the gap in living standards was slowly closing.

An important social change affecting the lives of hundreds of thousands of Finns was the land reform known as the *Lex Kallio*, introduced by the leader of the Agrarian Union, Kyösti Kallio, who was

Minister of Agriculture between 1921 and 1922 before becoming Prime Minister in November 1922. Under this law landless peasants were assisted by the Government to buy small holdings from private owners of large estates or from companies, local communes or the church. Reserve powers of compulsory purchase were seldom used and the transfer of ownership was completed smoothly within a few years. The *Lex Kallio* was the culmination of a series of reforms which removed from the rural scene those two economically underprivileged groups, the *torpparit* and the *mäkitupalaiset* and created a class of independent smallholders.

The land reforms helped to bring social stability and economic progress to the Finnish countryside. The lot of the small farmers was further enhanced by the work of the co-operatives, which were given government help to enable them to market their produce and to benefit from advances in plant and animal breeding and the use of fertilizers. By 1938 almost all butter exports and two thirds of cheese exports were handled by the Co-operative Butter Export Association (*Valio*). Another great advance made during the inter-war period was the achievement of virtual self-sufficiency in cereals, vegetables and animal feeds. Comparing the period 1924 to 1928 with that of 1934 to 1935, self-sufficiency in cereals increased from 56 per cent to 82 per cent; in vegetables from 54 per cent to 77 per cent; and in animal feedstuffs from 77 per cent to 90 per cent.

8

Finland in the Second World War

The Winter War

The impressive progress made by Finland during the first two decades of independence was threatened by the gathering war clouds which loomed over Europe in the late 1930s. Although many Finns hoped that they could escape the conflagration by declaring their neutrality, this illusion was finally shattered on 30 November 1939 when the Red Army invaded, ostensibly in the name of a 'Peoples Republic,' established by the Soviet government in the border town of Terijoki and headed by the founder of the Finnish Communist Party, O. V. Kuusinen.

The reasons for the invasion lay primarily in the larger strategic interests of the Soviet Union and had little to do with the real or imaginary threat which tiny Finland was supposed to present to its giant eastern neighbour. Stalin was obsessed by the fear of a German attack on the Soviet Union, possibly assisted by other capitalist powers. The Anti-Comintern Pact, signed in November 1936 by Germany and Japan and joined a year later by Italy, signalled Hitler's intention to destroy international communism.

The Finnish frontier came to within 32 kilometres of Leningrad, the chief seaport and second city of the Soviet Union. Finland had begun its independent life as an ally of Germany. Pro-German sentiment was still strong in senior military circles and amongst elements of the ruling classes. Mannerheim, who may not have shared the pro-German sentiments of some of his fellow officers, was nevertheless a dedicated anti-communist. He had become chairman of the Defence Council at President Svinhufvud's invitation in 1931 and was promoted to the rank of Field-Marshal in 1933, the only man in

Finland to hold this newly created title. The line of pill boxes and defence fortifications which were hastily constructed across the Karelian Isthmus in 1939 to provide some form of defence between the Soviet border and Viipuri, was known as the Mannerheim Line. The Soviet leaders shared the fears which all Russian leaders have felt since the time of Peter the Great – namely that a hostile power might use Finland as a base for an attack upon Leningrad. In the eighteenth century the potential enemy was Sweden. In the 1930s the threat came from Germany.

In August 1938 an official of the Soviet embassy in Helsinki, B. Yartsev, raised with members of the Finnish government the possibility of a German landing in Finland as a prelude to an invasion of the Soviet Union. He offered Soviet assistance to repel such an incursion, but was rebuffed by the Finns. At the same time, similar overtures were being made to the three small Baltic republics, Estonia, Latvia and Lithuania, which had, like Finland, once formed part of the Tsarist empire. In June 1939 Britain and France were engaged in talks in Moscow, at which the Soviet leaders raised the question of a German attack through the Baltic and suggested that action should be taken – even against the wishes of the governments of the Baltic states – to give the Soviet Union the guarantees it felt necessary for its security. When these negotiations broke down, Stalin tried to buy time by means of a direct approach to Germany. The secret clauses of the Nazi–Soviet pact of 23 August 1939 gave both dictators the assurances which they needed at that time. Spheres of influence were marked out in Eastern Europe. The Soviet Union was to have a free hand in Finland, Latvia and Estonia as well as in Poland east of the rivers Narew, Vistula and San and in Bessarabia. The Germans would have Lithuania and most of Poland. In September 1939 after the German invasion of Poland an adjustment was made, assigning territory in Lithuania to the Soviet Union's sphere of influence in return for a larger German zone in Poland. The Soviet government had little difficulty in persuading the three Baltic states to agree to its terms for bases on their territory. This was the first step to their absorption into the Soviet Union. Vilna was ceded to Lithuania from Poland in October 1939 but Lithuania was incorporated into the Soviet Union in August 1940, as were Latvia and Estonia.

The situation in Finland was different. Stalin issued a summons for talks in Moscow on 5 October 1939 and Paasikivi was sent to open negotiations a week later. The Soviet demands were for a strip of land in the Karelian Isthmus; the fortified island of Koivisto, lying in the approaches to Viipuri; the Hanko peninsula on the south west tip of Finland; and part of the Petsamo area in the Arctic. Paasikivi returned to Helsinki for instructions and went back for two further rounds of discussion, which ended on 9 November without agreement. The Finns were divided about their response to the Soviet demands. Mannerheim, aware of the state of Finnish defences, wanted a flexible and conciliatory approach. 'We would have needed at least a year's intensive work to be anywhere near ready,' he wrote on 6 November to his friend G. A. Gripenberg, the Finnish Minister in London. The Minister of Defence Niukkanen and the Foreign Minister Eljas Erkko were against concessions. Finland had offered only minor adjustments to the eastern frontier, and nothing on Hanko, and Stalin decided that further negotiation was useless, so he authorized military action.

A frontier incident was manufactured on 26 November, when allegations were made that Finnish artillery had fired on Soviet troops across the border near Mainila. This was used as an excuse for breaking off diplomatic relations; tearing up the 1932 non-aggression pact and invading Finland. The first town in the Karelian Isthmus to be captured was a small coastal settlement, Terijoki. This became the seat of a puppet government presided over by O. V. Kuusinen. 'Poika' Tuominen, the secretary of the Finnish Communist Party, had been chosen to be Prime Minister of the Terijoki government, but he was in Stockholm when the summons came. He refused the offer and called upon the Finnish workers to defend their country against the Soviet invasion. In fact, most Finnish workers needed no special instructions from the Communist Party to persuade them that their duty lay in taking up arms against the aggressor. The Finns displayed an impressive national unity in their lonely resistance to the Red Army. Winston Churchill in a BBC broadcast on 20 January 1940 expressed the admiration of the world for the tenacious courage of the fighting Finns. 'Only Finland, superb, nay sublime in the jaws of peril, Finland shows what free men can do. They have exposed, for all the world to see, the military incapacity of the Red Army . . . Everyone can see how communism rots the soul of a nation, how it makes it abject and hungry in peace and proves it base and abominable in war.'

The fine words spoken by Churchill and the moral support which Finland received during the Winter War from a wide range of political and military personalities in western Europe, ranging from Sir Walter Citrine, the secretary of the British TUC, to Edouard Daladier and Per Albin Hansson, the Prime Ministers of France and Sweden, and even to Colonel Vallaton, the Speaker of the Swiss Parliament, could not disguise the fact that Finland was fighting alone with its back to the wall. Little material help could be expected from outside.

By February 1940 it was apparent that the sheer weight of numbers was telling against the courage of the Finns. On 22 February Colonel Jean Ganeval from France and Brigadier C. G. Ling from Britain arrived in Finland to explain an Allied plan for sending an expeditionary force to Finland. It involved an expedition through the Arctic regions of Norway and Sweden which would, if necessary, violate the neutrality of those countries if their governments did not agree to the passage of troops through their territory. The newly arrived British minister, Gordon Vereker, who presented his credentials to President Kallio in an air raid shelter during a Soviet bombing raid on Helsinki, urged the Finns to fight on until help arrived – possibly in mid-April. Vereker talked of 20,000 men taking over the northern sector of the Russian front. In the House of Commons, during a debate on the German invasion of Norway, on 7 May 1940, Mr Attlee stated 'We were informed 19 March that we had a force of 100,000 men ready to go to Finland.' However, as Tanner records in his account of the Winter War, the Finns knew that the Allied plans were vague and 'lacked firmness' and that both Norway and Sweden might obstruct the scheme to violate their neutrality. Despite Vereker's efforts the Finns decided to proceed with peace negotiations. They knew from Mannerheim's reports that their troops could not hold on much longer and they suspected that Allied promises would amount to little more than too little arriving too late – in fact, all aid short of help!

The Russians knew this too. They had argued during the debates in the League of Nations which resulted in their expulsion on 14 December 1939 that they were not at war with Finland, but were intervening on behalf of the Terijoki government of the Finnish Democratic Republic, but in January had indicated that they would negotiate with the government in Helsinki. On 12 March 1940 the Finns signed the Peace of Moscow with the country with whom they were supposed not to be at war.

The terms of the Peace of Moscow inflicted grievous losses of territory on Finland. The Soviet frontier was pushed westward to approximately the line of the Peace of Uusikaupunki (Nystad) in 1721. The Karelian Isthmus, including the port of Viipuri, the whole of Lake Ladoga and a large part of Karelia passed into Soviet hands. There was also a frontier rectification to Finland's disadvantage in the Salla area which eliminated a salient which had brought the Finnish frontier to within 80 kilometres of the Leningrad to Murmansk railway. The Finns also agreed to construct a line linking Kemijärvi to the new Soviet border, thus giving a direct link between the White Sea port of Kandalaksha and the head of the Gulf of Bothnia, at Kemi. In the Petsamo area, Finland lost part of the Fisherman's Peninsula but was allowed to retain the port of Petsamo. The Hanko Peninsula was leased to the Soviet union for thirty years, thus providing a naval base controlling the northern approaches to the Gulf of Finland. The two sides also agreed that neither would conclude any alliance directed against the other.

Over 400,000 Finns living in the ceded areas were allowed to move into Finland, taking with them what possessions they could carry as they trekked westward to become homeless refugees. Their fellow countrymen rose magnificently to the occasion, and worked very hard to provide new farms, shelter and employment for the displaced persons. Under the Rapid Emergency Resettlement Act passed in June 1940, 330,000 hectares of land were acquired for resettlement of farmers from Karelia.

Finland had lost over 10 per cent of its territory. Twenty-five thousand of its menfolk had been killed and almost 45,000 wounded, of whom 10,000 were permanent invalids. However, Finland was not occupied by the Red Army. Its democratic political system remained intact and the resilience and unity of its people gave hope for the future, despite the terrible mauling which they had suffered. The Soviet Union could have pressed home its advantage but it chose not to do so. Was this a tribute to the gallantry of the Finns – a fear that occupied Finland would have been a troublesome colony to subdue? This is a speculation for which no convincing answer has been given.

In retrospect, some Finns have argued that their decision not to accept the proffered Anglo-French assistance not only saved Finland from a worse fate but also saved Britain from annihilation at the hands of the Germans. Supposing, the argument runs, that Britain and France had sent their expeditionary force to arrive in April 1940, as suggested. It would have arrived in time to meet Hitler's invasion of Norway. The fall of France was only two months away. Air Chief Marshal Dowding had made it clear as early as January 1940 that Britain could spare no fighters, and only twelve Blenheim bombers for the proposed Finnish front. The Soviet Union had 2,500 planes at its disposal, compared with the 300 available to the Finns. If Britain had found itself at war with both Germany and the Soviet Union – who were then allies – in the spring of 1940, what would have been the outcome of the Battle of Britain, six months later? This is one of the 'ifs' of history which no one can answer.

The uneasy peace

In the first six months after the conclusion of the peace of Moscow the situation in the Baltic area worsened greatly from Finland's point of view. Germany completed its occupation of Denmark and Norway. The Baltic republics were incorporated into the Soviet Union and many people feared that Finland would suffer the same fate. Soviet pressure on Finland was limited, however, to three main topics. In July they successfully demanded the right to send troops and military supplies across the Finnish railway system to the base at Hanko. At the same time Molotov raised the question of Soviet access to the nickel mines near Petsamo, which were then worked by a British–Canadian concessionaire, the Mond Nickel Corporation. The area had been occupied by the Red Army during the Winter War but was returned to Finland in March 1940. The Finns successfully played for time and managed to fend off the Soviet demand until June 1941, when the German army moved in from Norway, at the beginning of the German attack on the Soviet Union.

Petsamo – or rather its outport Liinahamari – was Finland's only link with Britain and the United States which was not subject to German control. Finland was able to import some grain, sugar and fuel oil from the USA with the consent of the Royal Navy. Although the highway from Rovaniemi, the capital of Lapland (and the nearest railhead) to Liinahamari had a poor, waterbound macadam surface and two river crossings by primitive ferries, it was able to keep some contact with the outside world until 14 June 1941, when the Royal Navy decided to end the concession which it had previously allowed, on the grounds that Finland had become a German satellite.

A third area of Soviet pressure was over the Åland Islands, where Molotov demanded either that they should be demilitarized, or that if they were fortified, the Soviet Union should share the work with Finland. The islands had been demilitarized under a League of Nations agreement in 1921 which had confirmed Finnish sovereignty over them despite Swedish claims. In May 1939 a joint Finnish–Swedish proposal for the defence of the islands was turned down by the League of Nations, after opposition from the Soviet Union. In 1940 the Finns were forced to accept the right of Soviet inspectors to visit the islands to ensure that they remained unfortified.

In these incidents the Soviet Union was forcing the Finns to go beyond the terms of the peace treaty, but this could be understood in the context of Stalin's obsession with security and his suspicion that Finland might be colluding with his so-called ally, Germany, to get its revenge for the defeat of March 1940. What was more disturbing to the Finns was the campaign waged against Väinö Tanner, who had become Foreign Minister in December 1939, and other ministers in the coalition government headed by Risto Ryti, which led in August 1940 to their resignation. Tanner was Kuusinen's old enemy – a right-wing Social Democrat who commanded more support from the Finnish workers than did the Communist Party. Kuusinen had the ear of Stalin and it is probable that his influence was behind the campaign.

It was inevitable that in the situation which existed in 1940 and 1941 the Finns should look to Germany for help. The first stage of their collaboration was an agreement in the autumn of 1940 which allowed German military personnel to pass through Finland and to establish supply bases in Lapland. In return, Germany promised military equipment for the Finnish army. On the face of it, this agreement was no greater infringement of neutrality than the comparable treaty between Sweden and Germany for troop transit facilities of June 1940. In reality they were entirely different: Sweden made her agreement reluctantly under heavy German pressure, but Finland's leaders welcomed the German proposal with enthusiasm and no pressure was needed.

It soon became apparent, however, that Finland was slowly being drawn closer to Germany. Many Finns remembered Germany's help in 1918 and many were also convinced that the future of Europe would be decided by Germany. The sentiments expressed in the newspaper *Suomen Sosiali-demokraatti* on 21 July 1941 by Väinö Hakkila, the Social Democrat MP who was Speaker of the Eduskunta, were shared by many Finns. 'That nation in Europe which is most fit for battle and the most efficient, the German nation, is now crushing with its steel army our traditional, ever treacherous and ever deceitful enemy.' This was written a month after the attack on the USSR had begun but it was obvious for some months before that Finland was preparing to join in when the time came for Hitler to settle his old scores with Stalin. By January 1941 Mannerheim had decided that Finland's security depended on collaboration with Germany, and the civilian leadership readily followed his line. Increasingly close contacts between the Finnish and German military commands culminated in May 1941 in a visit by General Heinrichs, Mannerheim's Chief of Staff, to German headquarters in Salzburg and Berlin. These meetings worked out the basic plans for Finland to participate in a possible German attack on the Soviet Union.

By the time war came again to Finland in June 1941 there was a new President of the Republic. Kyösti Kallio, the old Agrarian leader who had been elected in 1937, was worn out by the strain of the Winter War and had suffered several strokes. On 19 December 1940 he was preparing to go into retirement and at a ceremony at Helsinki railway station, when Mannerheim, Ryti and members of the government were preparing to say farewell, the 67-year-old President collapsed and died in the arms of the Commander in Chief. He was immediately succeeded by the Prime Minister, Risto Ryti.

By June 1941 Finland's leaders were committed to participate in Hitler's aggression against the Soviet Union. Mannerheim's undoubted distaste for many aspects of Nazism did not hold him back from acceptance of what he saw as both a necessity and a unique opportunity to secure Finland's future. Most ordinary Finns, who had no information about their leaders' commitments, accepted them readily when the time came as the natural response to the injustice of the Winter War. Hitler announced on 22 June 1941 'In alliance with their Finnish comrades, the victors of Narvik stand on the shores of the Arctic Ocean.' Mannerheim, in an order of the day to his troops on 10 July spoke of 'a holy war' and of liberating the people of Karelia. This implied that Finland's war aims went beyond the mere recovery of territory lost in 1940, and looked forward to a 'Greater Finland' which would embrace the whole of Soviet Karelia. Amidst the euphoria it was hardly noticed that Paasikivi, until then Finnish Minister in Moscow, quietly returned home to withdraw from public life, until he was called back again in 1944 to negotiate yet another peace treaty with the Soviet Union.

The Continuation War, 1941–1944

Although the President and the Commander in Chief appeared to have illusions about the creation of a 'Greater Finland', the Eduskunta unanimously expressed the view in a resolution of 29 November 1941 that Finland wanted no more than the restoration of its 1939 frontiers.

The German army operated mainly in Lapland, some of the troops advancing in the Arctic section from bases in Norway. After initial successes the front became stabilized on a line which fell short of Murmansk and the White Sea. In the southern sector the Finns advanced as far as Lake Onega and the Soviet Karelian capital of Petrozavodsk (Äänislinna). The Finnish advance in the Karelian Isthmus was held at the pre-war frontier line on 1 September, but in the area between Lakes Ladoga and Onega on 21 October the Finns reached the river Svir, well inside Soviet Karelia. In answer to a parliamentary question on 10 October Anthony Eden, the British Foreign Secretary, fired a warning shot across the bows of the advancing Finns. He stated that: 'If the Finnish Government persist in invading purely Russian territory, H. M. Government will be forced to treat Finland as an open enemy, not only while the war lasts but also when peace comes to be made.'

Mannerheim made it plain from the outset that he did not want Finnish troops to take Leningrad. The Germans who besieged Leningrad for over a year after 5 December 1941 came not from Finland but from German bases in Estonia and from the Baltic Republics. Once the Finns had established their positions in the winter of 1941 they remained virtually unchanged until 1944. They cut the mainline of the Murmansk railway at Petrozavodsk, but the Russians were still able to get supplies from the ice-free Arctic port via the branch line, which skirted the southern shore of the White Sea from Belomorsk to its junction with the Archangel to Vologda line, which ran well clear of the front. In the territories which were re-occupied over 270,000, or 70 per cent, of the refugees who had fled to Finland in 1940 returned to the homes they had been forced to abandon.

The realization that Germany was likely to lose the war permeated into the consciousness of the Finnish government and people during 1942. The USA was bombed into the war at Pearl Harbor in December 1941, at about the same time as the Finnish army achieved its maximum advance eastward. There was a great fund of goodwill towards Finland amongst the American people – partly because of the large Finnish-American communities in Minnesota, Michigan and the Dakotas, and partly because Finland had been the only European country to honour in full its debts to America after the First World War. The US government was reluctant to declare war on Finland and was able to avoid doing so for as long as there was a stalemate on the Finnish-Russian front. In fact, although Britain declared itself to be at war with Finland, America did not do so. Neither country engaged in serious hostilities against Finland.

By 1943 most Finns were convinced that they were on the losing side, and efforts were made to extricate the country from the war. This was an extremely delicate operation, as German troops were in Finland in sufficient strength to discourage any independent moves by the Finns to make a separate peace. In December 1943, when the Germans were in retreat across Russia after their defeat at Stalingrad, Urho Kekkonen, a leading member of the Agrarian Party, made a speech in Stockholm in which he advocated a policy of 'good neighbourliness' with the Soviet Union (the hereditary enemy) as being the only basis on which Finland could preserve its freedom and independence. Kekkonen was expressing a view which was gaining ground among the Finnish public. The government was reconstituted in order to exclude the representatives of the pro-German IKL (Peoples Patriotic League), which had only 8 representatives in parliament. The new Prime Minister, Professor Edwin Linkomies (1894–1963) began to put out cautious peace feelers. In February 1944 a motion passed by the Eduskunta urged the government to seek terms 'which would permit us to withdraw from the war.' In March Paasikivi was sent to Moscow to start negotiations but the terms offered, which included a Finnish promise to expel or intern the Germans by the end of April and for the levying in Finland of a war indemnity of $600 million, were considered unacceptable by the Linkomies government.

In June the Red Army launched an offensive on the Karelian front and Mannerheim warned the government that his troops could not hold the line. Ribbentrop, Hitler's Foreign Minister, arrived in Helsinki on 25 June and pressured President Ryti into signing an agreement promising that Finland would not make a separate peace, in return for immediate German military assistance.

Ryti had been re-elected President in March 1943 by means of the special procedures permitted under the 1919 constitution. He signed the agreement with Ribbentrop in his personal capacity, without submitting it to the Eduskunta. When Ryti resigned on 1 August 1944 it was held that the agreement lapsed. On 4 August Mannerheim was elected President. He immediately ordered peace negotiations and on 5 September an armistice was declared. Finland had broken off diplomatic relations with Germany on the previous day.

The first session of the armistice conference was held in Moscow 14 September. Finland was represented by the Prime Minister Antti Hackzell, Foreign Minister Karl Enckell and Generals Heinrichs and Walden. The Soviet delegation was headed by Molotov, supported amongst others by Marshal Voroshilov and Maxim Litvinov. Sir Archibald Clark Kerr, the British Ambassador in Moscow, headed the British delegation but his only contribution was to interject at appropriate moments statements such as 'I am in complete agreement with Mr Molotov', or 'I wish to confirm Mr Molotov's statement.'

The conference completed its work on 18 September and an agreement was signed which required Finnish troops to withdraw to the 1940 lines and to disarm all German troops on Finnish soil. Finnish forces were to return to peace time dispositions by the end of the year, when it was assumed that the Germans would have been expelled or rounded up. Hanko was returned to Finland, in exchange for a 50 year lease of the Porkkala area, a peninsula on the coast some 40 kilometres west of Helsinki. Petsamo was also to be handed over to the Soviet Union. A war indemnity of $300 million (at 1938 prices) was to be paid to the Soviet Union in specifically named goods over a period of six years. It has been estimated that the real cost to Finland of the direct reparations and other payments to the Soviet Union and others amounted to $600 million at 1938 prices.

The terms of the armistice agreement of September 1944 were incorporated into the Paris Peace Treaties signed by the Allied Powers on 10 February 1947. The Peace Treaty with Finland also confirmed the demilitarization of the Åland Islands and set limits on the size of Finland's armed forces – a land army of 34,400 men, a navy of 4,500 with a maximum tonnage of 10,000 GRT and an airforce of 60 planes with 3,000 men. Finland would not be allowed to manufacture or possess atomic weapons.

The Finns successfully complied with the requirement to expel the Germans, losing 1,000 dead in the process. The operation took longer than expected, because the Germans in Lapland resorted to scorched-earth tactics, and fighting continued in the Arctic Circle on the Norwegian border until VE Day.

It has been estimated that Finland lost 85,000 dead between 1939 and 1945 (2 per cent of the total population), of whom 90 per cent were young men between the ages of 20 and 30 years. A further 50,000 were permanently injured. This appalling total of human loss was in addition to the loss of territory and the material losses through reparations payments, the devastation of towns caused by war and the loss of productive capacity in the ceded territories. A further burden was the problem of resettling the flood of refugees, who, for the second time in four years, were forced to move out of Karelia.

9
Finland in the post-war world: the political situation

The Soviet Union insisted that Finland should suppress all traces of fascism and put on trial those responsible for dragging the country into the war. At the same time the anti-fascist groups which had been suppressed previously – notably the Communist Party – should be allowed to operate freely within the political system.

Paasikivi became Prime Minister in September 1944 and, under the presidency of Mannerheim until 1946, he directed the political life of Finland during the difficult years of adjustment. The prestige of Mannerheim was an indispensible asset which helped to educate Finns to the realities of their new situation. Mannerheim realized that Finland could no longer pose as a bastion of Christian civilization against the barbarian hordes of bolshevism. There was no more talk of crusades against the hereditary enemy. Instead there was a sober appreciation that, if Finland was to survive and prosper as a democratic society, a way must be found to live at peace with the giant eastern neighbour. Paasikivi had always realized this. As a Compliant in the Tsarist times and as a negotiator of peace settlements with the Soviet Union over a period of 25 years, he had always been consistent in his assessment of reality. This conservative-minded banker echoed the sentiments of Engels in accepting the maxim that 'Freedom is the recognition of necessity'. Words which recognize this sentiment are carved below the rugged granite block which stands in Helsinki as his monument. He would not allow a statue in his likeness, such as the fine equestrian effigy which commemorates Mannerheim.

Another leader who helped to convince the Finns of the need to find a *modus vivendi* with the Soviet Union was Urho Kekkonen

(1900–86), whose original position had been implacably anti-Soviet. He was one of the three MPs who voted against accepting the Peace of Moscow in 1940 and he maintained his view during the early part of the Continuation War. His speech in Stockholm in 1943 was the first public sign of a change of attitude. Almost twenty years later, addressing a meeting of Finnish MPs, he was able to say 'Whoever is for Kekkonen is for friendship with the Soviet Union and whoever is against Kekkonen is against friendship with the Soviet Union.'

Political life revived with remarkable speed during the autumn and winter of 1944. The Communist Party, which had been illegal for quarter of a century, suddenly re-appeared as a legal party within two weeks of the signing of the armistice. Two thousand members attended a conference in Helsinki on 4–5 October and the leaders who were elected to prepare the party for the forthcoming elections immediately entered into negotiations with some of the left-wing socialists who were dissatisfied with the Social Democratic Party (still led by Tanner) with a view to forming a broad left-wing electoral alliance. This initiative bore fruit on 29 October in the birth of the Finnish People's Democratic League (*Suomen Kansan Demokraattinen Liitto* – or SKDL). One of the founder members of the SKDL was a group known as *Vapaa Sana* (Free Speech), after the name of a newspaper founded in July 1940 by the veteran left-wing socialist Karl Wiik in protest against the continuation in peace time of the censorship which had been imposed during the Winter War. From its first issue, *Vapaa Sana* attracted the bitter opposition of Tanner and the majority of Social Democrats, and the antipathy was mutual. *Vapaa Sana* attacked the pro-German policy of some Social Democrats, and its supporters were accused in turn of being agents of the Soviet Union. Supporters of the paper were expelled from the Social Democratic Party and in August 1941 six who were MPs and a seventh who was chief administrator of Helsinki were arrested on charges of treason. Sentences of from three to six years in prison were handed down by the Supreme Court in September 1942. They were all released in 1944 and were able to resume their political activities.

Another group of left-wing socialists who were expelled from the Social Democratic Party in early 1945 and who joined the SKDL were members of a group called the Social Democratic Opposition, led by a former Minister of Finance, Mauno Pekkala. Their offence was to advocate an electoral pact between the SKDL and the Social Democrats. Later SKDL was joined by left-wing youth and student groups, women's organizations and others, but the hard core was the nucleus of Communist Party members, who claimed 40 of the 49 seats which SKDL won in the elections of March 1945. This electoral victory was a great blow to the Social Democrats, who saw their membership of the Eduskunta drop from 85 at the last election in 1939 to 50 in 1945. Paasikivi formed a coalition government in which the main partners were the Social Democrats with 50 seats and the Agrarians and SKDL who each had 49 seats.

One of the first tasks of the new administration was to carry out the terms of the armistice agreement concerning the elimination of allegedly pro-fascist organizations. IKL had already been disbanded. A few other militantly anti-communist and pro-German societies were banned. Emergency legislation was introduced to bring to trial the 'war guilty' (*sotasyylliset*). Paasikivi did not relish the necessity of passing retrospective legislation in order to bring to trial a group of former ministers – including five former Prime Ministers, but he was pressed on the one hand by the Allied Control Commission – in practice by the Russians – and by the left wing in his Cabinet, and felt that he had no choice in the matter. Ex-President Ryti, Väinö Tanner and Edwin Linkomies were the most prominent of those who were sentenced on 21 February 1946 to terms of imprisonment as being 'war guilty'.

These questions were part of the overriding issue in Finnish political life during the early post-war years – the regulation of the country's relations with the Soviet Union. The Finnish President is given wide responsibilities over foreign policy by the 1919 Constitution. Mannerheim used his powers as fully as possible considering the constraints imposed by the presence of the Control Commission, headed by the Soviet representative, Andrei Zhdanov, who was charged with the responsibility of ensuring that Finland carried out its obligations under the Armistice agreement. He believed that there were times when the President must say no, courteously but firmly, should Zhdanov make unreasonable demands.

Mannerheim saw it as his duty to fulfil the armistice requirements concerning the expulsion of the Germans, but he realized that the timetable set in Moscow in September 1944 for completing this operation was totally unattainable in view of the determined resistance which Colonel Siilasvuo encountered from the German Mountain Army in Lapland. He managed, however, to prevent the Red Army from intervening, as they had the right to do, if the timetable was not kept. Mannerheim felt that in some respects Paasikivi was too ready to submit to Soviet demands, although it later became apparent that there were limits to Paasikivi's compliance. In the autumn of 1945 Mannerheim's health deteriorated and he was forced to take a holiday in Portugal. Paasikivi was left in charge and eventually, in March 1946, he succeeded Mannerheim as President.

Although Paasikivi was respected in Moscow he also had great authority in Finland and he was able to use his position with great skill in order to set Finland on a course which it has successfully followed ever since. The fundamentals of the 'Paasikivi line' are independence, neutrality and friendship with the Soviet Union. He appeared to know how far it was necessary to comply with Soviet wishes on certain matters which were not considered vital to Finnish interests but also to stand firm when Soviet demands encountered the bedrock of national independence and the integrity of Finnish democracy.

His policy produced tangible benefits within a short time. Even during his premiership in December 1945 the period for delivery of reparations payments was extended by two years and in 1948 the value of the outstanding balances was halved. When Finland finally discharged its debt in 1952 there was a smooth transition from forced deliveries to normal trading relations. One of the reasons for Finland's economic success in the post-war world has been its ability to use Soviet trade as a factor of stability when its trading partners in western Europe have been affected by recession. In 1956, the final year of Paasikivi's second term of office, the Soviet Union handed back to Finland the base at Porkkala which had been leased for 50 years under the 1944 agreement.

The crucial year in Paasikivi's first period as President, from 1946 to 1950, was 1948. The international situation darkened when the

Cold War between the Soviet Union and its wartime allies intensified. In February the Czechoslovak crisis resulted in a seizure of power by the Communists. The Soviet grip tightened on Romania and Hungary. In June the Yugoslav Communist Party was expelled from the Cominform and Stalin launched a vitriolic campaign in a vain attempt to force Tito out of office. At about the same time the four-power administration of occupied Berlin broke down and the Soviet blockade of the city began.

Many Finns feared that their country was next on the list of those which were to be forced to accept the status of a Soviet satellite. The possibility of a Soviet–Finnish Treaty of Friendship, analogous to those with Hungary and Romania, which led to their absorption into the Soviet sphere of influence had been discussed with Zhdanov, Mannerheim and Paasikivi as early as 1945; and between Molotov and the Finnish Prime Minister, Mauno Pekkala, in November 1947. In February 1948 Paasikivi received a latter from Stalin which outlined a proposed mutual assistance treaty 'which would be similar to the treaties between Hungary and the Soviet Union and Romania and the Soviet Union', but in the event the treaty which Paasikivi signed on 6 April 1948 differed in several important respects from those with the east European satellites. It bore the title Agreement of Friendship, Co-operation and Mutual Assistance, (see Appendix C) and is known by its Finnish initials as the YYA Treaty. It is short, consisting of only eight articles and it appears on the face of it to be a simple and straightforward document. Yet it has given rise to much misinterpretation and has been used as the basis for the misconception known as 'Finlandization' which certain western politicians and journalists use as a code word for subservience to the Soviet Union.

In fact it is based on a realistic assessment of mutual interest, between two countries of unequal size and power, which in no way infringes the sovereignty of the smaller partner. The preamble records Finland's desire to 'remain outside the conflicting interests of the Great Powers'. Article I pledges that, should either Finland or the Soviet Union be attacked *through Finnish territory* by Germany or any state allied to Germany, 'Finland will, true to its obligations as an independent state, fight to repel the attack *within the frontiers of*

Finland . . . and if necessary with the assistance, or jointly with, the Soviet Union'. Such assistance, however, will only be given '*subject to mutual agreement*' (emphasis added). Article II provides for the parties to 'confer with each other' if an attack appears to be threatened. Article III pledges support for measures to maintain 'international peace and security in conformity with the aims and principles of the United Nations'. The remaining Articles require that neither party will 'conclude any alliance or join any coalition directed against the other'; that each will refrain from interfering in the internal affairs of the other and that they will work 'in a spirit of cooperation and friendship towards the further development and consolidation of economic and cultural relations.' The treaty was initially intended to last for ten years, but was subsequently extended until it was superseded by the new treaty between Finland and the Russian Republic in 1992.

It is important to note that the YYA Treaty did not confer on the Soviet Union the right to intervene militarily in Finland unless there was mutual agreement. It did not require Finland to go to war automatically in defence of the Soviet Union; and it did not require Finnish forces to operate anywhere else but in Finland.

The only occasion on which the Treaty has been invoked was in 1961, when Khrushchev proposed consultations under Article II because of the deployment of German forces on NATO exercises in the Baltic. At the time the tension between the great powers was at its height, following the building of the Berlin Wall. President Kekkonen was in Hawaii at the time at the end of an official visit to Canada and the United States. He did not consider that the presence of German forces in the Baltic justified Khrushchev's fears. A month after receiving the note he flew to Novosibirsk to meet Khrushchev and to persuade him to drop the matter. He deftly turned the so-called Note Crisis to his advantage by letting it be known that Khrushchev would not feel any need to press the issue if Kekkonen, rather than his Social Democrat sponsored opponent, Olavi Honka, were returned in the presidential election. Honka withdrew his candidature.

The YYA Treaty was perhaps the greatest achievement of Paasikivi's presidency, but there were other issues in which his skill and determination helped to stabilize the position of Finland, both at home and abroad. In the light of what happened to the other eastern neighbours of the Soviet Union culminating with the coup in Prague in February 1948, the years 1945–48 in Finland have commonly been characterized as 'the dangerous years'. It seemed possible that the Soviet Union, exploiting the powerful communist movement in Finland, would contrive a seizure of power, as in Czechoslovakia. But most observers now agree such comparisons are deceptive, and that the conditions in Finland were not favourable for such a development. The Finnish communists had never succeeded in penetrating, or neutralizing, the main institutions of government, the army, the police, the bureaucracy and the judiciary. Nor did they seriously attempt to raise a paramilitary force of their own. Further in 1947–48, the leadership of the Party was paralyzed by internal feuding. Stalin seems to have rejected direct Soviet intervention in Finland, providing his basic aim – to prevent Finland moving into the American bloc – could be secured by other means. Paasikivi's strategy was to satisfy Stalin of Finland's continuing non-alignment by negotiating the YYA treaty, while firmly opposing any threats of internal subversion. His immediate aim was to safeguard the parliamentary election due in 1948. When rumours of a communist coup in Finland, almost certainly groundless, were at their height in April 1948, Paasikivi put the army and police on the alert. When, shortly after, the communist Minister of the Interior, Yrjö Leino, who was suspected of trying to subvert the police, was given a vote of no-confidence in the Eduskunta, and failed to resign immediately, Paasikivi dismissed him, and supported the government in facing down a communist-inspired strike movement which demanded Leino's re-instatement. The communist leaders backed off from a confrontation and put their hopes on the results of the election. When this was held in July 1948, SKDL suffered a major setback, their representation fell from forty-nine to thirty-seven seats, and the Social Democrats overtook them as the largest party of the Left with fifty-four seats. SKDL was excluded from the new government formed after the election and was kept out of office for the next eighteen years. The Soviet media were noisily critical of this development, but Paasikivi was adamant that he would not allow that to influence the internal politics of the country.

Paasikivi had invited K. A. Fagerholm to form a minority Social Democratic administration, which held office until the presidential elections of 1950. In these elections Urho Kekkonen and Mauno Pekkala stood as candidates against Paasikivi, who was returned with a clear majority on the first ballot. The Soviet leaders mistrusted the Finnish Social Democrats and showed their displeasure in various ways. This did not prevent Paasikivi from including them in several governments. Fagerholm was a target for abuse in *Pravda* for his advocacy of Nordic co-operation, especially after Norway and Denmark had joined NATO.

'The history of Finland's independence is full of examples of how the "idea of the North" is used in aggressive policies against the Soviet Union', *Pravda* commented in October 1951, adding that Fagerholm 'unrestrainedly extolled so-called Northern cooperation' which Finnish ruling circles were pursuing with their Scandinavian partners 'at the behest of the American–British warmongers'. Fagerholm stood against Kekkonen for the presidency in 1956 on the retirement of Paasikivi and was defeated by only two votes in the electoral college.

As far as the Soviet Union was concerned, the evil genius of Finnish Social Democracy was Väinö Tanner, O. V. Kuusinen's old enemy from 1918. Tanner's base in Finnish working-class politics came not only from his position in the Party but also from his commanding position in the co-operative movement, *Elanto*. He was also chairman of the International Co-operative Movement from 1927 until his trial as 'war guilty' in 1945. The fury of the Soviet leaders and of the left in Finland knew no bounds when, in 1958, the Social Democratic Party chose him as their chairman. The 'Tannerites' who held the majority of positions within the party had fought bitterly against left-wing elements in the trade union and co-operative movements, and although the two groups had shared power in several governments, there was always an uneasy relationship between them. There is an interesting side light on this relationship in a letter written in 1947 by Dennis Healey, then International Secretary of the British Labour Party, to Väinö Leskinen, the Tannerite Secretary of the Social Democrats, expressing concern at recent news from Finland: 'I understand that since the trade union elections the Communists have become increasingly provocative, making it almost impossible for the Social Democrats to maintain even the appearance of friendly relations with them'. He urged Leskinen to do all in his power to ensure that the Social Democrats should do nothing to upset the Soviet Union during the next few months, as it might delay the ratification of the Paris Treaties.

After the exclusion of SKDL from government in 1948 there was no restraint in the battle for the soul of the labour movement. Communist-led strikes in 1949 were supported by the Prague-based World Federation of Trade Unions (WFTU), and in 1951 the Social Democrat majority at the conference of the Trade Union Federation (SAK) forced through a resolution disaffiliating the Finnish unions from the WFTU. There were further damaging strikes in 1956, which even led to unproven allegations of a plan for a communist coup d'etat. In the following year SAK affiliated to the pro-western International Confederation of Free Trade Unions (ICFTU).

This led to a split in the Social Democrat movement: the anti-Tanner minority broke away under the leadership of Emil Skog and formed their own party and for some years seriously weakened the non-communist Left in Finland. This continued until Tanner retired, and a new Social Democrat leader, Rafael Paasio, was willing to face realities, toned down the party's militant anti-communist stance, and opened contacts with the Soviet Embassy. The Social Democrats made their peace with Moscow, and were released from the tacit anti-Soviet blacklist which kept them from office. Paasio was then able to create a new opening to the Left by inviting SKDL to join the government he formed in 1966. Ele Alenius, the non-communist Chairman of SKDL, together with two communists, were given minor posts in a four party coalition. This paved the way for a healing of the rift in the trade union movement, the renewed strength of which gave it the self-assurance to enter into negotiations which have since provided Finland with a more rational and efficient system of wage bargaining than exists in most capitalist countries.

The degree of union organization in Finland is higher than in most western nations. The government, the unions and the employers engage in annual negotiations, which include the whole range of economic policies, from wage and salary levels to welfare benefits, taxation policy, the cost of living and even the terms of trade. Bargains once struck are legally enforceable. Legislation has also been introduced through the Law on Cooperation within Enterprises, to give workers statutory rights of representation on boards of management. Strikes have not been abolished. However they have been contained within a framework of agreed rules, which prevented the recurrence of the disastrous labour struggles of the 1950s.

No sooner had the rift between left and right within the labour movement been closed in one direction than a new schism appeared on the far left. Disagreement broke out within the Communist Party following the Soviet intervention in Czechoslovakia in 1968. A pro-Soviet group led by Taisto Sinisalo, a former dockers' leader from Kotka, and an SKDL MP, attacked the majority Communist Party leader, Aaltonen and the non-communist SKDL chairman, Alenius, for their allegedly anti-Soviet stance. Sinisalo found a platform for his views in the left-wing newspaper *Tiedonantaja*, which became the mouthpiece of the hard-line communists. The quarrel was contained for most of the 1970s, although Sinisalo's attacks became even more vitriolic as the official party line drifted towards Euro-communism and as the left-wing socialists in SKDL became ever more uneasy about their role in the left-wing alliance. The Social Democrats, freed from their Tannerite image, shifted imperceptibly to the left, picking up support from disillusioned SKDL voters. After re-entering government in 1966, SKDL went into steady electoral decline. The Communists finally split in 1986, and the 1987 elections the Sinisalo faction fought under the banner of the Democratic Alternative, winning four seats. SKDL managed to hold on to 16 of their 27 seats. The internal threat to Finland's political stability from a popular communist movement with mass support had been eliminated.

Finland's history from 1956 to 1981 was dominated by the twenty-five-year presidency of Urho Kekkonen. Once he had consolidated his grip on the levers of power inside Finland and established himself in Soviet estimations as a reliable collaborator, he became, literally, the indispensable man who acquired quasi-dictatorial power. Kekkonen was a ruthless and cunning power broker and manipulator, but he had a principled political strategy. He started from Paasikivi's acceptance after 1944 that Finland's survival must be built on an exclusive, special relationship with the Soviet Union. But with Paasikivi that strategy had been defensive and limited, based on the hope that if Finland was meticulous in observing her treaty obligations, the Soviet Union would respect her western political system and domestic autonomy. Kekkonen had a broader vision, based on his apparent belief that in the long run the Soviet Union might prove to be the winner in the Cold War. He believed that if Finland adopted a more pro-active policy, and demonstrated her usefulness as a good neighbour, Finland could win a wider freedom in international politics. Kekkonen's aim for Finland was to secure a recognized status as a neutral, non-aligned power, which was willing to use its good relations with both sides in the Cold War to help alleviate international tensions. The strategy accepted Finland's special relationship with the Soviet Union, based on the YYA treaty, but if the strategy succeeded, the dangerous provisions of the treaty about political consultation and military cooperation need never be invoked.

There was a price to be paid for this. Since the Russian archives have partially opened it has been revealed how close the Finnish links with Moscow became. There were two lines of communication, based on the Soviet Embassy in Helsinki: the 'official line' through the ambassador to the Soviet government, and the more important 'political line' through the KGB resident direct to the Politburo. In effect all important political initiatives by Finland were notified in advance to Moscow and then evaluated in the light of the Soviet response. This gave the Soviet Union an informal veto power which extended into domestic politics. Individuals or groups who were classified in Moscow as anti-Soviet were effectively marginalized in Finnish public life. In the same way material judged offensive to the Soviet Union could not appear in the media or be published in Finland. Thus the writings of Solzhenytsin, and even the memoirs of the discarded communist leader, Leino, could not be published there. A process of self-censorship, guided by indications from Moscow, was operating. There were other deleterious effects of the system. As Kekkonen gathered almost total authority into his own hands, an inevitable corruption of public life set in. This was compounded by the necessity for everyone in official positions to affirm in public their commitment to Soviet–Finnish friendship and their total confidence in the policies of the Soviet Union, which few Finns sincerely believed in.

But the gains for Finland were undeniable. The Soviet leaders had identified Kekkonen as the man they could do business with. It is now known that Soviet money helped to fund his election campaigns. Once installed as President, Kekkonen's role as facilitator in resolving the 'night frost' crisis of 1958 strengthened his credentials. The supreme test was the 'Note Crisis' of 1961, the only occasion when the Soviet Union proposed formally to activate the consultation procedures in the YYA treaty. Aspects of this episode are still obscure, but it is certain that Kekkonen and the Soviet leaders were jointly trying to ensure his re-election as President in 1962. It emerged that the price for the Soviet Union withdrawing its proposal for consultation under the YYA was the re-election of Kekkonen. Once this was assured by the withdrawal of the united opposition candidate, Olavi Honka, the crisis was easily resolved at a private meeting between Kekkonen and Kruschev at Novosibirsk. This produced a remarkable payoff for Finland, because it was announced that the Soviet Union would trust Finland to act as a 'guard dog' who would take the initiative if consultations were required. This meant in effect that the responsibility for activating the YYA treaty passed to Finland. From then on Kekkonen went from strength to strength. This culminated when Finland hosted the European Security Conference which produced the Helsinki Accords in 1975. Finland's status as an honest broker in the Cold War was seemingly accepted by both sides. By this stage the Soviet confidence in Kekkonen was such that the leaders were asking his advice in framing their own relations with the West. Kekkonen's achievement enabled Finland to play a full part in the United Nations and the Nordic Council from the 1950s, to associate with EFTA in the 1960s and to share her weapons procurements between East and West; while in addition Finland got privileged access to Soviet markets and could negotiate the advantageous trade deals which made a substantial contribution to the economic takeoff after 1960.

By 1981 Kekkonen's mental powers were declining to the point where he had to be replaced. The Soviet Union had its favoured candidate in Ahti Karjalainen, but the Finnish electorate chose the

Social Democrat, Mauno Koivisto, and this was accepted by Moscow without adverse comment. Koivisto was a realist with a gritty integrity, one of the few Finnish politicians who had confronted Kekkonen on a major issue and won. He was committed to changing the style of the presidency and restoring a proper constitutional balance in internal politics. But foreign policy was unchanged and the lines of communication to Moscow were are busy as ever. As perestroika developed under Gorbachev, the possibility of revising Finland's relations with the Soviet Union emerged. The Russian hold was relaxed, Gorbachev was the first Soviet leader who acknowledged publicly that Finland was a neutral power, while Soviet interventions in internal politics gradually ceased. But Koivisto was cautious: for example, despite strong pressure from Finnish public opinion he declined to encourage the secessionist demands of the Baltic Republics, and urged them to pursue their aims within the framework of the Soviet Constitution, a reticence that Gorbachev appreciated. It was 1991 before Koivisto decided the time had come to request a revision of Finland's treaties with the Soviet Union, on the grounds that with the changed international situation many of their provisions were obsolete. This resulted in 1992 in a new treaty between Finland and Russia, which put their relations on a normal international footing and replaced the YYA treaty and the special relationship. Looking back on the years from 1944 to 1992 it is apparent that, on balance, Finland is one of the great success stories of post-war Europe, and despite recent economic difficulties, partly caused by the collapse of the Soviet Union, this looks set to continue.

10

The economy of Finland in the twentieth century

At the end of the Second World War the Finnish economy was seriously crippled. Apart from the losses in manpower and equipment which were directly attributable to the war, there was the disruption to foreign trade, which had begun in 1939, even before Finland itself was involved in the war. Its two major trading partners, Britain and Germany, were prevented by war from taking Finnish exports of timber and paper products. In 1939 over 40 per cent of imports came from Britain and Germany and the two belligerent powers bought between them over 50 per cent of Finland's exports. After the United States entered the war in 1941 the trickle of raw materials and fuel oil which had been brought through dried up completely. The textile industry lost its supply of raw cotton and although it was able to continue production for a time by using the stockpiles which had been built up; and although great ingenuity was shown in utilizing substitute materials, the industry was soon in crisis. As the war proceeded machinery began to wear out and could not be replaced. Some supplies for essential war industries were imported, with German permission, and Sweden was able to send a limited amount of iron ore. The cost of the war had imposed a heavy burden upon state finances and there was a large balance of payments deficit.

Apart from these deprivations, which were 'normal' to a wartime situation, there were certain special disabilities which Finland faced in 1945. The loss of Viipuri and the manufacturing centres of Karelia deprived Finland of a third of its hydroelectricity, a quarter of its chemical pulp production, 12 per cent of its productive forests and

9 per cent of its arable area. In addition there was the millstone of reparations payments to the Soviet Union which were a first charge upon the economy. Finland's political situation after 1944 – of dependency on the Soviet Union – prevented the government from seeking economic assistance for reconstruction from the West except on a limited scale. Even though Finland was invited to attend the initial discussions in Paris in 1947 which led to the launching of the US financed Marshall Plan, the government decided (despite a recommendation to the contrary from the Foreign Relations Committee of the Eduskunta) to decline the invitation. The Marshall Plan having become the source of serious differences among the Great Powers, Finland, desiring to remain outside the areas of Great Power politics, 'regrets that it does not find it possible to participate.' There was, however, no such objection to Finnish membership of the IMF and the World Bank, which Finland joined in 1948, seven years before its admission to the United Nations.

The position regarding reparations payments was not entirely negative. Soviet insistance on payments being in metal goods, engineering products, ships and electric cables stimulated the growth of these industries. The initial Soviet demands went beyond the capacity of the country to produce these products and it was necessary to import raw materials and semi-finished products, mainly from Sweden, in order to meet the targets. A strike of Swedish metal workers in 1945 put these deliveries in jeopardy. There was an intensive programme of investment, much of it state financed, to bring the Finnish metal industry up to a level where it could meet its obligations. Even before the debt had been fully discharged, however, a five-year Finnish–Soviet trade agreement, signed in 1950, provided for free deliveries to replace forced reparations payments, and in subsequent years Finland became a major supplier of metal products to the Soviet Union. In 1953 the Soviet Union surpassed Britain as Finland's major trading partner, supplying 21.4 per cent of imports and receiving 25.4 per cent of exports. The growth of the metal-using industries was stimulated first by the reparations payments and then after 1952 not only by trade with the Soviet Union but also by the diversification of products to satisfy markets in the OECD countries. In 1950 the share of metal goods in Finland's export trade amounted to 10.9 per cent of the total. It leapt to 20.9 per cent in 1953. Although this level was not maintained during the first few years, there has been a steady growth to the present figure of over 30 per cent. There has been a corresponding decline in the share of exports from the forest-based industries, although the total volume of all exports has steadily increased. There was a temporary boost to Finland's foreign trade during the Korean War, when the United States and other countries stockpiled metal goods, paper products and chemicals – all of which Finland was able to supply.

By the mid 1950s Finland had recovered from the effects of the war and was poised for a major restructuring of its economy to meet the challenge of survival in the post-war world. There were some major problems to overcome, especially in the field of labour relations and in changing the role of agriculture in the economy. For a time it seemed that Finland was suffering from what became known as the 'English disease' of stagflation, made worse by strikes and balance of payments problems. In 1956 there was a drop in production of 2 per cent which was caused by a combination of strikes, a severe winter and a down turn in world trade. By 1959 these difficulties had been largely overcome and Finland began to prosper. In the mid 1960s the national income per capita exceeded that of Britain for the first time. It has steadily pulled ahead during the last two decades, so that today Finland is among the top ten industrial nations in the world and is beginning to catch up on its wealthy Scandinavian rivals.

This has been achieved without the windfall of the discovery of a new energy source, as happened in Norway, or with any of the internal or external factors which have assisted the others. Sweden, for example, has a stronger base of raw materials and has benefited from its neutrality during the Second World War, which enabled it to emerge in 1945 with its industrial base undamaged by the war. By joining the EEC in 1973 Denmark was able to maintain its export trade with Britain and western Europe.

Finland became associated with EFTA in 1961, through the Fin-EFTA agreement, and became a full member in 1986. In 1973 a trade agreement with the EEC gave Finland many of the economic advantages of membership with none of the political overtones which would have called into question its neutral stance. Earlier in the same year an agreement with Comecon – the only such agreement between a western-type market economy and the communist-led economic group – emphasized Finland's position outside the major world power groupings.

The secret of Finland's success has been its ability to specialize in the production of goods and services which make the best use of its limited material resources. Emerson might have been writing about Finland when he said 'if a man write a better book, preach a better sermon, or make a better mouse-trap than his neighbour, though he build his house in the woods, the world will make a beaten path to his door.' Finland's 'better mouse-traps' include ice-breakers, glassware, ceramics, pharmaceutical products, high-quality textiles, pre-fabricated houses, sports equipment, electronics, cruise liners and a whole host of other specialized products in which skill, design, originality and flair account for more than bulk, volume and mass-production capacity.

The ship-building industry has been one of the great success stories. Even before the war Finland had an internationally recognized expertise in the production of ice-breakers. It was a condition of survival in world trade that Finland should be able to keep its ports open for as long as possible during the long winter freeze-up of its coastline. The first specially commissioned ice-breaker was launched in 1890. In 1939 there were seven ice-breakers in commission in the Gulf of Finland and the Gulf of Bothnia. Two of these were taken as reparations by the Soviet Union. The privately owned Wärtsilä yard at Helsinki resumed the construction of ice-breakers in 1954 and since that time has produced a continuous supply of modern ships for domestic use and for sale to the Soviet Union, the United States, Canada, Argentina and Chile. Wherever ships encounter ice their ability to keep on sailing depends to a great extent on the products of Finnish shipyards, both private and state-owned, which manufacture about two thirds of the world's ice-breakers. Knowledge of the special problems encountered in high-latitude marine conditions has led to other forms of specialization – for example, in offshore rigs for Arctic oil drilling operations and shallow draught ice-breakers for use in rivers in the Russian Arctic. Finnish shipyards are not only concerned with vessels for working in ice-blocked seas. They supply a range of ships, from bulk ore carriers and container vessels to luxury liners. The largest cruise liner built in the last two decades is the pride of the P and O fleet, the 45,000 tonne Royal Princess, launched – ahead of schedule – at the Wärtsilä yard in 1984 and now in service on the Caribbean–Pacific cruise circuit.

The special steels used in the shipbuilding industry are supplied by the state-owned Rautaruukki steel works, situated on the Bothnian coast near Raahe, in latitude 60°40′N, almost in the Arctic Circle. It is one of the most modern steel works in Europe, with a lower energy input per ton of steel produced and a higher output per worker than any of its competitors. It receives its raw material (concentrated ore) from a mine and processing plant at Kostamus, in Russian Karelia. A joint Finnish–Soviet project involved the building by Finnish construction workers of a railway across the Russian border to link the mine with the steel works, and the installation by Finnish engineers of the specialized pelletization plant which concentrates the ore.

On a much smaller scale than Rautaruukki, the glass and ceramics industry, which is based on a long-established tradition of high quality craft work, supplies ornamental glassware from the Iittala works near Hämeenlinna and ceramics from the Arabia works in Helsinki, which are world famous in the luxury markets of the United States and western Europe. Artists like Tapio Wirkkala and Kaj Frank were released from commercial pressures to enable them to design their products in complete artistic freedom. The measure of the success of this far-sighted policy can be gauged by the record of Finnish successes at the Milan Triennale, where Finnish designers won more prizes than any other country except Italy in each of the four exhibitions held between 1951 and 1963. A similar record of success has been achieved by those who now carry on the work of the pioneers – not only in glass and ceramics but also in textiles, furniture and jewellery.

The role of project exports in the Finnish economy is of growing importance. The Finns sell their expertise in a range of industrial fields, including the construction of hotels in Russia, conference centres in Africa and Asia, paper-making factories in Britain and eastern Europe, hydro-electric schemes in the United States and railway engineering in Latin America. In 1982 Finnish project exports earned over one billion dollars in foreign currency and directly employed over 5,000 Finnish specialists, as well as many thousands of locally engaged workers on the sites abroad. In order to service this activity, banking, insurance and technical services have been developed. One of the most interesting firms which is employed in consultancy work is that created almost single-handed by Jaakko Pöyry, whose international design consortium operates in every continent.

The Finnish economy in 1945 was based primarily on agriculture and forestry. Since the 1960s it has become more and more concerned with high technology, quality design and the provision of services. Agriculture now engages less than 7 per cent of the population, although production of dairy produce, eggs, beef and pork is above the level of domestic demand and over 70 per cent of home needs in bread, grains and vegetables can be satisfied. The problem of overproduction of dairy produce has been tackled by a government-financed scheme to persuade farmers to take early retirement. This has been partially successful. The number of milk suppliers has been cut from the peak of 240,000 in 1965 to under 90,000 but because of the increased efficiency of those still working, milk production is still too high. Output of cheese has doubled since 1965, absorbing some of the surplus liquid milk, but Finland still has problems with agricultural overproduction.

In the forestry industry there has been a shift from wood production to the manufacturing of paper and of chemical byproducts. There has also been an increase in the processing of waste wood for use in power stations and for other fuel-saving purposes. The forests are still Finland's greatest natural asset, however, and the ingenuity of Finnish scientists in finding new uses for wood products continues to keep Finland in the fore-front of the world's timber-producing nations. Timber, paper and wood products account for 37 per cent of all exports. This leaves over 60 per cent for other items, of which metal and engineering goods are the most important, representing 31 per cent of the value of exports in 1986.

Finland's lack of domestic fuel resources means that it is necessary to import large quantities of oil and natural gas, mainly from Russia. The state oil corporation, Neste, is responsible for the refining and bulk distribution of this fuel, and it also manufactures petrochemicals. Finnish–Soviet trade agreements are based on the assumption that the accounts will roughly balance. This has meant that on occasions Finland has imported more oil than was necessary to satisfy domestic demands. Neste has either re-exported the refined products or has developed an export trade in petrochemicals. Natural gas is brought in by a pipeline which was completed in the 1970s, from across the Russian border. In 1977 the first of Finland's nuclear power stations was opened at Loviisa, to the east of Helsinki. A second reactor was opened on the same site in 1980. Both were built to Russian designs. The nuclear material is supplied by Russia and the spent fuel is sent back for disposal. Two other reactors, built near Rauma, are of different design and obtain their fuel from non-Russian sources. Here the waste is sent eastward for disposal. Since the disaster at Chernobyl in April 1986, there has been considerable controversy about the wisdom of expanding Finland's nuclear power capacity. The official view is that, given the limits on other power supplies – hydro-electricity, processed peat and wood and imported oil – Finland has no option but to go ahead with its nuclear programme. The success of the Greens in the 1987 general election, when they increased their seats from two to four in the Eduskunta, suggests that not all Finns accept the official view.

The continuous growth of the Finnish economy from the 1950s had, by the 1980s, made Finland one of the most affluent societies in the world, easily surpassing the United Kingdom. This period of expansion ended abruptly in 1991. One factor was the collapse of the Russian market; by 1990 Finnish exports to Russia had fallen to 40 per cent of their previous best level. At the same time Finland had introduced unregulated financial markets, which created an economic boom based on a massive expansion of consumer credit. The wave of borrowing, secured on property values, was fuelled by an inflation rate which caused real interest rates to be low, or even negative. Further the forest industries, the core of the Finnish economy, were meeting new competition from Third World countries.

Both government and people had been slow to recognize how world economic conditions were changing and the crisis of 1991 caught them unprepared. The sharp downturn in exports forced a devaluation of the Finnish mark in November 1991, which in turn

Finland's greatest contribution to twentieth-century civilization, however, lies simply in the fact that it has survived intact as a nation state dedicated to the principles of parliamentary democracy and that it has been able to maintain a welfare state with a high (and steadily rising) national living standard, despite the battering it has endured from a hostile world during the brief period of its national independence. The hope which Finland's example gives to small nations faced with apparently overwhelming odds is Finland's greatest contribution to human welfare. The civic genius which enabled the country to extricate itself from an apparently hopeless situation in 1944 – to snatch victory from the jaws of defeat – must owe something to luck, but it owes much more to the people of Finland and to their leaders. They shed their romantic illusions about a 'Greater Finland', a bastion of Christian civilization standing against the ravening hordes of barbarism, represented by their traditional enemy, Russia. Few nations can abandon the myths by which a generation has lived and which have sustained the people during the formative period in their history, and face soberly and without illusions the bleak truth that the only road to survival leads in the opposite direction from that which has been previously followed. The romantic nationalism of the nineteenth century which played a vital part in the formation of the Finnish nation could offer no comfort or support in the world of the mid twentieth century; although it had served its purpose during two previous centuries, firstly in sustaining the nation during the later stages of Russian occupation and then in providing a core round which the new nation could rally.

The story of the resettlement of the post-war refugees is one aspect of the way in which a united and determined people showed that it is possible for a small and militarily weak nation to learn to live alongside a giant and at times predatory neighbour without losing its sense of national identity. Finland has managed to do this without following the course which many small and medium-sized nations have felt constrained to follow. Finland has resisted the pressures from all sides to line up in a military alliance with one or other of the great powers. Austria and Sweden are other European nations which have shown that neutrality is not, as in the view of Mr Dulles, an 'immoral' posture but is in fact a viable option for small nations. Norway and Denmark chose to join NATO, and Romania and Hungary had no option but to join the Warsaw Treaty. Finland's neutrality was a fragile growth in 1944, although there was a tenuous pre-war tradition of Scandinavian neutrality, and it has passed through many phases. In Paasikivi's time it was a protective reflex action, and the only alternative to the adoption under Soviet pressure of a satellite status analogous to that of Hungary. Even then it paid some small dividends to Finland, in the scaling down of reparations payments and the return of the Soviet base at Porkkala. After 1956, under Kekkonen, Finland developed its neutrality more positively and confidently, with the ability to initiate policies and to undertake activities which had some influence on the world stage. Finland has played a notable part in the peace-keeping activities of the United Nations, supplying military commanders, observers and administrators for UN operations in Africa, Kashmir, Suez, Lebanon and Cyprus. Helsinki has been the home for conferences, peace organizations and international meetings at both unofficial and intergovernmental levels concerned with detente, European security and disarmament. The Helsinki Conference on Security and Cooperation in Europe (CSCE) was a culmination of years of patient diplomacy conducted by Finnish diplomats, although of course the Conference could not have taken place without the concurrence of the major powers. There are many who seek to depict Finland's role as that of a messenger boy for the self-interested and power-hungry giants. Nevertheless, it was Kekkonen who recognized that the moment was ripe, and it was widely recognized that the widening of the scope of participation to bring in the United States and Canada, and therefore to give a worldwide rather than a purely European character, owed much to the personal efforts of the Finnish President. It was fitting that he was able to invite the leaders of 30 countries to be guests in Alvar Aalto's magnificent Finlandia Hall in the heart of Helsinki. The fact is that the 'Helsinki Process' – the term used to describe the developments before and since 1975 in the slow unfolding of a new era in power relationships – is now accepted as a major contribution to the influence which a small nation can have in improving the climate of international relations. Of course, Finnish foreign policy is conceived in terms of Finnish national interest. This is true of all nations. Not all, however, can shed their illusions – whether of past imperial glories or of the hope of revenge for past wrongs – and recognise the truth of the dictum 'Freedom is the recognition of necessity.' Since 1989 and the collapse of the Soviet Union, Finland has been re-evaluating its international position, but has so far held to the cautious pragmatism that served well after 1944. It has affirmed its policy of non-commitment, despite membership of the European Union, and decided not to seek membership of NATO, at least for the present.

National identity

Finland has been a country of outward migration for most of its modern history. The land is too poor to attract large numbers of new settlers and from the nineteenth century onwards there have been times when many young Finns faced the stark reality of 'emigrate or starve'. Thus for a long time there was no need for an immigration policy. Today, however, there is a strict immigration policy, the main purposes of which are defensibly economic. Finland has never been in a position to allow the relatively open-door immigration policies which have enriched the national cultures of such countries as Britain, Germany and the United States; approximately 90 per cent of the Finnish population is still Lutheran and white. There are, however, some ethnic minorities in the country, including the descendents of a group of Muslims from Asian Russia who settled in Helsinki in the nineteenth century.

The dominant question in Finnish national identity in the nineteenth and early twentieth century was the role of the numerically small but economically powerful Swedish-speaking minority, who numbered 13 per cent of the population in 1900 and who now account for about 6 per cent. The rise of Finnish nationalism inevitably brought the Finnish and Swedish speakers into conflict. It should be said from the outset that the Finland–Swedes are not Swedes in any other sense than that of language. They are citizens of Finland and their loyalties are wholly engaged as Finns. They know and feel no obligations to Sweden. It should also be understood that a high proportion of the Swedish speakers have always been farmers and fisher folk and have not formed part of the often outspoken urban middle class who felt themselves threatened by the rising tide of Finnish national sentiment. In the 1930s, relations between the two linguistic groups reached a low ebb, with fighting breaking out between university students of the two language groups. However, the advance of the Finnish language to a position of equality with Swedish was accomplished before independence and the cause of the Finnish language was often advanced by far-seeing Finland–Swedes. Many of the early Finnish national writers and politicians spoke Swedish as their mother tongue and many others were bilingual.

The law at present protects the use of Swedish in official transactions in mixed communes. When motoring through Finland the traveller gets advance warning of the linguistic state of the next commune on the road by looking at the village name board. If the majority is Swedish speaking the name appears first in Swedish form, followed by its Finnish equivalent – for example, 'Pargas / Parainen' in a commune where 61 per cent are Swedish speakers. If the Swedish minority is below a certain figure, the name appears first in Finnish and then in Swedish – for example, 'Sarkisalo / Finby' where Swedish speakers number only 15 per cent of the population. The Åland Islands have a special status which allows positive discrimination in favour of Swedish speakers. The status of the Åland Islands is the subject of an international treaty, signed at the end of the First World War, which entrenched the use of Swedish, as well as guaranteeing the demilitarization of the islands. There have been cases in the 1970s and 1980s when the refusal of trading and residence permits to Finnish speakers has given rise to public controversy, but these have been minor disturbances on the surface. Swedish-speaking persons conscripted into the Finnish Army may elect to serve in Swedish-only units and in some universities there are still split departments in which instruction is given in each language separately. Swedish schools are provided under the state system in communes where the numbers justify it and it is always open to Swedish-speaking parents to found schools for their children which, like the British voluntary-aided schools for religious communities, attract state subsidy. There are several such schools in the Helsinki area.

The great test of loyalty to Finland to which the Swedish speakers were subjected came during the Winter War and the subsequent Continuation War. Finnish–Swedes rallied to the cause of Finland and defended their homeland with the same tenacity and courage as was shown by their Finnish-speaking cousins. Thereafter there could be no lingering doubts about their loyalty to Finland.

There are two other minority groups in Finland around whose presence some tensions have been generated – the gypsies and the Sami. Both are numerically small groups in Finland (as they are elsewhere in Scandinavia) and because of this they have tended to be ignored. In the post-war world they have found their voice – and are often outspoken – and have challenged the majority to examine its conscience. The slow encroachment of the Finns on the grazing grounds of the Samis' reindeer herding areas might be justified in terms of economic efficiency, but it has paid scant regard to the social needs of the indigenous population. Moreover, in recent years the misuse of the environment in the delicate ecosystem of the Finnish northlands has not only done ecological damage but has also further undermined the Sami way of life. The culminating disaster (and this of course cannot be blamed upon the Finns) has been the poisoning of the pastures by radioactive fall-out from Chernobyl.

The gypsies form a sometimes vociferous minority who have joined with their cousins in Sweden and Norway to form a Scandinavian 'black' movement which is demanding greater recognition of gypsies' civil rights and is showing some signs of winning concessions.

Another minority group, the treatment of which has slightly tarnished the image of Finnish tolerance and liberality, are the conscientious objectors to military service. However, it should be stated at the outset that Finland has well deserved its reputation as a just and free society. In the assessments made by such bodies as Amnesty International of the degree of freedom in various countries, Finland always appears towards the top of the list. There was some consternation, therefore, when Amnesty condemned Finland in the early 1980s for its illiberal policies towards objectors to military service. (Finland has a system of compulsory military service in common with all European countries except Britain and Ireland.)

There has long been a recognition that those with a genuine conscientious objection to bearing arms could serve their time in some form of non-military social service. There were attempts made, not always successfully, to ensure that those choosing this alternative did not gain an unfair advantage over those who entered normal military service. The problem arose in the 1980s when a small number of Jehovah's Witnesses refused to render any compulsory service to the state, and two of them went to prison. Amnesty took up their case and they were effectively supported by a campaign backed up by that intrepid champion of human rights, the late Ketil Bruun, a left-wing sociologist who had no sympathy with the religious views of the Jehovah's Witnesses, but who firmly believed in their right to differ from the majority. All cases of civil liberties must be tested against the worst possible scenario. In this case the standard of Finnish toleration slipped a little, but was soon restored, and although some Finns have a slightly dented conscience over the affair, it can reasonably be said that Finland can still hold its head high in the community of nations as a champion of civil liberties.

In examining many aspects of Finnish economic, social and cultural life it is apparent that one unusual feature of modern Finland is the relative absence of those invisible social barriers which inhibit the full development of the human spirit. Finns do not seem to be unduly concerned about whether a project is funded by the state or by private enterprise. The boundaries between co-operative, local authority, domestic and even foreign initiatives in the promotion of new ideas in all spheres of life are blurred and appear to be untrammeled by dogmas of either the left or the right.

The relative absence of class distinctions in education, in everyday social life and in the protocols of public life forcibly strikes a visitor from Britain who spends any length of time in Finland. Of course, there are hierarchies of wealth, and amongst some of the older generation of Swedish speakers there are snobberies which hark back to the days of the Swedish nobility and even to the German Baltic barons. In everyday life, however, the pragmatism of 'taking people as one finds them' is the general rule. This may be explained partly by the fact that Finland never had any hope or expectation of being an imperial power, rather than any inherent virtue of the Finns. When placed in positions of power in historic times individual Finns have shown themselves capable of wielding the weapons of repression with as much skill as members of any other nation. The treatment of the Sami people and of gypsies in the twentieth century has at times been characterized by obtuseness and by a willingness to subordinate the long-term interests of the downtrodden minority for the short-term interests of the majority. On the other hand, Finns have shown themselves to be capable of acts of far-seeing generosity in their progressive social policies when the plight of the minorities has been drawn to the attention of the ruling majority. Without the existence of an overseas empire or of a native monarchy and aristocracy there was no soil in which the roots of racial, social or class superiority could grow. When Finns become involved in the affairs of the Third World they do so without memories of an imperial past to cloud their relationships with the peoples of Africa and Asia. Finnish missionaries have made an impression on the peoples of east Africa and Namibia, largely because, although obviously of European stock, they have generally been free of the taint of white supremacy. Their work in Namibia, which still continues, may have brought them into conflict with the white administration but it is probably true that the work of the UN in Namibia, through Martti Ahtisaari (until recently Special Representative of the Secretary General) was made easier because of the pioneer work of his fellow Finns who were missionaries there when the Germans were in command at Ludentz Bay before the First World War.

Family life

Outwardly the position of women in Finnish society is as near to the ideal as can be found in any developed industrial democracy. Finland was the first country in the world to give equal voting rights to men and women in elections to the national parliament – in 1906 – although women in New Zealand had won the right to vote on equal terms with men in local elections in 1893. The first women MPs took their seats in the Eduskunta in 1907 and as many as 19 were chosen out of a total membership of 200 – a percentage not yet achieved in Britain or in many other developed countries. Today over a quarter of Finnish MPs are women, compared with a total percentage of 53 in the population at large. The tradition which developed in the nineteenth century in rural Finland, by which the younger girls went to school whilst the boys were taken into farm work once they had acquired the elementary skills of reading and writing, persists. Throughout the twentieth century more than half the secondary school pupils have been girls. More recently, in 1981, 64 per cent of students taking university examinations were women. Women play a part in Finnish public life which is far more important than it is in most other countries – and women are not confined to traditional 'women's jobs' in welfare and the caring services. There are women in business, in forestry and in engineering. Although their numbers are still low compared with those of the men, they are still well ahead of their sisters in other countries. There is, of course, legal equality between men and women and equal pay legislation has been in force in most occupations throughout the post-war period. Nevertheless, women's earnings are still no more than 75 per cent of those of men – compared with only 65 per cent in Britain – because women tend to be employed in the less skilled and lower-paid occupations. There are also historical–sociological factors which help to explain the lower economic status of women in some parts of Finland. There are sections of the Finnish economy which are still stuck in the labour conditions of Tsarist Russia. One only has to stand in awe watching muscular Finnish women in late middle age handling huge boulders of crystalline limestone on the conveyor belt of the limestone mine at Montola in Savo, to realize that Maxim Gorkii died less than sixty years ago.

Since the Second World War many women have remained active in agriculture (34 per cent, compared with only 19 per cent in Britain) because they have continued to maintain the family smallholding, which by itself would be incapable of sustaining the whole family, whilst the men become wage earners in forestry or in local industry. The family farm provides a valuable supplement to the diet, and many Finnish families have a far healthier regime because the mother is able to pick fresh fruit and vegetables which she has grown herself.

The heavy loss of life which Finland sustained during the bleak years between 1939 and 1945 bore more heavily on the male than on the female population. The processes of demographic recovery have by now restored the 'normal' sex-ratio balance to the population, but for a generation after 1945 Finnish women bore a heavier responsibility as bread winners than would have usually been the case. One example might be given to illustrate this point from amongst the many contemporaries known to the author when a student in Finland in the 1950s. (The names are, of course, fictitious). Jussi was born in 1927 in Sortavala, on the shores of Lake Ladoga. His father died during one of the enforced migrations which the family had to endure as the fortunes of war swept away their old home and the community which sustained it. Jussi and his three older sisters survived, and the mother, a tough Karelian woman of peasant stock and with an immoveable faith in the need to maintain the bedrock of the nation – the rural family – made certain that her family prospered, whatever privations she had to endure to ensure its survival. Helped by voluntary welfare agencies and state assistance, she was able to see all her children through university. She took a job as a residential cook in a hospital, which gave her and the family a roof over their heads and a basic supply of food. She earned the cash to provide her children with some of the extras which enabled them to lead the lives of normal university students. Fortunately, class divisions amongst Finnish students are less rigid than those in Britain, and the Finnish student 'regional associations,' which were a survival from the old mediaeval guilds, gave loans and other forms of assistance on a basis which was neither patronizing nor mean. Jussi belonged to the Satakuntalainen Osakunta, the association which coincided with the historic province of Satakunta, in the lower Kokemäki valley, around Pori. This was because the first hospital in which his mother had worked when the family first settled upon their ejection from their Karelian home was at Pori. The *osakunta* owned some of the prime shopping frontage in Mannerheim Street, Helsinki, and was very wealthy. (It would be like a Yorkshire student association in London owning half of Oxford Street.) Their chairman was Edwin Linkomies, a former Prime Minister, and he and many politicians, businessmen and other pubic figures continued to play an important role in political life – sometimes a reactionary one – but at the same time were also able to provide a grants and welfare system for their members which was independent of the state. Their role has drastically diminished in Finland today. However, the point is made in some detail, not only to illustrate a curious survival into twentieth century Finland of a once important mediaeval institution, but also to show how poor Finnish students in the post-war world were able to pay their way through higher education. Another factor was the well-established continental system of working one's way through college. When Jussi's mother died in the 1960s she had been able to boast that all her children had been given a start in life comparable with that of the children of the rich. One became a leading research scientist, another a senior official in the state-run sugar corporation and the others became teachers.

Social services

The self-help system which affected higher education also had some bearing on the other social services. However, the high level of provision for public housing and Finland's world-wide reputation for excellence in the fields of public health, mother and child welfare, care for the aged, pensions and social security payments, depends upon the intervention of the state. This begins early.

Compensation of workers injured in accidents at work began in 1895. By 1968 this had extended to included free medical care for the disabled, disablement pensions and a daily wage allowance of up to 75 per cent of previous earnings for those permanently injured. In addition to help provided by the state and the commune, there were also voluntary schemes, operated by trade unions, co-operatives and private firms. The huge increase in the need for medical care for the war-disabled resulted in the state taking a larger share in responsibility for public health. Finland was also one of the pioneers of family allowances – both in cash and in kind. At first, when the system began in 1937, there was a means test and benefit was only payable to families with four children or more if both parents were alive, and for single parent families with two children or more.

In 1944 a system of state-financed home-funding loans was started, which paid interest-free loans to couples under 30 years of age. The burden of repayment was reduced if the couple had a child and the debt was totally expunged if more than four children were born. In recent years the state has taken more and more responsibility for family welfare and Finland now has one of the most generous systems of payments for mother and child care anywhere in the world. An aspect of the earlier system of payment of maternity benefit in kind survives in the present arrangements for maternity grants. Expectant mothers can, if they choose, receive a 'maternity package' of basic clothing, which is worth Fmk 1,300 (the cash payment is Fmk 580). In 1981, 55,000 such packages were distributed.

In addition to provision made by local authorities there are several nation-wide health schemes to cover such national health problems as alcoholism, rheumatism, tuberculosis and so forth. The collaboration of state, voluntary agency and local authority, which was common in Britain in the nineteenth and early twentieth century – and which still persists – is also well understood in Finland. The elimination of tuberculosis, once a scourge of the whole of Scandinavia, was achieved by the combined efforts of these various elements. In 1930, 27 Finns in every 10,000 died of tuberculosis. By 1950 this had fallen to 9 and today the disease is virtually unknown in the native Finnish population. The 'Children's Castle' (*Lasten Linna*), built in 1948 by the Mannerheim League for Child Welfare, with state assistance, is no longer needed for its original purpose. For a time it continued to cater for TB patients from the Third World, but it is now a general hospital within the system of public health and welfare arrangements. The links between the Finnish church and certain African countries have meant that Finland, despite its remoteness from the scene of battle, has been drawn into the world-wide struggle against poverty, ignorance and disease in a way which may seem surprising.

Alcoholism

Alcoholism is a scourge which affects Finland and the other Scandinavian states to a greater extent than may be the case in other developed countries. In pre-war days there were strong temperance movements, especially amongst the workers in the trade unions and co-operatives. This resulted in the introduction of prohibition in 1919, which lasted for over a decade, but was repealed in 1933. The failure of the experiment was brought about partly by the enormous boost it gave to the criminal classes to smuggle supplies of alcohol under the noses of the inadequately staffed coastguards. It might have worked if there had been a less complacent attitude on the part of the influential middle classes, who delighted in finding loopholes in the rather tattered defensive curtain which had been erected to protect the people from the demon drink. An English writer in the early 1930s described how she sat in the lounge of the Kampi hotel in the city of Helsinki, sipping vodka from teacups which waiters filled from small teapots. She had, that morning, visited an illicit liquor store on one of the islands near Helsinki. Whilst she sat getting steadily more and more tipsy on Finnish 'tea', her hosts of the morning were placing in her room six bottles of her favourite French wine!

The abandonment of prohibition did not mean that there was a 'free for all' in the supply and consumption of alcohol. A state monopoly in the distribution of alcohol – through Alko shops – was established, together with strict controls over the production, importation and advertising of alcoholic drinks. These controls began to be relaxed in respect of beers and table wines in the 1960s and will have to be further modified in consequence of entry into the European Union.

Finnish drinking habits are very different from those which apply in England. Until recently it could be said that Finland's drinking patterns coincided more closely with those prevalent in Scotland before the laws were relaxed in the 1970s. Spirits rather than beer are the favourite drinks, and the Finnish habit – which dies hard – is for the father to arrive from work on Friday night having first visited the Alko shop, and to spend a part of the week-end engaged upon emptying the bottles which he has brought home, sometimes as a solitary drinker or in company with a group of his male friends. Of course, this is not a picture of normal family life in Finland. Alcoholics do not form the majority of the population, but the problem of alcoholism is still a major socio-medical problem. It may contribute to the pattern of male domination in the family, which nullifies to some extent the progressive thrust of the feminist movement, and which forces some Finnish women into a position in which their legal rights are not fully observed in practice.

One aspect of the alcohol problem in which the Finns show some similarity to their Scandinavian neighbours is the universal condemnation of drunken drivers. In view of the attitude of many people in Britain to the problem of drunken driving which was expressed in 1987, at the time when several MPs and other figures in the public eye were convicted of drink-drive offences, it is instructive to note that none of those involved would have had a shred of credibility left had they committed the offences in Finland. Ahti Karjalainen, a former Prime Minister and Foreign Minister and a possible candidate in the Presidential elections of 1981, lost all prestige as a public figure when convicted of being drunk at the wheel of his car. His fall from all positions of power and influence compares with the experience of a former British Foreign Secretary whose drinking habits seemed to offer no barrier to his political career.

Sport

Finland's prowess on the international sporting scene first became apparent in the early Olympic contests, even before independence was won. Paavo Nurmi was ready to take his place in the 1916 Olympic team when the Games were cancelled because of the war. Willi Kolehmainen had already blazed the trail for Finland by winning the 5,000 and 10,000 metres track events, and the marathon at Newark, New Jersey in 1912. Paavo Nurmi, the Flying Finn, dominated the athletics track during the 1920s. At Antwerp he won the 10,000 metres team and individual gold medals, and a silver medal in the 5,000 metres. The pre-eminence of the Finns in athletics was maintained throughout the 1930s, with men like Iso Hollo and L. Lehtinen carrying off many of the long-distance records. At this time, even Urho Kekkonen, later to become President of Finland, had a reputation in long-distance running and cross-country skiing which extended outside the borders of Scandinavia. The winning streak in long-distance running was resumed after the staging of the

1952 Games in Helsinki. Although the phenomenal performances of the ex-policeman from Helsinki, Lasse Virén, in 1972 and 1974 have been called into question after accusations of drug taking, there are still many Finnish names appearing in the championship tables of European and world athletics contests. In the 1984 Winter Olympics at Sarajevo, world records were broken by Marja-Liisa Hämälainen, who took the world by storm with her exciting performances in the Nordic ski events.

The life-style of many Finns, which is far closer to nature than that of the peoples of other more apparently sophisticated societies, may help to explain Finland's performances in international athletics; but this argument cannot also be used to explain the pre-eminence of Finland in motor sports, where drivers such as Timo Mäkinen, Hannu Mikkola, Ari Vatenen and Timo Salonen have become famous amongst the followers of rallying and cross-country motor racing. It may be that the ability to practise on the ice of frozen lakes and to roar through the forests of Finland has given the motor-racing enthusiasts opportunities which those who live in more densely populated and urbanized environments lack. The Rally of a Thousand Lakes is an international event.

The enjoyment of outdoor activities is still a part of the Finnish way of life, even though most Finns are urban dwellers and are as prominent as Germans and Swedes in the annual rush to the Mediterranean sun which preoccupies a large proportion of middle-class Europe. A very high proportion of Finns, however, own summer houses on islands or on lake shores, and the whole family often migrates to the summer house for several weeks, leaving the breadwinner to cope with the problems of the office or the factory by commuting to and from the summer cottage. The summer house has its sauna, its fishing boat on the lake and its outside earth closet. It is often primitive in relation to the life style of the city flat, but it brings Finns into a close relationship with nature and gives tired professional people the opportunity to rest and relax. This may explain why so much modern architecture and design in Finland shows an ability to co-operate with nature and to bring together artificial and natural products in a way which stamps modern Finnish products with a unique character.

Design

The attachment of Finns to the natural beauty of their environment is reflected in the design of their towns. They appear to have a gift for blending the most modern styles of architecture with the preservation and use of natural features. Helsinki is a city which has grown around a planned, neo-classical centre, designed by the German architect C. L. Engel in the early nineteenth century. As it has grown outward from its original nucleus, new buildings have been erected which , while displaying originality and modern concepts of design and technology, still blend harmoniously with the older structures. Eliel Saarinen (1873–1950), who was the architect of the Helsinki railway station, completed in 1914, used local granite in a way which was forward-looking but entirely appropriate to its setting. In 1922 Saarinen settled in America, becoming president of the Cranbrook Academy of Art and Director of the City Planning Department of Chicago. In this position he exercised a great influence on the design of buildings throughout America. In the granite towers of Helsinki railway station one can see the outline of the skycrapers built in New York and Chicago in the 1930s.

The most famous Finnish architect of the twentieth century was Alvar Aalto (1898–1976), a versatile artist whose influence extended from the design of public buildings to private houses and interior decoration. Although he never completely abandoned his Finnish roots, he spent much of his time after 1940 in the USA and western Europe. He was Professor of Experimental Architecture at the Massachusetts Institute of Technology from 1942 to 1947, and designed buildings in Germany, France and Iraq. The contributions he made to industrial architecture in Finland include the Sunila pulp and paper mills at Kotka, and factories and industrial estates at Anjala, Varkaus and Karhula. His last great work was the Finlandia conference centre in Helsinki, which was finished in time to provide the venue for the Helsinki Conference on European Security, held in 1975. Both Saarinen and Aalto were impelled to leave Finland because they needed the scope which their homeland could not provide for them. They were the first of many Finnish architects who found it necessary to work abroad.

The momentum of architectural creativity has been maintained during the difficult post-war years. One of the most exciting buildings to be erected anywhere in Europe since the Second World War is the Temple Church (*Temppeliaukio*) designed by Timo and Tuomo Suomalainen. It resembles a large, partly sunken, igloo, hollowed out from a residual mass of rock near the centre of Helsinki. The domed roof is arched by burnished copper, through which light is admitted through a tracery of shapes. The walls are of rough-hewn granite, from the rock on which the city is built. The altar and reading lectern are of bronze and copper and the seating is of natural pine. Art and nature are in harmonious equilibrium in this most attractive church.

To designers and architects outside Finland the best known post-war creation has been the garden city of Tapiola, some 16 kilometres to the west of Helsinki. The original intention was to create a self-supporting satellite town which would offer enough work to discourage residents from commuting to and from Helsinki. Alas, as the bumper to bumper lines of cars attempting each morning to enter Helsinki city centre from the west bear daily witness, this aspect of the Tapiola plan did not succeed. After 30 years it is still, however, a showplace for modern design techniques in blending different types of building – terrace houses, small town blocks, detached houses – in a way which is not only aesthetically pleasing but which provides a social mix of working-class and middle-class housing, from family accommodation to bachelor flats, and which helps to reinforce the relatively classless nature of Finnish society. The skill with which the elements of wood and water – forests, seas and lakes – penetrate into the artificial environment of the town is also a lesson which has not been learned in many of Britain's post-war satellite towns.

The argument often used in Britain, that money was in short supply and that returning ex-servicemen had to be found some sort of accommodation as quickly as possible, does not justify the ugliness of some post-war housing estates in Britain. Finland, too, had overwhelming economic constraints, but successfully overcame them. One aspect of the Finnish post-war housing situation which is worthy of mention is the ARAVA scheme, by which the state guaranteed interest-free loans to would-be house purchasers, and where private, state and local authority agencies worked together to provide well-designed but cheap accommodation.

The life-enhancing creative arts in which the Finns have excelled extend to other fields of design. The excellence of Finnish pottery, glassware, furniture, textiles, interior decoration and industrial design owes much to the far-seeing policies of Finnish manufacturers. One of the reasons for this may be that, in its remote position in relation to the main markets of Europe, and with its limited resources, Finland could not hope to compete in the mass production of consumer goods for the markets of western Europe and north America. The only way forward was to move up-market and to sell to those who were more interested in quality than in quantity. As early as the 1870s the School of Decorative Arts in Helsinki was promoting exhibitions at home and abroad, and artists were encouraged to give free rein to their talents in an environment where long-term benefits were given priority over the short-term advantages of rapid turnover and immediate profitability. Firms such as Arabia, Iittala and Nuutajärvi, manufacturing ceramics and glassware, combined the production of large scale goods – sanitary ware and tableware for everyday use for the home market – with high quality, individually designed works of art for the luxury export market. Finnish artists have carried off prizes at the Milan Triennale in most years since 1951. In the four exhibitions held between 1951 and 1963 Finnish designers won more prizes than any other country except the host nation, Italy. Names such as Kaj Frank, Tapio Wirkkala and Timo Sarpaneva are in the forefront of post-war designers in ceramic and glass ware.

Such a reputation is not gained by the promotion of a small elite of top quality designers. It must grow from a tradition of long duration during which the whole community has learned to appreciate the values of good design. It is a tradition which began in Finland before independence and which has blossomed in the last few decades, just as the Finns have grown in self confidence, realizing that good design is not only aesthetically satisfying but is also commercially profitable.

Literature

The Finnish language may erect obstacles to the appreciation of Finnish literature in the outside world but in spite of this handicap the literature of Finland has been one of the important strands in the fabric of modern European culture. The impact made by *Kalevala*, especially after 1849, when the Finnish Literature Society published a second edition based on Lönnrot's 1835 compilation, was immense. By the end of the century it had appeared in more than 30 translations. Longfellow was influenced by the German translation when he wrote his epic, *Hiawatha*. A virtual *Kalevala* industry came into existence, inspired by the Literature Society, which houses in its archives more than one and a quarter million lines of *Kalevala* poetry. The study of folklore and oral traditions throughout the world was enriched, and is still being enriched, by the scholars who draw on this storehouse of traditional folk culture.

Finnish literature was deeply affected by *Kalevala* during the rest of the nineteenth century. As the Finns strove to find their voice in the world of European culture they naturally turned to their folk roots. The greatest of the lyric poets, Eino Leino (1878–1926), used folk themes to illustrate the plight of contemporary humanity. He also translated Dante's *Divine Comedy* into Finnish verse.

There are two main themes in Finnish literature which appeared before the Second World War – that drawn from folklore and that based on more recent historical experience. The works of Runeberg and Topelius draw on the history of the Finns during the wars with Sweden and Russia in the eighteenth and early nineteenth centuries. *Tales of Ensign Stål* by Runeberg and *Tales of a Field Surgeon* by Topelius deal respectively with the action of Finnish troops in the war with Russia (1808–9) and with the history of two families over generations since the Thirty Years' War in the seventeenth century. Although both authors wrote in Swedish, they are numbered amongst the pioneer figures of modern Finnish literature. Aleksis Kivi (1854–72) is regarded as the father of Finnish literature, because he not only wrote the first Finnish novel, *The Seven Brothers* (1870), but was also the originator of both tragic and comic Finnish drama. It is appropriate that his statue sits in front of the Finnish National Theatre and that his plays are still performed there.

Many great works of Finnish literature draw on the recent history of Finland during periods of great national crisis. Amongst the authors best known abroad are F. E. Sillanpää (1888–1964), who was awarded the Nobel Prize for Literature in 1939. His powerful account of the struggles of rural communities during the last decades of Russian rule – *Meek Heritage* – and the traumatic events of the civil war, covers a similar period in time to that dealt with by Maxim Gorkii in *The Artamonovs*, and deserves to take its place alongside the Russian classic as a cry from the heart of the poor and downtrodden of all times and nations. Sillanpää's other famous works include *Fallen Asleep While Young* (1931) and *Man's Way* (1932), both of which explore the plight of young Finns in restricted and stultifying rural communities, although they are as much concerned with individual psychological problems as with the sociological setting. Much of Sillanpää's work is drawn directly from his own experience, and his charming evocation of a young man's first love in *Midsummer Evening* is one of the most touching love stories ever written.

Historical works of a more directly political character, arising from recent Finnish history including the Civil War, are exemplified by Joel Lehtonen (1881–1934), whose work would doubtless have taken its rightful place in the forefront of modern historical fiction if it had not suffered the constraint of appearing in Finnish. Väinö Linna's *Unknown Soldier* (*Tuntematon Sotilas*, 1954) has achieved some fame outside Finland, having been made into a successful film. It is a story of a patrol of Finnish troops fighting the Russians on the Karelian front during the Second World War. It has also been performed at the Tampere Summer Theatre in an unforgettable natural open air setting in which the auditorium rotates as the audience follows the soldiers through the forest and down to the lake shore. The powerful anti-war sentiments of the *Unknown Soldier* have led critics to compare it with Erich Maria Remarque's *All Quiet on the Western Front*. Linna's work has greater depth and subtlety than that of his German predecessor. Unfortunately the experiences of a small nation fighting for its life on the fringes of Arctic Europe make less impact on the reading public than does the clash of Titans across the fields of Flanders during the First World War.

One Finnish writer who has successfully overcome the limitations of language is Mika Waltari (1908–79) who broke into the international best-seller class in 1945 with his *Sinhue the Egyptian,* a skilful and well-researched piece of historical fiction which recreates the world of ancient Egypt. Other works of Waltari, some in a different genre from that of Sinhue, probably entered the publishers' lists in the USA, Britain and Germany on the coat tails of Sinhue. Though they may not have achieved best-seller status they are still highly regarded on both sides of the Atlantic as important works of 'middle brow' literature.

Music

If the Finnish language places obstacles to the appreciation of literature, no such inhibitions hamper the enjoyment of music. It is not necessary to have a dictionary at hand to listen to Sibelius. His work, of course, dominates the musical scene during the first half of the twentieth century. Although he began as one of the early circle of Finnish patriots (including the poet, Leino and the painter, Gallen-Kallela) who met regularly during the 1890s in the Café on Esplanadi, he soon overstepped the confines of Finland and became a dominant figure in modern European culture. The early works, of which the Lemminkäinen Suite is typical, are consciously drawn from *Kalevala,* just as the paintings of Akseli Gallen-Kallela and the poems of Eino Leino openly acknowledge their source of inspiration. The best known and most often played of these early works is 'The Swan of Tuonela', a depiction of the swan which haunts the dark waters of the Lake of Tuoni across which the dead souls are transported to the other world.

The later works of Sibelius (1865–1957) are less obviously grounded in the folk traditions of Finland. He became a man for all seasons and for all nations, and although his individuality owes much to his Finnish background, he acquired an international reputation. His genius overshadowed most of his Finnish contemporaries during the early inter-war years. In the 1920s and 1930s Yrjö Kilpinen wrote songs which have been compared to those of Anjo Wolf. The piano compositions of Selim Palmgren (1878–1951) earned him the title 'the Chopin of the North.' A younger contemporary, Uuno Klami (1900–61) may have derived inspiration from Ravel and Stravinsky, but his vigorous compositions are unmistakeably grounded in the folk traditions of Finland. The authentic voice of Finland may be heard in the music of Leevi Madetoja (1887–1947), whose opera *The Ostrobothnians* (*Pohjalaisia*) is based on an episode of Finnish history during the Russian occupation. Madetoja captures the harshness and forlorn desolation of both the natural and the human environment of the Ostrobothnian lowlands. This work and Merikanto's *Juha* are two modern operas which catch the authentic voice of Finland.

Since the Second World War the Finns have begun to make an impression on the world of music not only through their composers but also through their orchestras, opera and ballet companies and their solo performers. The great musical festivals, like that at Savonlinna, have brought Finnish music to the notice of the rest of the world. In 1987 there were as many as 150 music festivals, large and small, taking in jazz, opera, chamber music and every form of instrumental composition, all on offer to the visitor to Finland. Names such as Kim Borg, Martti Talvela and Paavo Berglund have appeared regularly on concert programmes throughout the world during the last few decades, and seasons of Finnish music in the United States and Britain have helped to convey the true richness of the musical life of Finland. The production at Covent Garden in London in 1987 of Auli Sallinen's opera, *The King Goes Forth to France*, was notable in that the work was jointly commissioned by the BBC, Covent Garden and the Savonlinna Festival.

The Church

The Lutheran Evangelical Church which claims the allegiance of more than 90 per cent of Finns is, like many religious bodies in the late twentieth century, a mere shadow of its former self. Yet it is more vital than so-called state churches in many other countries. The spate of church building since the Second World War is testimony to the vigour of a progressive church which is building for the future. Its stock of buildings includes some of the finest examples of modern architecture anywhere in the world. The Kalevala church built at Tampere in 1966 by the romantic individualist Reima Pietila, the startling Temple church in Helsinki (1969) and the stark modernity of Juha Leiviska's church of St Thomas (1975) at Oulu are examples of contrasting styles of architecture chosen by Lutheran parish communities.

The lively debates which take place within the church between the traditionalists and the liberal reformers included such issues as sexual morality, drink, race relations, the role of women in society and the role of the church in politics. At the time of his appointment Archbishop Vickström was asked which were, in his view, the most important questions facing the Church in the 1980s. He replied 'First of all, peace.' This involved consideration of the position of the military in Finnish life, the right of conscientious objectors to choose non-military forms of national service and the problem of Finland's sale of arms to other countries. 'The second question is . . . justice in the world and Finland's aid to developing countries'. He felt that Finland's contributions were far too low (0.3 per cent of GNP). The third question concerned the injustice of unemployment and the need to establish the right to work.

It is perhaps because the Bishop's order of priorities lies closer to that of the state than is found in many other nations that Finland enjoys relative social calm in a world where turmoil and confrontation are the order of the day. In both its internal domestic arrangements and its relations with the rest of the world Finland holds up a model of a country where violent extremes are unknown and where calm common sense, combined with hard work, a sense of humour – and a touch of good fortune – combine to produce a society in which the act of living may be practised in a congenial environment.

APPENDIX A

Alexander I's Act of Assurance, Porvoo Diet, March 1809

This document was read by Tsar Alexander I to the members of the Four Estates (some 125 in number) representing the various classes in Finnish society. It finally released the Finns from their allegiance to the Swedish Crown and provided Finland with a constitutional framework which regulated the affairs of the Grand Duchy until the overthrow of Tsar Nicholas II in 1917. The Finns considered that, in return for their recognizing the Tsar as their lawful monarch, they had been promised Russian acceptance of the Finnish Constitution, but later Tsars held that no human agency could usurp the God-given right of the Tsars to rule as absolute monarchs.

We, Alexander I, by the Grace of God Emperor and Autocrat of all the Russias, etc., etc., etc., Grand Duke of Finland, etc., etc., etc., do make it known: That Providence having placed Us in possession of the Grand Duchy of Finland, We have desired, by the present Act, to confirm and ratify the religion and fundamental laws of the Land, as well as the privileges and rights which each Estate in the said Grand Duchy in particular, and all the inhabitants in general, be their position high or low, have hitherto enjoyed according to the Constitution. We promise to maintain all these benefits and laws firm, unchanged, and in full force. In confirmation whereof We have signed this Act of Assurance with Our own hand.

Given . . . March 15, 1809. Alexander

Decree of April 4, 1809

We, Alexander I . . . do make it known: That when We convoked Finland's Estimates to a General Diet, and received their oath of allegiance, We desired, on that occasion, by means of a solemn Act . . . proclaimed in the sanctuary of the Supreme Being, to confirm and secure to them the maintenance of their religion and fundamental laws, together with the liberties and rights that each Estate in particular, and all of Finland's inhabitants in general, have hitherto enjoyed.

In hereby promulgating the Act mentioned above to Our faithful Finnish subjects, We also desire to inform them that We having agreed to conform to and to maintain the traditional customs of this land. We consider the oath of allegiance, of the Estates in general, and of the Deputies of the Estates of the Peasants in particular, taken in the name of their fellows as well, as to be good and binding on all the inhabitants of Finland, without exception.

Fully convinced that this good and loyal people will ever cherish towards Us and Our successors the same fidelity and firm affection which has ever distinguished it, We shall for Our part not fail to give this nation, with God's aid, continuing proof of Our constant fatherly solicitude for its happiness and prosperity.

APPENDIX B

The Bolshevik recognition of Finland's independence in 1917: documents exchanged between the government of Finland and the Council of Peoples' Commissars and the Central Executive Committee of the Congress of Soviets, December–January 1917–18 (NS)

(a) Letter of the Finnish government requesting recognition of Finland's independence, 30 December 1917 (NS)

To the Council of Peoples' Commissars

The people of Finland earnestly hope that the great people of Russia, victoriously enduring the trials of this present time, will find a great and happy future in pursuing the road to freedom . . . within the people of Finland the conviction of every nation that has risen to self-consciousness, that it can only be sure of preserving the conditions necessary for its survival and fulfill its national and social destiny when fully politically independent, has grown irrevocably . . . on this basis the Government of Finland turns to Russia, requesting that it should recognize the political independence of Finland, which the Diet and Government of Finland have regarded it their duty to proclaim for the people of Finland and their mission. Finland expects this recognition from Russia, in whose name it has often been proclaimed that freedom is the right and the honour of every people. Nature has situated the peoples of Finland and Russia as close neighbours. The people of Finland sincerely hopes that this relationship of friendship and mutual respect will always prevail between these nations, and is convinced that the complete freedom of both nations provides the best assurance that this hope will be realised.

(b) Resolution of the Council of Peoples' Commissars, 31 December 1917 (NS)

In reply to the proposal of the Government of Finland that the Republic of Finland be recognized as independent, The Council of Peoples' Commissars, in full accordance with the principle of the right of nations to self-determination, has decided to propose to the Central Executive Committee:

(a) that the political independence of the Republic of Finland be recognized, and

(b) that there shall be established a special Committee of representatives of both parties, to prepare proposals for those practical measures which follow from the separation of Finland from Russia.

W. Uljanov (Lenin), L. Trotski, G. Petrovski, J. Stalin, I. Steinberg, V. Carelin, A. Schlichter

(c) Minute of the Central Executive Committee of the Soviet of Workers', Soldiers' and Peasants' deputies, 4 January 1918 (NS)

At its meeting of the 22 December 1917 the Central Committee of the Soviet of Workers', Soldiers' and Peasants' deputies decided

(1) To recognize the political independence of the Republic of Finland.

(2) In joint negotiations with representatives of the Government of Finland and the Working Class of Finland to set up a special Committee to prepare those practical measures, which arise from the separation of Finland from Russia.

J. Sverdlov	V. Avanesov
Chairman	*Secretary*

APPENDIX C

Agreement of Friendship, Co-operation and Mutual Assistance Between the Republic of Finland and the Union of Soviet Socialist Republics, 6 April 1948

This is the text of the YYA Treaty – Sopimus ystävyydestä, yhteistoiminnasta ja keskinäisestä avunannosta (Friendship, Co-operation and Mutual Assistance) – which was in force up to 1992 and which provided the basis for Finnish–Soviet relations from 1948–1992. Despite attempts by the critics to use the term 'Finlandization' to imply otherwise, the YYA Treaty confers no automatic right for the Soviet Union to intervene militarily or politically in Finnish affairs. Nor does it require Finnish forces to fight outside their own borders. Article 2 requires the two partners to consult each other in certain clearly defined circumstances. On the one occasion when Khrushchev perceived such a threat, in 1961, his view was rejected by President Kekkonen and no action was taken under the terms of the treaty.

The President of the Republic of Finland and the Presidium of the Supreme Soviet of the USSR;

Desiring further to develop friendly relations between the Republic of Finland and the USSR;

Being convinced that the strengthening of good neighborhood relations and cooperation between the Republic of Finland and the USSR lies in the interest of both countries;

Considering Finland's desire to remain outside the conflicting interests of the Great Powers; and

Expressing their firm endeavour to collaborate towards the maintenance of international peace and security in accordance with the aims and principles of the United Nations Organization:

Have for this purpose agreed to conclude the present agreement and have . . . agreed to the following provisions:

Article 1

In the eventuality of Finland, or the Soviet Union through Finnish territory, becoming the object of an armed attack by Germany or any state allied with the latter, Finland will, true to its obligations as an independent state, fight to repel the attack. Finland will in such cases use all its available forces for defending its territorial integrity by land, sea, and air, and will do so within the frontiers of Finland in accordance with obligations defined in the present agreement and, if necessary, with the assistance of, or jointly with, the Soviet Union.

In the cases aforementioned the Soviet Union will give Finland the help required, the giving of which will be subject to mutual agreement between the Contracting Parties.

Article 2

The High Contracting Parties shall confer with each other if it is established that the threat of an armed attack as described in Article 1 is present.

Article 3

The High Contracting Parties give assurance of their intention loyally to participate in all measures towards the maintenance of international peace and security in conformity with the aims and principles of the United Nations Organization.

Article 4

The High Contracting Parties confirm their pledge, given under Article 3 of the Peace Treaty signed in Paris on February 10, 1947, not to conclude any alliance or join any coalition directed against the other High Contracting Party.

Article 5

The High Contracting Parties give assurance of their design to act in a spirit of cooperation and friendship towards the further development and consolidation of economic and cultural relations between Finland and the Soviet Union.

Article 6

The High Contracting Parties pledge themselves to observe the principle of the mutual respect of sovereignty and integrity and that of non-interference in the internal affairs of the other state.

Article 7

The execution of the Present agreement shall take place in accordance with the principles of the United Nations Organization.

Article 8

The present agreement shall be ratified and remains in force ten years after the date of its coming into force. The agreement shall come into force upon the exchange of the instruments of ratification, the exchange taking place in the shortest time possible in Helsinki.

Provided neither of the High Contracting Parties has denounced it one year before the expiration of the said ten-year period, the agreement shall remain in force for subsequent five-year periods until either High Contracting Party one year before the expiration of such five-year periods in writing notifies its intention of terminating the validity of the agreement.

In witness hereof the Plenipotentiaries have signed the present agreement and affixed their seals.

Done in the city of Moscow on the sixth day of April, 1948, in two copies, in the Finnish and the Russian languages, both texts being authentic.

Bibliography

The following list is not intended to be particularly systematic or representative – the readership at whom this book is directed is already well served by Screen's bibliography (see below). Rather is it meant as a selective guide to English-language sources which the author has found helpful in writing about Finland and which readers may find illuminating in their further study of the country, its history and its spirit.

BIBLIOGRAPHICAL GUIDES

Aaltonen, H. *Books in English on Finland.* University of Turku, 1964.

Books from Finland published by Helsinki University Library quarterly since 1967, is a guide for the English speaking reader to Finnish literature and translations.

Groennings, S. *Scandinavia in social science literature.* Indiana University Press, Bloomington, 1970.

Nyman, Kristina. *Finland's war years 1939–1945: a list of books and articles concerning the Winter War and the continuation war.* Society of Military History, Helsinki, 1973.

Screen, J. E. O. *Finland.* (World bibliographical series, vol. 31.) Clio Press, Oxford, 1981.

Articles on all aspects of Finnish history appear in a variety of Scandinavian journals in English. These are conveniently covered by *Index Nordicus*, a cumulative index to English-language periodicals on Scandinavian studies, compiled by Janet Kvamme, prepared under the auspices of the American – Scandinavian Foundation and published by G. K. Hall, Boston, 1980. Journals indexed include *Co-operation and Conflict, Scandinavian Economic History Review, Scandinavian Political Studies, Scandinavian Review, Scandinavian Studies,* and *Scandinavica.*

COUNTRY AND PEOPLE

Bacon, W. *Finland.* Hale, London, 1970.

Highway to the wilderness: a sojourn beyond the Arctic Circle. Vanguard Press, New York, 1961.

Facts about Finland. Otava, Helsinki, current edition.

Forssell, H. *Sea Finland: Finnish seafaring from early history to the future.* National Board of Antiquities, Helsinki, 1985.

Hall, Wendy. *The Finns and their country.* Parrish, London, 1967.

Halmesvirta, A. *The British conception of the Finnish race: nation and culture 1760–1918.* Jyväskylä, 1990.

Ingold, T. *The Skolt Lapps today.* Cambridge University Press, 1976.

Irwin, J. L. *The Finns and the Lapps: how they live and work.* David and Charles, Newton Abbot, 1973.

Jackson, J. H. *Finland.* 2nd ed. Allen and Unwin, London, 1940.

Kallas, H., Nickels, S., eds., *Finland: creation and construction.* London, 1968.

Mead, W. R. *Finland.* Benn, London, 1968.

Nickels, S. *Traveller's guide – Finland.* Rev. ed., Cape, London, 1977.

Nickels, S., Kallas, H., Friedman, P., eds. *Finland: an introduction.* 2nd ed. Allen and Unwin, London, 1973.

Nicol, Gladys. *Finland.* Batsford, London, 1975.

Sentzke, Geert. *Finland: its church and its people.* Luther-Agricola Society, Helsinki, 1963.

Siuruainen, E., Aikio, P. *The Lapps in Finland.* Society for the Promotion of Lapp Culture, Helsinki, 1977.

Stenius, G. ed. *Introduction to Finland.* Söderström, Porvoo, 1963.

Stoddard, T. L. *Area handbook for Finland.* U.S. Government Printing Office, Washington, 1974.

Sutherland, H. *Lapland Journey.* Bles, London, 1938.

Sykes, J. *Direction north: a view of Finland.* Hutchinson, London, 1967.

Toivola, U. ed. *Introduction to Finland.* Söderström, Porvoo, 1960.

Look at Finland is a general magazine for foreigners on all aspects of Finnish life, published quarterly in Helsinki by the Finnish Tourist Board and the Ministry of Foreign Affairs.

STATISTICS

Statistical yearbook of Finland. Tilastokeskus, Helsinki, 1878 to date.

Yearbook of Nordic statistics. Nordic Council/Nordic Statistical Secretariat, Stockholm, 1964 to date.

GEOGRAPHICAL BACKGROUND

Fullerton, B., Williams, A. F. *Scandinavia.* 2nd ed. Chatto and Windus, London, 1975.

Jones, M. *Finland: daughter of the sea.* (Studies in historical geography) Dawson, Folkestone, 1977.

Koutaniemi, L., ed. *Characteristics of the North: proceedings of the XIX Conference of Finnish Geographers.* Oulu, Geographical Society of Northern Finland 1984.

Mead, W. R. *An economic geography of the Scandinavian states and Finland.* University of London Press, 1959.

Mead, W. R., Jaatinen, S. H. *The Åland Islands.* David and Charles, Newton Abbot, 1975.

Mead, W. R., Smeds, H. *Winter in Finland.* Evelyn, London, 1967.

Platt, R. R., ed. *Finland and its geography.* Duell, Sloan and Pearce, New York, 1955.

Sømme, A., ed. *The geography of Norden.* Heinemann, London, 1968.

Suomi: a general handbook on the geography of Finland. [Fennia 72] Geographical Society of Finland, Helsinki, 1952.

For special contributions to the study of Finnish geography there are two periodicals which carry articles in English or English summaries: *Fennia* and *Terra,* both published by the Geographical Society of Finland since 1889.

The official map-making organisation is the National Board of Survey (*Maanmittaushallitus*) which produces a regular series of topographical maps on a scale of 1:20,000 as well as a wide range of specialist maps. It has also produced the largest scale atlas of the country, *Finland in maps* on a scale of 1:250,000, published in a handy volume of 224 pages by Weilin and Göös, Helsinki, 1979.

HISTORY

PREHISTORY

Burnham, R. *Who are the Finns? A study in prehistory.* Faber, London, 1964.

Hajdu, P. *Finno-Ugrian languages and peoples.* Deutsch, London, 1975.

Kivikoski, E. *Finland.* (Ancient peoples and places) Thames and Hudson, London, 1967.

Zvelebil, M. *From forager to farmer in the Boreal zone: reconstructing economic patterns in prehistoric Finland.* 2 vols. British Archaeological Reports, Oxford, 1981.

GENERAL

Derry, T. K. *A history of Scandinavia: Norway, Sweden, Denmark, Finland and Iceland*. Allen and Unwin, London, 1979.

Engman, M., Kirby, D., eds., *Finland: people, nation, state*. London, 1987.

Jutikkala, E., Pirinen, K. *A history of Finland*. Rev. ed., Heinemann, London, 1979.

Klinge, M. *A brief history of Finland*. Otava, Helsinki, 1981.

Let us be Finns: essays on history. Helsinki, 1990.

Warner, O. *The sea and the sand: the Baltic 1630–1945*. Cape, London, 1945.

Wuorinen, J. H. *A history of Finland*. Columbia University Press for the American–Scandinavian Foundation, New York, 1965.

Nationalism in modern Finland. Columbia University Press, New York, 1931.

FINLAND IN SWEDISH HISTORY

Roberts, M. *Gustav Adolphus: a history of Sweden 1611–1632*. 2 vols. Longmans, London, 1953–58.

The age of liberty: Sweden 1719–1772. Cambridge University Press, 1986.

Roberts, M., ed. *Sweden's age of greatness 1632–1718*. St Martin's Press, New York, 1973.

EIGHTEENTH TO TWENTIETH CENTURIES

Copeland, W., *The uneasy alliance. Collaboration between the Finnish opposition and the Russian underground 1899–1904*. Helsinki, 1973.

Hovde, B. J. *The Scandinavian countries 1720–1865: the rise of the middle classes*. 2 vols. Chapman and Grimes, Boston MA, 1943; reprinted, Kennikat Press, Port Wellington NY, 1972.

Huxley, S. D., *Constitutionalist insurgency in Finland*. Helsinki, 1990.

Kirby, D. G., ed. *Finland and Russia 1808–1920: from autonomy to independence; a selection of documents*. Macmillan for the London School of Slavonic and East European Studies, 1975.

Luntinen, P., *F. A. Seyn 1862–1918: a political biography of a Tsarist imperialist as Administrator of Finland*. Helsinki, 1995.

Paasivirta, J. *Finland and Europe: international crises during the period of autonomy, 1808–1914*. Hurst, London, 1981.

Polvinen T., *Imperial borderland: Bobrikov and the attempted russification of Finland 1898–1904*. London, 1995.

Puntila, L. A. *The political history of Finland 1809–1966*. Heinemann, London, 1975.

Screen, J. E. O., *The Finnish army 1881–1901*. Helsinki, 1996.

TWENTIETH CENTURY – GENERAL

Barros, J. *The Åland Islands question: its settlement by the League of Nations.* Yale University Press, New Haven, 1968.

Hamalainen P. K. *In time of storm: revolution, civil war and the ethnolinguistic issue in Finland.* State University of New York Press, Albany NY, 1979.

Hannula, J. O. *Finland's War of Independence.* Faber, London, 2nd ed. 1939.

Harmaja, L. *Effects of the war on economic and social life in Finland.* Yale University Press, New Haven, 1933.

Kirby, D. G. *Finland in the twentieth century.* Hurst, London, 1979.

Finland in the 20th century. London, 1979.

Lyytinen, E. *Finland in British politics in the first World War.* Suomalainen Tiedeakatemia, Helsinki, 1980.

Odhe, T. *Finland: a nation of co-operators.* Williams and Norgate, London, 1931.

Penttilä, R., *Finland's seach for security through defence.* London, 1991.

Smith, C. J. *Finland and the Russian Revolution 1917–1922.* University of Georgia Press, Athens GA, 1958.

Upton, A. F., *The Finnish revolution 1917–1918.* Minneapolis, 1980.

Wuorinen, J. H. *The prohibition experiment in Finland.* Columbia University Press, New York, 1931.

1939–1945

Chew, A. F. *The white death: the epic of the Soviet – Finnish Winter War.* Michigan State University Press, East Lansing MI, 1971.

Condon, R. *The Winter War: Russia against Finland.* Pan, London, 1972.

Engle, E., Paananen, L. *The Winter War: the Russo-Finnish conflict 1939–40.* Sidgwick and Jackson, London, 1973.

Jakobson, M. *The diplomacy of the Winter War: an account of the Russo-Finnish conflict 1939–40.* Harvard University Press, Cambridge, MA, 1961.

Krosby, H. P. *Finland, Germany and the Soviet Union 1940–1941: the Petsamo dispute.* University of Wisconsin Press, Madison, 1968.

Lundin, C. L. *Finland in the Second World War.* Indiana University Press, Bloomington, 1957.

Nevakivi, J. *The appeal that was never made: the Allies, Scandinavia and the Finnish Winter War 1939–40.* Hurst, London, 1976.

Palm, T. *The Finnish–Soviet armistice negotiations of 1944.* Almqvist and Wiksell, Stockholm, 1971.

Tanner, V. *The Winter War: Finland against Russia 1939–1940.* Stanford University Press, 1957.

Upton, A. F. *Finland 1939–1940*. Davis-Poynter, London, 1974.
Finland in crisis 1940–1941. Faber, London, 1964.
Wuorinen, J. H. *Finland and World War II 1939–1944*. Ronald Press, New York, 1948.

HISTORICAL MEMOIRS AND BIOGRAPHIES

Gripenberg, G. A. *Finland and the great powers: memoirs of a diplomat*. University of Nebraska Press, Lincoln NE, 1965.
Jagerskiöld, S. *Mannerheim: Marshal of Finland*. Hurst, London, 1986.
Korhonen, K., ed. *Urho Kekkonen: a statesman for peace*. Otava, Helsinki, 1975.
Mannerheim, C. G. E. *The memoirs of Marshal Mannerheim*. Cassell, London, 1953.
Raikkonen, E. *Svinhufvud, the builder of Finland: an adventure in statecraft*. Wilmer, London 1938.
Rintala, M. *Four Finns: political profiles: Mannerheim, Tanner, Ståhlberg, Paasikivi*. University of California Press, Berkeley, 1969.
Saari, E. *Paavo Ruotsalainen: the George Fox of Finland*. Friends Home Service Committee, London, 1978.
Screen, J. E. O. *Mannerheim: the years of preparation*. Hurst, London, 1970.
Tokoi, O. *Sisu, "Even through a stone wall": autobiography*. Speller, New York, 1957.
Tuominen, A. *The bells of the Kremlin: an experience of Communism*, ed. P. Heiskanen. University Press of New England, Hanover NH, 1983.
Tuominen, U., Uusitako, K. *J. K. Paasikiviei: a pictorial biography*. Otava, Helsinki, 1970.
Warner, O. *Marshal Mannerheim and the Finns*. Weidenfeld and Nicolson, London, 1967.

FINNS IN AMERICA

Hoglund, A. W. *Finnish immigrants in America 1880–1920*. University of Wisconsin Press, Madison 1960.
Jalkanen, R. J., ed. *The Finns in north America: a social symposium*. Michigan State University for Suomi College, Hancock, 1969.
Karni, M. G., Ollila, D. J., eds. *For the common good: Finnish immigrants and the radical response to industrial America*. Tyomies Society, Superior, Wisconsin, 1977.
Kolehmainen, J. I., Hill, C. W., *Haven in the woods: the story of the Finns in Wisconsin*. Madison, Wisconsin, 1965.

Virtanen, K. *Settlement or return: Finnish emigrants (1860–1930) in the international overseas return migration movement*. Migration Institute, Turku, 1979.

POLITICS

Alapuro, R., *State and revolution in Finland*. Berkeley, California, 1988.

Arter, D. *Bumpkin against bigwig: the emergence of a green movement in Finnish politics*. University of Tampere, 1978.

Politics and policymaking in Finland. Wheatsheaf, Brighton, 1987.

Berglund, S., Sundberg, J., eds., *Finnish democracy*. Helsinki, 1990.

Hiden, M. *The Ombudsman in Finland: the first fifty years*. Institute of Governmental Studies, University of California, 1973.

Hodgson, J. *Communism in Finland: a history and interpretation*. Princeton University Press, 1967.

Nousiainen, J. *The Finnish political system*. Harvard University Press, Cambridge MA, 1971.

Nyholm, P. *Parliament, government and multi-dimensional party relations in Finland*. Societas Scientiarum Fennica, Helsinki, 1972.

Paastela, J., *The Finnish Communist Party in the Finnish political system*. Tampere, 1991.

Pesonen, M. *An election in Finland: party activities and voter reactions*. Yale University Press, New Haven, 1968.

Rintala, M. *Three generations: the extreme right wing in Finnish politics*. Indiana University Press, Bloomington, 1962.

Sinkonnen, Sirkka. *Women's increased political participation in Finland*. European Consortium for Political Research workshop, Berlin, c/o University of Essex, 1977.

Törnudd, K. *The electoral system of Finland*. Evelyn, London, 1968.

Upton, A. F., and others. *The Communist Parties of Scandinavia and Finland*. Weidenfeld and Nicolson, London, 1973.

FOREIGN RELATIONS

Allison, R. *Finland's relations with the Soviet Union 1944–84*. Macmillan in association with St Antony's College, Oxford, 1985.

Jakobson, M. *Finnish neutrality: a study of Finnish foreign policy since the second World War*. Evelyn, London, 1968.

Kekkonen, U. *Neutrality: the Finnish position; speeches by Dr Urho Kekkhonen, President of Finland*. Heinemann, London, 1970.

Kiljunen, K. *Finnish aid in progress: premises and practice of official development assistance.* Institute of Development Studies, University of Helsinki, 1983.

Maude, G. *The Finnish dilemma: neutrality in the shadow of power.* Oxford University Press for the Royal Institute of International Affairs, London, 1976.

Mazour, A. G. *Finland between East and West.* Van Nostrand, Princeton, 1956; reprinted, Greenwood Press, 1976.

Miljan, T. *The reluctant Europeans: the attitudes of the Nordic countries towards European integration.* Hurst, London, 1977.

Möttölä, K., Bykov, O. N., Korolev, I. S., eds. *Finnish–Soviet economic relations.* Macmillan, London, in association with the Finnish institute of International Affairs, 1983.

Polvinen, T. *Between east and west: Finland in international politics 1944–1947.* University of Minnesota Press, Minneapolis, 1986.

Ries, T., *Cold will: the defence of Finland.* London, 1988.

Vloyantes, J. P. *Silk glove hegemony: Finnish–Soviet relations 1944–1974; a case study of the theory of the soft sphere of influence.* Kent State University Press, Kent OH, 1975.

Yearbook of Finnish Foreign policy. Finnish Institute of International Affairs, Helsinki, 1973 to date.

ECONOMICS

Hjerppe, R., *The Finnish economy 1860–1985: growth and structural change.* Helsinki, 1989.

Jucker-Fleetwood, E. *Economic theory and policy in Finland 1914–1925.* Blackwell, Oxford, 1958.

Kanniainen, V., Lilleberg, J. *On external and internal factors in the explanation of inflation: the Finnish experience 1962–1974.* Department of Economics, University of Helsinki, 1980.

Kaukiainen, Y., *A history of Finnish shipping.* London, 1993.

Kiljunen, K. *Finland in the changing international devision of labour.* UNIDO, Vienna, 1985.

Knoellinger, C. E. *Labor in Finland.* Harvard University Press, Cambridge MA, 1960.

Laakkonen, V. *The co-operative movement in Finland 1945–1974.* Department of Co-operative Research, University of Helsinki, 1977.

Myllyntaus, T., *Electrifying Finland. The transfer of a new technology into a late-industializing economy.* London, 1991.

Singleton, F. *The economy of Finland in the twentieth century*. University of Bradford Press, 1987.

Valkonen, M., *The central organization of Finnish trade unions 1907–1987*. Helsinki, 1989.

ECONOMIC MONITORS IN ENGLISH

Bank of Finland. *Yearbook and Monthly Bulletin*, Helsinki, 1921 to date.

Economic Intelligence Unit. *Quarterly economic review of Finland and annual supplement*. London, 1953 to date.

Finland, Ministry of Finance, Economics Department. *Economic survey: supplement to the Budget proposal, submitted by the Government to Parliament*. Helsinki, annual.

Finnish Foreign Trade Association. *Finnish foreign trade*. Helsinki, 1930 to date, 8 issues per year.

Kansallis-Osake Bank. *Economic review*, Helsinki, semi-annual.

Union Bank of Finland. *Annual Report* and quarterly bulletin *Unitas*, Helsinki.

The Organisation for Economic Co-operation and Development is the major international monitor of its member countries, including Finland, and issues an annual volume *Economic survey: Finland*. It also issues less regular reviews of economic aspects of specific sectors – titles include:

Agricultural policy in Finland (see below)
Environmental policies in Finland
Water management in Finland
Manpower policy in Finland
Reviews of national policies for education: Finland (see below)
Reviews of national science and technology policy: Finland
Social sciences policy: Finland (see below)

AGRICULTURE

Mead, W. R. *Farming in Finland*. Athlone Press, London, 1953.

Organisation for Economic Co-operation and Development. *Agricultural policy in Finland*. Paris, OECD, 1975.

Talman, P. *Dairy Farming in Finland: geographical aspects of the development, typology and economics of Finnish dairy farming*. Department of Geography, University of Oulu, 1978.

Varjo, U. *Finnish farming: typology and economics*. Akadémiai Kiadó, Budapest, 1977.

Yearbook of forest industries. Central Association of Finnish Forest Industries, Helsinki.

SOCIAL STUDIES

Central Organisation for Traffic Safety. *Reports.* Helsinki, 1965 to date. *Road traffic accidents in Finland.* 1964 to date, annual.

Harmoja, L., *The effects of the war on economic and social life in Finland.* New Haven, Conn., 1933.

Jallinoja, Riitta. 'Independence or integration: the women's movement and political parties in Finland.' In *'The new women's movement'*, ed. D. Dahlerup, Sage, London, 1986.

Kuusi, P. *This world of man.* Pergamon, Oxford, 1985.

Social Policy for the Sixties. Kuopio, 1964.

Lander, Patricia S. *In the shadow of the factory: social change in a Finnish community.* Schenkman, Cambridge MA, 1976.

Lönnqvist, J. *Suicide in Helsinki: an epidemiological and social-psychiatric study.* Psychiatria Fennica, Helsinki, 1977.

Natkin, R., Sulkunen, P. 'The suburban pub in Finland: a woman's viewpoint / a male domain.' In *Public drinking and public policy,* Addiction Research Foundation, Toronto, 1985.

Organisation for Economic Co-operation and Development. *Social sciences policy: Finland.* Paris, OECD, 1981.

Social Research Institute of Alcohol Studies. *Reports.* Helsinki, 1960 to date.

Social policy for the sixties. Kuopio, 1964.

Sulkunen, I., *History of the Finnish temperance movement: temperance as a civic religion.* New York, 1990.

Sweetser, F. *Metropolitan and regional society of Helsinki.* Societas Scientiarum Fennica, Helsinki, 1973.

Verkko, V. *Homicides and suicides in Finland and their dependence on national character.* Gads Forlag, Copenhagen, 1951.

Wynn, Margaret. *The protection of maternity and infancy: a study of the services for pregnant women and young children in Finland.* Council for Children's Welfare, London, 1974.

EDUCATION

Finland, Ministry of Education. *Educational development in Finland 1984–1986: report to the 40th session of the International Conference on Education,* Geneva, 1986.

Finnish Society for Research in Sports and Physical Education. *Physical education and sports in Finland.* Söderström, Porvoo, 1979.

Iiasalo, T. *The science of education in Finland 1828–1918.* Societas Scientiarum Fennica, Helsinki, 1979.

Organisation for Economic Co-operation and Development. *Reviews of national policies for education: Finland.* Paris, OECD, 1982.

A current view of Finnish educational developments and their implications for lifelong education can be gained from the useful periodical *Adult education in Finland* published in English by the Society for Popular Education, Helsinki, quarterly from 1964 to date.

DESIGN AND THE ARTS

Smith, J. B. *The golden age of Finnish art: art nouveau and the national spirit.* Otava, Helsinki, 1975.

Modern Finnish painting and graphic art. Weidenfeld and Nicolson, London, 1970.

Richards, J. M. *800 years of Finnish architecture.* David and Charles, Newton Abbot, 1978.

Fleig, K., ed. *Alvar Aalto.* Thames and Hudson, London, 1975.

Wikberg, N. E. *Carl Eric Wikberg.* City of Helsinki, 1973.

Hertzen, H. von, Spreiregen, P. D. *Building a new town: Finland's new garden city Tapiola.* MIT Press, Cambridge MA, 1971.

Sarpaneva, T. Brunn, E., Kruskopf, E. *Finnish design 1875–1975: a hundred years of Finnish industrial design.* Otava, Helsinki, 1975.

Design in Finland: a survey of modern Finnish design. Finnish Foreign Trade Association, Helsinki, 1961 to date, annual.

Konya, A., Berger A. *The international handbook of Finnish sauna.* Architectural Press, London, 1973.

Cowie, P. *Finnish cinema.* Tantivy Press, London; Finnish Film Foundation, Helsinki, 1976.

Hillier, J., ed., *Cinema in Finland: an introduction.* British Film Institute, London, 1975.

Richards, D. *The music of Finland.* Evelyn, London, 1968.

Layton, R. *Sibelius,* Rev. ed. Dent, London, 1978.

Sibelius and his world. Thames and Hudson, London, 1970.

Tavastjerna, E., *Sibelius.* 2 vols., London, 1976, 1986.

LITERATURE

Ahokas, J. *A history of Finnish literature.* Indiana University Research Center for the Language Sciences, for the American–Scandinavian Foundation, 1973.

Rubulis, A. *Baltic literature.* University of Notre Dame Press, Indiana, 1970.

Wilson, W. A. *Folklore and nationalism in modern Finland.* Indiana University Press, Bloomington, 1976.

Bosley, K., *The Kalevela.* Oxford, 1989.

Kuusi, M., Bosley, K., Branch, M., comp. *Finnish folk poetry, epic: an anthology in Finnish and English.* Finnish Literature Society, Helsinki, 1977.

Lönnrot, E., comp. *Kalevala: the land of the heroes;* translated by W. F. Kirby. Athlone Press, London, 1985. [this translation originally published 1907].

The Kalevala, or poems of the Kalevala district; translated by F. P. Magoun. Harvard University Press, 1963, reprinted 1985.

Kivi, A., *Seven Brothers.* tr. A. Matson, Helsinki, 1952.

Kolehmainen, J. I. *Epic of the north: the story of Finland's Kalevala.* Northwestern Publ. Co., New York Mills, Minnesota, 1973.

Dauenhauer, R., Binham, P. *Snow in May: an anthology of Finnish writing 1945–1972.* Fairleigh Dickinson University Press, Rutherford NJ, 1978.

Laitinen, K., ed. *Modern Nordic plays: Finland.* Twayne, New York, 1973.

Carpelan, Bo. *Room without walls,* illustrated by Hannu Taina. Forest Books, Chingford, 1987.

Haavikko, Paavo. *Selected poems.* Penguin, Harmondsworth, 1974.

Leino, Eino. *Whitsongs.* Menard Press, London, 1978.

Linna, Väinö. *The unknown soldier.* Collins, London, 1957; Söderström, Porvoo, 1975.

Runeberg, Johan Ludvig. *The tales of Ensign Stål.* Söderström, Helsinki, 1952.

Sillanpää, Frans Eemil. *Fallen asleep while young: the history of the last offshoot of an old family tree.* Putnam, London, 1933.

People in the summer night: an epic suite. University of Wisconsin Press, Madison, 1966.

Topelius, Z. *The sea king's gift, and other tales from Finland.* Muller, London, 1973.

Waltari, Mika. *Sinuhe the Egyptian: a novel.* Putnam, London, 1949.

Although Fred Singleton, with remarkable fortitude, completed the main text of this book before his death, he was unable to complete the bibliography to his satisfaction, and asked me to prepare it for him. He had made some bibliographical notes and, having worked closely with him for many years, I knew what materials he had been referring to, and what he had found particularly useful. From this base and from other sources this bibliographical listing has been compiled, with additional assistance from the staff of the Library at the University of Bradford. It should therefore be recorded that, while it was a privilege to be asked to undertake the task, any errors or imbalance in the bibliography are entirely my own.

JOHN J. HORTON
Deputy Librarian
University of Bradford

Index